Lame Habits

Of

Truly Good People

A small book filled with big ideas about what it means to be human

Published by The Pacific Book Group, Honolulu, Hawaii
Please address any correspondence to: www.GudrunCarstairs.com

Library of Congress Control Number: 2008940812

ISBN: 978-1-60145-653-3

Printed in the United States of America

Photograph of the author by Calvin Winbolt

The author of this book does not give medical advice or prescribe the use of any technique given in this book, either directly or indirectly, as a form of treatment for emotional, psychological or medical problems without the advice of a professional in the psychotherapeutic or medical field.

The intent of the author is only to offer information of a general nature, not to offer a specific diagnosis, prescription or cure. Although one may find he insights and exercises offered in this book very helpful, this book is sold with the understanding that neither the author nor publisher are engaged in presenting specific psychological, emotional or medical advice. Each person has unique needs, and this book cannot address these individual differences.

In the event that the information given in this book is used otherwise, the author and the publisher assume no responsibility for such actions.

Lame Habits

Of

Truly Good People

A small book filled with big ideas about what it means to be human

Gudrun C. Carstairs

The Pacific Book Group
Honolulu, Hawaii

I dedicate this book to my husband, Robert, who through his steadfast loving support gave me the time and space to write.

And, I dedicate this book to my daughter, Tiana, who is my daily inspiration.

Acknowledgments

I am deeply grateful to the many people that have walked through my door over the years and contributed in their own invaluable way to this book. I couldn't have done it without the insights, questions and challenges that they brought my way. I thank each and every one of you!

I find it difficult to fit a list of all the many people that have touched my life and encouraged me to write on this page. However, I want to express a special thank you to Patricia Dawn, Gary Kerwin, Gail Muese, Gail Honda, and Shama Stewart for lending a helpful hand along the way.

A heartfelt thank you to the teachers that have helped me find my voice and inner knowing. Thank you to Duncan McCallister and Chuck Spezzano for being there when I needed guidance. Many others spoke to me through their books. They inspired me to follow in their footsteps.

My love and appreciation goes to my parents, Oskar and Amanda Bachmann, my sister, Barbara, my brothers, Oskar, Karl and Peter. Deep inside I always felt, that if I really needed them, they would come to my rescue (as I would for them).

Thank you to the friends that over the years crossed my path and were there when I needed them most. Our paths may have parted, but all of you have a special place in my heart. You each added in your own unique way to shaping, both me, and this book.

Table of Contents

First Thoughts

Human relationships are often complicated. As humans, our approach to life is governed by an underlying sense of vulnerability. We feel misunderstood and take offense where none was intended. We are afraid to be hurt and lose what is dear to us. Our everyday responsibilities and demands for a better life overshadow our inner experience. Truly, inner change and social change go hand in hand. A better world begins with our personal attitudes and relationships.

What is truly important to us? Why did we do what we did? Are our thoughts and actions guided by fear? Do we believe that safety lies in the power to dominate, hoard, take and control? Or, do we carry a belief in a common wish for *good* existing in all of us? Do we recognize this *"call for love"*[1] even if it is voiced in warped ways? As the fallible humans we are, we seem to ask for what is important to us through criticism, attack, blame and at times violence. We relinquish responsibility and pretend that we don't have choice. We take and don't give.

Do we believe in affirming our responsibility towards each other and our planet beyond the boundaries of ethnicity, religion, culture and geography? Or, do we believe that others are out to get us. They are out to take what we have and want. Their main purpose in life is to bother and deprive us!? We have to make a choice. We can choose to live life either fear-based with its entire multitude of manifestations. Or, we can choose to live life love-based, with a vision of inclusivity, tolerance and equality. *Then our outlook is governed by a belief that there is enough and that we are enough.* A belief that we deserve and that what is ours will come to us.

This book is an attempt to outline the commonalities that govern our thinking, seeing, feeling, reacting and choosing in our personal lives.

[1] Foundation for Inner Peace, *A Course in Miracles*

What we pass on to our children not just economically and environmentally, but also emotionally will make the world a better or worse place to live. If our past experiences and the conclusions we drew have the power to color and often determine how we experience others and ourselves in the present, wouldn't it be wise to know about the *how* and *why*? Only then can we have a conscious sense of our attitudes towards others and the world today.

The roots of societal injustice and ecological selfishness can be found in this inner world as well. After all, the people in power are foremost people. Our alienation from our inner self, from one another and an attitude of seeing others solely in terms of what others or the earth can do for us, begins early on. It leads to our inability to see ourselves as part of a bigger picture. We trade consideration for selfishness. Our world remains small and consumed with our own needs, wants and concerns. We become unable to find meaning and purpose in our everyday day. Life becomes a drudgery of routines. We feel threatened by rejection, opposition and loss.

For many people their deeper source of discontent is the outcome of a sense of disconnection and alienation. They carry a deeply rooted sense of vulnerability that everything could be taken away. They fear to be unhappy. The routines of their everyday life are boring and feel empty. *"I don't have time to do what I really want!,"* they will say. Our society is consumed with endless attempts to find satisfaction and safety through increasing our economic wealth and societal status and our physical well-being and appearance. Our body becomes a marketing tool. Relationships become a means to avoid feeling alone. Buying things becomes an attempt to buy happiness; we dream of retirement to finally do what we want to.

Material affluence gives us an illusion of fulfillment. If money compensates for the alienation and emptiness we experience then it will produce an estrangement from what truly holds purpose and meaning for us. Cash in the bank can't provide us with a higher meaning for our lives. By the same token, there is nothing noble about living in a state of financial lack. Lack keeps us stuck in surviving life instead of living life.

Still very young, we were taught to focus on what had practical and monetary value. What was useful was more important and in apparent contradiction to what was our truth. Some of us may carry a legitimate anger at authorities, personal and spiritual, for failing us. Much horror was and is committed in the name of religion. However, if we are not in touch with the inner dimensions of life and ourselves, we too easily slip into the trap of attempting to seek on the outside what only can be found on the inside. We lose ourselves in a frantic search for money, power, success, health, safety and pleasure. It is up to us now to shoulder the responsibility to improve what was laid into our childhood cradle. It is our responsibility to do better then our parents and other authorities did by us.

Life does hold suffering and the physical world and the people we interact with do set up limitations. Our relationships and the world we live in are *the ultimate personal growth testing ground* to face and overcome these limitations. A challenge entered by all but only truly faced by a few. As humans we tend to cope out, hide and show an overpowering aversion to taking responsibility for us. We retreat into a state of self-absorption of viewing others as vehicles to advance our own personal interests. We desperately attempt to avoid the vulnerability that comes with living in a physical body; we intertwine physical vulnerability with psycho-emotional vulnerability. Each day we must choose who we will be today. Awareness needs to be translated into new action. And, as humans we will fail, no matter how sincere or lofty our intentions and visions are. *This is a book about having the courage to admit to our human fallibility and hopefully eventually embrace our and others humanity with grace.*

How do we complicate our life and the people in it? The principles that govern what we think, see, hear, feel, experience and ultimately do can be understood. Awareness gives us choice or it's lack limits choice and makes our reactions predictable. If we hope to produce true relationship, societal and global change, we must work to get our own house in order first. Choice is that moment when I tell myself: *"There is another way of looking at this!"*[2] Our new vision of living in a shared world of societal justice, ecological responsibility

[2] Foundation for Inner Peace, *A Course in Miracles*

and world peace rests on our personal healing, our own harmonious relationships, our inner sense of self-worth, our daily generosity, not just monetary but emotional generosity of forgiving our and others humanity.

As humans we are subject to making poor choices without realizing it. Our mind creates its own world, our world, constantly. It establishes our own heaven or hell every minute of the day. So not always immediately apparent, we are all harmed by destructiveness directed at any individual, group, nation and the environment anywhere on this planet. Our own pain, aggression and carelessness thrown out at the world have a *boomerang* effect. The human race is mutually interdependent, if we like it or don't. We have a responsibility for each other, our neighbor's children and the stewardship of this planet. Our attitude of governing our personal and political lives from fear needs to give way to governing from a shared platform of understanding, caring, respect and valuing of each other. For this, we do not need to reject each other's differences nor rational thinking and scientific understanding.

It is in our personal self-interest to live in relationships, communities and nations that are not only economically but also emotionally satisfying.

Gudrun

We see ourselves as right and good and others as wrong.

Needing to Be Right has its Roots in Fear

Feeling right, we feel justified; the problem is…it doesn't solve the problem.

Just as a dog will answer a threat with a *snarl*, most people answer a perceived threat to their self-image with a defensive gesture. Our initial reaction to conflict becomes: *"I am right (innocent/good) and you are wrong!"*

Our reaction may be a quiet inner withdrawal or a loud outer protest. To see someone else as wrong when their way of thinking or being in the world goes against our ideas and values seems automatic. We carry a picture in our mind about what we believe is best and right. When they, at times unknowingly, threaten this picture, we move to defend and attack. That we do this makes us human. What we do about it matters! That our upset is based in a deeply rooted sense of vulnerability producing fear is not necessarily obvious.

He said, "I am going out for a cup of coffee." She was sitting there helping their son with his history homework. Later on, she would be taking him to his afternoon sports activity and as usually make time to watch.

Resentment welled up inside of her. She felt that she was carrying more than her share. He had left already before she was able to gather her thoughts and feelings. Her first reaction was to accuse him. She felt right and justified.

We don't recognize our need to be right as fear.

Feelings of *vulnerable, unsure and inferior* have been safely pushed out of our conscious awareness and as such out of our experience, at least so it seems. Once caught in reacting without deeper understanding it is hard to take positive action towards what we *want.*

We become afraid that we will be stuck with what we *don't want*. We are afraid that somehow we will be denied what is precious to us, be harmed and made less. This moves us to be tempted to blame, complain and accuse. We act superior when we feel inferior and unsure. We become intolerant when we feel threatened.

Our fears have ancient roots. Living in a physical body and in a physical world we are subject to physical laws. This creates uncertainty, limitations and, at times, a feeling of being terribly vulnerable. *Bad things happen to truly good people.*

And, truly good people often complicate their own and others' lives with limiting and destructive attitudes. Being right asserts our space. It forms an invisible box with walls that we can touch.

It gives us an illusion of safety. Things are clear, known, tangible and we experience order. This appears to guarantee and safeguard our (and at times others') emotional needs or physical well-being.

She took a moment to step back from her feelings and realized that she could simply ask him for what she wanted: to have him take their son to sports and invite her out for a cup of coffee occasionally!

He was making space for himself...she had a right to do the same for herself and for them as a couple. She didn't need to make him wrong or become defensive out of fear of not being valued or not important to him.

There is a difference between knowing what we know and feeling righteous.

The difference lies in how we feel energetically. When we feel righteous our energy withdraws from others, closes and attacks. Then our own convenience, our fears and hang-ups govern our thinking and experiencing. Our mind closes. We can attack without words. Our energy speaks volumes. Attack is the best defense! We become invested in convincing them that *we are right and they are wrong.* Without being immediately aware of it, we feel they challenged us or what is dear to us.

We assume that they see us as not important, acceptable, respectable, worthwhile listening to, smart, capable, attractive, etc., and that our best interests are disregarded.

Insisting that things are either *right or wrong* is akin to believing into a simplistic form of *good and bad.* It returns us to the world perception of our early childhood. Our energy and thinking polarizes and we move to equalize things. It seems as if the other has taken a step to upset the power balance of the relationship.

We do not realize that no matter what the other has done or didn't do, it is our own mind that is questioning ourselves by accepting the perceived challenge when defending against it.

We can only truly "*turn the other cheek*" once we know ourselves. Turning the other cheek understood rightly is to resist attacking back in self-defense. It has nothing to do with allowing abusive behavior. Self-awareness allows us to break the predictable reaction cycle.

Truly feeling secure in knowing that we are right (for ourselves) and trusting (in ourselves), on the other hand, still allows us to hear another's opinion. We feel quietly confident. There is no challenge therefore there is no need for defense.

We have the power of our conviction. Many people in history have brought about change due to their conviction. They perceived an injustice and were willing to address it, even give their lives for its change. When we are guided by our conviction, we leave no stone unturned.

Once we become capable of seeing commonalities, we can easily grant others the right to disagree. It even becomes tolerable if they defend and attack out of their vulnerabilities. We can see the attack for what it is, a cry to be reaffirmed. Our energy remains extended and open. We become capable of setting constructive boundaries.

What we react to is not necessarily what was said or done.

When her husband left to have his coffee she felt threatened without realizing it immediately. She took his leaving to have a cup of coffee as: "He doesn't want to spend time with me!" "He is being selfish and doesn't care enough to consider my needs." "I am not truly important to him!"

We react to what we think was implied or intended and what we fear could result. And to confuse things even further, at times, we are right about one aspect of what is going on. Maybe he was being a bit selfish at that moment.

Relationships hold a delicate energetic balance. When we become a little too selfless our mate will balance our energy by being just a bit on the selfish side. Seeing his selfishness becomes the stepping-stone to making assumptions: *"...he doesn't care enough to consider my needs".* Once we take this extra step one of our deepest sensitivities has been assaulted.

Seeing how we are contributing to what is going on and staying away from assumptions would mean we have to take responsibility for our side of it. Instead, it is much easier to have a litany of accusations and justifications that prove that we are right and are unjustly treated.

We demand change of the other. We are in essence saying that they have caused us or intend to cause us harm of some form. We feel threatened and our mind closes. *Our box has been rattled. They* upset the order of things!

Fear thinking takes what is another step.

The problem is, others feel their actions are justified as much as we do. They too carry assumptions about what they think should happen. And they do not want to see themselves as having caused harm. At times, they dare to believe that harm was (or could be) caused them instead.

We draw conclusions because of this...or that... It is in attaching our personal meaning, and mistaking this meaning for a fact, that we begin to complicate our lives.

- Stay away from what you think the reasons for someone else's behavior are and instead identify what feelings are being triggered for you. (Change "He doesn't value me," to "I don't feel valued".)
- If one of your deepest needs or sensitivities has been challenged recognize that it is much older than what is happening in the present...connect present to past. You have temporarily lost your ability to truly see the other.
- Ask questions instead of making accusations! We often confuse facts with assumptions based in our personal meaning. Would you rather be right or happy?
- Don't give into the temptation to ask for a positive through a negative.

Tell the other how it affects you emotionally without blame! Showing your soft underbelly in an intimate relationship is essential and leads to more closeness...as long as you don't use it to make the other feel guilty and the other will not use your disclosure against you.

We tend to feel righteous when we view the world through the perspective of our fear and pain.

At the bottom of every upset rests a form of fear. Our present-day perception becomes distorted by our unresolved past. Our vulnerabilities dictate what we see and do. Victimization makes for good stories...we feel outraged or sympathize with the injustice the victim had to endure.

We have made it a habit to ask for a positive through a negative. We ask through our complaints, demands, blame, lies and hurtful actions. We are tempted to withdraw and punish, threaten to leave, blame and criticize hoping to be seen in a positive light in return and get what we want. Initially, we may feel justified and right in doing so. Again, this makes us human.

Little do we realize that our emotional well-being as adults is much more self-sufficient than we have come to believe. True, others can cause us emotional stress with their ignorance, carelessness or ill intention, yet this is different from harm.

What is true for our physical well-being with a body subject to physical laws does not automatically hold true for our emotional well-being. The children's rhyme "Sticks and stones can hurt my bones but words can never hurt me", communicates the truth about our adult emotional life.

We habitually surrender ourselves to the fear that we can be victimized emotionally.

This makes us shrink back, doubt, hesitate and overly careful in our interactions with others. And, it leads us to defend ourselves by blaming and accusing. On an emotional level it is the interpretations we put on things that make them so to us. Our mind begins to focus on what we *don't want*.

Using the above example, accusing her husband of being selfish and uncaring, will put him on the defensive. Chances are that he will not hear her accusations as a wish for togetherness. It is much more likely that he will begin to withdraw even more since now spending time with his wife has become a demand.

The more we believe that we can and will be harmed the more we tend to experience ourselves as harmed. It becomes a self-fulfilling prophecy. Undigested experiences have a subtle effect on how we walk, talk, behave and what we expect to have happen. Attempting to protect ourselves by *assuming that we know what is right or wrong* in our interactions with others often becomes our hidden attempt to bolster our shaky self-image. It becomes our feeble attempt at self-protection.

The walls we build for protection also keep out the love and success we crave. The more unsafe people feel the more right they feel they have to be and the more rigid, controlling, cut off and closed-minded they become.

Feeling threatened triggers a deep sense of needing to stay in control.

All our alarm bells go off and we respond with the most immediate defense available to us. It may be fight, flee, or ignore. The defensive strategy we use typically has brought us some form of success and safety in the past. In other words, it is known, tried and tested and therefore convenient.

It doesn't take any deliberation, which means valuable time and offers at least some measure of protection. It allows us to regain our sense of power, stay in control, or put off the threat. It offers a mask behind which to hide temporarily.

Behind this mask, we don't have to face our true feelings about the situation or ourselves. We don't have to be *wrong* or feel unworthy of love and approval. Behind this mask, we don't have to face other people's reactions and stand in the fire of their anger or pain. Behind this mask, we don't have to dare to fight for change or challenge someone we might regard as more powerful.

The wife felt threatened and her first reaction was to blame her husband for making her feel upset. Blaming him reestablished a sense of being in charge. It allowed her to avoid being in touch with her deeper sense of insecurity.

The courage to admit to our true intentions, fears and desires, to look ourselves squarely in the face, is rare. If we don't foster it, we hinder our own maturity and the happiness and growth of our relationships. When our soul's need to evolve beckons and we ignore or distort its call then fate might drag us kicking and screaming down the path we could have gone willingly. A lack of awareness about our underlying fears and motivations keeps us locked in repetitive surface struggles.

We Need to be Right if We Need to be Seen as Good

We all strive to continually establish and re-establish a positive self-image.

We were raised to be good. To the degree that we lack self-acceptance of our shortcomings, we become invested in being seen as (and see ourselves as) *only* loving, good, selfless, caring, smart, etc. *To be right* supports the good picture we carry about ourselves. Often our good intentions unwittingly turn into hurtful actions.

Righteousness leaves us prone to invade another's space in an obvious or subtle way under the banner of being good and right. It closes our mind. We cannot any longer see the other. All we see is what we believe to be right.

Righteousness pushes. Anger is a natural reaction to when someone else has overstepped the line. We have lost ourselves when we retaliate by attacking or withdrawing. We may get to feel right in return which feels good and makes us feel powerful for the moment. The price we pay is a loss of our sense of connection. Our world splits itself into *"I and you"*. This creates distance and alienation.

Have you noticed that people tend to raise their voices when either they are physically far apart and feel they need to bridge that distance or when they are angry? One could conclude that one aspect of feeling angry is feeling far apart and distant.

The energy underlying anger can be used to destroy or to create.

Remember scrubbing your house last time you were *mad?* It is an energy that wants to move *towards. "What outcome do we hope to accomplish?"* When we deny our anger, we tend to surrender where we should have fought or fight where we should have surrendered.

"How do we truly feel?" "What do we truly want?" Unless we honestly answer these questions, we will react or act out. *"What are*

the different ways that we defend against a feared reality?" "What is this ideal picture we are so desperate to uphold?"

Justifying and claiming ourselves as only good, innocent and right in a conflict and seeing others as wrong and bad protects the good picture we are set to maintain of ourselves. It is a desperate cover-up. It fosters the arrogant assumption that we know what is right and wrong for others. It creates an illusion of order and safety.

We have been taught that when we are good we are loved, loveable and loving.

As a result, we have confused and entwined good behavior with being loved. Love now is conditional and dependent on our good or socially acceptable behavior. This leads to hiding our bad thoughts, feelings, actions and intentions. Being good becomes a hidden attempt at guaranteeing that we deserve to be loved.

Love does not any longer exist as an independent state of being; it has to be earned and can be forfeited. We become caught in using *doing good* and *being good* for all kinds of hidden self-serving reasons that we cannot any longer acknowledge. Good then isn't any longer an expression of our inner state of being or a choice and natural extension of self. It comes with an agenda. We hope to gain something.

The mother was shopping for new clothes. Her little boy sitting in the shopping cart was unusually quiet. Suddenly he asked: "Mommy, am I being a good boy in the store?" "Yes, the mother said, "You are being a good boy!"

We have learned to confuse our and others' inner state of a preexisting innocence and worth with a human version of good that we were taught growing up. Problems arise when our human values and morals that were taught to us become super-imposed onto this preexisting inner state. Innocence is a deeper state of our inner being untouched by right and wrong or good and bad.

Once innocence and good become entwined and confused, we become afraid.

Of course, others behave in hair-raising ways at times. By pouncing on the bad out there (in others), we don't have to look at it or acknowledge it in here (in ourselves). This keeps our self-image intact. There is a difference, however, in seeing their behavior and judging them for what we see. As long as we confuse inborn innocence with a version of *human goodness*, we have to defend against *human badness.*

When we judge, we further entwine inner innocence with human good and bad. Judgment of others supports the positive picture we hold about ourselves (in comparison) of being good and with it, we think, a right to all what's good in life. It often doesn't take much to shake our conviction and make us doubt. We remain vulnerable.

As long as we stay preoccupied with finding wrong in others, we don't have to be aware of and examine our own shortcomings or simply trust the hand of life. We now *need* to be good so as to be loved and liked and deserving. What is good and socially acceptable is seen as right. Our *need* to be right, at least in part, is our need to be loved, loveable and loving. As long as we can see ourselves as right we experience ourselves as good.

The wife, in the above example, reasoned that her husband did what he did because he didn't value her or see her as important. After some self-exploration she realized that she had problems valuing herself and at times valuing him. Her past experiences had left her with a deep sense of not feeling important.

Her husband had become the mirror to reflect these feelings back to her. This is not to imply that he doesn't share some of the responsibility…we relate to others through our unresolved hang-ups.

We have internalized the values, morals and concepts given to us when we were young. Often we have done so and still do so with little discrimination. Children have to be taught to question (respectfully). Most of us were taught to *not* question but follow.

Righteousness renders us incapable of keeping perspective during a conflict.

Even people who commit the most hideous crimes were raised to be good or at least some version thereof. They may not have been taught and as a result may not have the ability to see a conflict through the eyes of others. When we cannot see the perspective of others, we cannot develop empathy. When we feel extremely isolated and alienated we lose our ability to care. In its extreme, we become socially handicapped and cannot function in healthy relationships.

All of us carry the tendency to become preoccupied with our perspective and experience and with what is wrong with others and what *they* need to do to fix it. Strong emotions dictate a polarized view of a situation. We become self-absorbed and unable to see a conflict through another's eyes. All we can see is our own loss and hurt and the injustice done to us. We can choose to step back from this self-absorbed view of life and others. No matter what the situation, there is always more than one perspective.

When we personalize other people's reactions, we take on what isn't ours.

The very moment that we personalize what others say or do about us or towards us, we become entangled. Now an alarm response triggers a series of assumptions, feared for outcomes and protective mechanisms. We lose our ability to recognize that what was said and done was most of all about them and not necessarily about us. We energetically take on someone else's problem and treat it as if it was ours. Both parties become blinded.

If the husband, in the above example, cannot take responsibility for his side and empathize with his wife's needs of feeling important to him, he is likely to react in a defensive manner. He will be triggered into relating from his own fears, self-accusations and insecurities.

Take a moment and recall a recent conflict you experienced with your husband, child, boss, friend, etc. If your reaction is one of frustration, blame, feeling justified, or hurt, instead of *hanging out* in your feelings try the following:

1. Take a breath;
2. Imagine yourself stepping back from your feelings and perspective (or in your mind, push your feelings and perspective away from you);
3. Turn your attention inside;
4. Ask yourself: *"What do I think was implied or intended?" "What am I afraid of?"*
   Repeat your questioning until you get a distinct *that's it* feeling. Is your fear realistic for what is happening in the present or is it an echo of the past? Is there a constructive action you can take? In other words, can you move towards what *you want*, instead of defending against what *you don't want?*
5. If the other person's behavior were actually a distorted call for love... *"What would they be asking for?"* Can you answer this request (without losing yourself)?

If we are told often enough as children that we are bad, etc., we tend to believe it.

If children feel they cannot succeed at being good, they may intentionally seek out to be *bad,* and stop caring if they are seen as good. They identify with being bad. Now they have a perception and reputation to live up to. When others tell them that they are good at something, they suddenly fail. They undermine what they know is important to others so as to set the facts straight. They may inadvertently go as far as endangering others and themselves. This *lose-lose* dynamic may be impossible to stop as long as it is not recognized for what it is.

Most of us will desperately continue to attempt to hide our bad intentions and actions and be and do good so as to be liked, loved and be seen as loveable and loving. In the world of duality (of good and bad), being good is *the escape* from our human wrongdoing. This wrongdoing is typically a version of having acted neglectfully according to the values we have internalized. The more cut-off we are from our inherent state of innocence, untouchable by what we do or don't do, the crasser our wrong-doing may become.

Being good in its multitude of versions (e.g. helpful, loving, selfless, generous, responsible, etc.) now becomes the accepted and desired personality ideal. It becomes the positive picture we are desperate to hold. We, in actuality, are now prone to become *do-gooders* out of fear of the dark opposite (hurtful, careless, selfish, stingy, irresponsible, etc.).

In the human world of duality good comes with bad. Therefore telling oneself *"I am a good person because I do good,"* or *"I am a good person and would have acted selfless if you only would have done such and such..."* comes with a hidden statement proclaiming the opposite.

The hidden statement will say: *"I don't really believe that I am a good person, so I have to prove that I am. I have to defend and justify my goodness. I have to get you to reaffirm me as good"...or at times, "I have to point out the bad in you so that by contrast it is obvious that I am good. Only then can I feel OK about myself."*

This is true even though there is much good that has come out of the actions of *do-gooders*. The universe has a way of even turning our hang-ups into a benefit.

Good is the glue that makes our harmonious living together possible.

All choices we make and the actions that flow from them have consequences. Our choices and actions produce consequences we like and therefore experience as good. Or, they produce consequences we don't like and therefore experience as bad. If we don't like the consequences we get, we have to re-examine the choices we made (thoughts, attitudes and actions).

Young children live in a black and white world of good and bad. Sadly, our parenting attitudes reinforce this thinking. Ideally, we would help them distinguish between good and bad actions apart from who they are. Our underlying essence of innocence and worth remains undisturbed no matter how much we fail as humans. Children need to be taught that good is preferable because its consequences support our harmonious living together. It makes life with others easier.

"Is he a good guy or a bad guy?," she asked the little boy clutching an action figure. "A good guy!," he replied without hesitation. "What do good guys do?," she asked. They fight the bad guys," he replied promptly. "Can bad guys ever be good?," she wanted to know. "No," he countered, "If you are bad, you are always bad!"

We are taught and raised to be good (selfless, kind, caring, honest, responsible, etc.). Only very few were taught as children that they are innocent in essence and that any judgment of good or bad belongs to their human interactions. Essence cannot be changed, behavior can!

We can learn to look beyond our own and others' human faults.

Original innocence is an eternal memory we carry at the deepest level of our psyche. Things become problematic when we attempt to bring this eternal version of innocence to our human lives. Lived out in the human realm of good and bad, it manifests itself for most people as an intense need to be good and right.

Our first reaction to any situation is typically to see our approach or ourselves as right and the other as wrong. We find plausible explanations and justified reasons for why we did what we did. To place fault on the other party becomes a form of approval seeking from others and us. *"I would never do, or think, such a thing,"* we declare.

When we accept our human faults we can learn to manage and look beyond the obvious. Our and their *bad* becomes nothing more then a distraction from seeing to the reality of who we and others are, *innocent in essence, all the while, possibly, quite faulty as humans.*

Needing to be Right Distorts Our Relationships

We look at our mates and our relationships and we find them lacking.

They lack patience, competence, passion, depth, meaning, sincerity, etc. the possibilities are endless. We are convinced it is they, not us, who are at fault! Little do we realize that our mind has the ability to throw its own unresolved anxieties, imbalances, fears, dashed hopes and unfulfilled dreams like a movie projector on a screen onto those around us. And others do the same with what they *assume to see* in us. We seldom question if we are right in what we see and assume.

We maintain that things can change by only changing *them,* ultimately by changing others. We all succumb to this notion at one time or another in our relationships. Our problematic issues follow us from relationship to relationship and continue to torture us as we receive *their effect from others.* This leads to accusing, attacking and blaming others. We are upset not just for the reasons that are apparent. The obvious cause of our upset feelings is just the tip of the iceberg.

We criticize our own unresolved issues in others.

Have you ever wondered why certain aspects in others' behavior are so irritating, while other shortcomings seem more amusing then anything? What are the things that you would find unacceptable in a mate? The answer, is the key to your own self-accusations, hang-ups and the taboos internalized or arrived at along the way.

The culprit is our internalized values and morals. We abide by them with a strange righteous seriousness. Human shortcomings become unforgivable sins. It is ingrained in us to respond from fear first. We have to teach ourselves to look at what disturbs us through the eyes of trust and love. Feeling right in our grievances or judgments creates separation. Maybe the other challenged one of our deepest values or touched one of our deepest hurts. In the end, we only ever forgive someone else for his or her human shortcoming. This part of them, and us, is their hurt part, their lost part, their immature part, the part that wasn't loved, accepted, or developed, the *shadow*.

And, since we know what we are looking for, we will always find it! We project our guilty feelings by finding something wrong so as to equalize things. Now, in comparison with their faults, ours don't look so black. We compensate by achieving and shining in one area so as to avoid looking at our failure and fear of risking in another. We explain and plead, placating, denying them the right to be angry or express their hurt.

Our defenses serve a double function. They are intended to convince others that seen rightly, we really are to be seen as good. They allow us to maintain an image of ourselves as a good person!

Loss of emotional connection is scary.

We are often aware of being able to physically feel a problem. It begins with a vague feeling of disconnection or a sense that something is wrong. Fear tempts us to withdraw. Righteousness tempts us to blame. Blaming our mate moves us into retaliating by doing the same or doing the opposite. If we experience the other as distant, we now either distance ourselves, or we attack or cling. What we typically don't do is identify *what we want* and take constructive actions towards it. Our thinking becomes preoccupied with *what we don't want.*

Once we have felt triggered, the simple and obvious, *ask for what you do want without blame,* appears impossible. Blaming our mate, we avoid looking at how threatening it feels to us for someone we love and depend on to distance himself from us. We avoid looking at the deeper connections and dynamics that now inhabit the present. Blaming allows us to feel justified in our attack or withdrawal. After all, *he/she* is distancing.

We avoid dealing with the other side of the experience that relates to us. If we truly picked up our cross and resolved the situation, first of all inside of ourselves, we would be faced with choices: admit to and resolve our unresolved feelings and fears, take action on our behalf, accept the limitations that exist, or leave.

In blaming we get to avoid and we get to stay even so (apparently) miserable. In blaming we avoid admitting to and exploring our vulnerabilities. We never transcend the surface level and therefore never find true relief. Yes, he/she may come around and pacify our feelings. However, true relief comes from a new sense of inner connection. Connection belongs to, is shared by and at the same time is independent of our mate.

Our partner may not sense the approaching tornado that is about to strike.

Men and women who are ill equipped to pick up on their partner's emotions won't sense when their partner feels alienated. They don't know how to meet their partner's emotional needs. So for them, until their mate says something, they stay oblivious.

Minimizing a problem is how many people deal with something uncomfortable. Ignore and avoid it and it will go away, they tell themselves! When their partner does raise the issue, they often feel annoyed and somehow guilty. The other ruined their happy day. They will blame their partner for making *a big deal over nothing.* Or, they feel reaffirmed in their low opinion of themselves as incapable mates. In their defensiveness they are tempted to feel right and justified either way.

In defending and finding wrong, we neglect the one thing that would have brought a solution: to be emotionally present to our partner. We neglect to simply inquire into their distress without taking our partners feelings or actions personal. This would reestablish the connection they and we seek. The resulting distance exasperates both of them. Both by-pass an opportunity to have the present be a place of healing instead of a reenactment of the past with its hurt.

Both partners whirling around in their own hurt lose their ability to see the others' "call for love".

Both want the same, to feel connected and loved, but the bridge between their two worlds seems impassable. Once we take on the blame that someone else may express towards us, we are lost.

Our essential *goodness* has been assaulted. We react and attack in self-defense.

To personalize and take on someone else's thoughts and feelings means to react to them as if they *were true*. We lose our awareness that what was expressed was most of all about the other person's unmet needs. We become caught in attempting to regain our sense of good by justifying, defending and blaming in response.

The effects can be measured as a physiological reaction in our body. All humans have remarkable blood pressure shifts that happen when they talk about something important. This is referred to as *"flooding"* by Dr. John Pittman, a psychologist at the University of Washington.

"...a psycho-physiological response which occurs in relationships where people express criticism and hostility, and refuse to engage emotionally. Flooding is primarily the rapid increase in heart rate by about 10 beats per minute. Some people experience such immediate severe flooding in response to emotional conflict that their heart accelerates 30 beats per minute in the space of a single heartbeat." (Dr. John Pittman)

"Engaging emotionally", means to be emotionally present.

We can only stay emotionally present when we don't perceive another's viewpoint or actions as a threat. This requires a firm belief in our underlying worth, invulnerability and innocence separate from our potential human fallibility. It allows us to inquire into someone else's thoughts, feelings and intentions and for the moment suspend our personal response to them. This is about what they think they need and want, not necessarily us. It requires the ability to listen underneath what is being said, for the *"call for love"* voiced by the other, no matter what twisted form it may take.

Next time try the following:

- Take a breath; Imagine putting an invisible energetic protective shield around yourself;
- Regard their complaints and attacks as a *"red herring"* attempting to distract you from what is really important;

- As you listen to their complaints or attacks try to listen for what they are asking you for underneath;
- Acknowledge what is being said, most of all, the underlying good intentions and/or concerns being voiced;
- Find a joint problem-solving step.

Trust into our own (and others') goodness and capabilities are an act of choice.

A choice we may have to make minute by minute. We can only make this choice if we are willing to level the playing field. We have to open our mind to the possibility that we are subject to human shortcomings as much as they are. This requires that we see them as *good in essence and deserving of a second chance*. Forgiveness of others failings requires a letting go of our righteousness. Forgiveness, however, does not necessarily mean we open ourselves to ongoing abuse. As long as they or we are caught up in our hang-ups hurtful behavior is inevitable. We relate to each other through our hang-ups as long as we have limited awareness of our inner life. Caught in our hang-ups our perspective remains self-absorbed. We are all subject to the dynamics of that law.

It is in our most intimate relationships that we are capable of reliving our deepest hurts. Healing and change has to take place inside of us first. Our and others actions will either strengthen the relationship or weaken it. People will be people. We can ask in this very moment for *what we want* instead of fretting over how they have failed and *what we don't want.* If we want something new and different we have to deal with what confronts us today in a new way. It is the only way to learn that we are bigger then our hurt.

Righteousness Turns Mistakes into Sins

We have been taught to see and judge our mistakes as sins.

Sins can only be corrected by someone else's forgiveness or God's forgiveness. Neither of those can we ever be totally sure of nor do we have any power over. This makes us dependent on others. And, if God is a father figure up in the sky, separate from us, we are dependent on God's mercy.

Sins ask for punishment. On the other hand, if we look at errors as mistakes instead of sins, they become an integral part of any learning process. We become capable of forgiving ourselves and in turn, we become capable of forgiving others. Mistakes now ask for correction instead of punishment, rejection, self-loathing and eternal condemnation.

When we don't learn from our mistakes there is a reason. Repeated mistakes are a hidden call to become more aware of the roots underlying our actions. Ultimately, they force us to develop a higher degree of self-awareness and self-love. When we do learn from our mistakes, we grow in maturity.

As children we learn to disown negative (bad) feelings, thoughts, intentions and actions. In doing so we reject one half of an interconnected energy. Now we are good, not out of choice, but out of fear. We learn that love is conditional. We are loved when we are good and punished, rejected and judged when we are bad. We learn to reject, judge and deny half of our and other people's human experience. Their and our bad behavior proves them and us as *unworthy!*

As humans we are all guilty and fallible, only the times and the degree will vary.

As I was taught in Catholic school "Forgive me, Lord, for I am a sinner!" The original Greek meaning of the word sin is *"to miss the mark"*, *"to miss the target"* (Greek: *"hamartia"*).

In the Aramaic Language and culture the term *hamartia* was an archery term. When the archer shot at the target and missed, whoever was keeping score then yelled the Aramaic word for sin. It meant, *"to fall short or miss".*

This correlates to losing ourselves in a fear-based perception of life. When we respond from love our energy extends and embraces, we are on track. We hit the goal and we are in alignment with our deeper nature. As a result, we feel quite tolerant of others' and our own shortcomings. We are in actuality beyond forgiveness...there is nothing to forgive since we don't perceive a sin.

Getting caught up in a fear-based perception of life is our human state of affairs most of the time. We have to choose daily and often minute-by-minute to either come from love-based extension or a fear-based protection. We have to reinvent ourselves: *"Who do I want to be in this situation?"* Of course, this requires awareness of our habitual emotional responses. We have to resist to succumbing to the lure of self-pity and feeling unjustly treated.

We have a right to be loved for who we are.

We begin to grow-up and mature when we learn what produces the consequences *we want*. Learning by trial and error produces a slow learning curve. We can speed up the process by consciously choosing relationship building actions and attitudes. This teaches us to meet others on common ground; instead of insisting they ought to see life through the perspective of our eyes. These lessons cannot be *forced* upon us. We have to arrive with our will intact. We draw a battle line, setting up the struggles in relationships that we experience, when we say *Not Me!* Now our dark wishes, unacceptable actions and intentions are denied and projected. This may offer us temporary protection, however, we become subject to the same measure of the judgment we met out.

The kindergarten teacher had a grave look on her face. She caught her son lying she told the mother. Her son had taken another child's toy and claimed it as his own she went on. When she confronted him, he insisted that it was his. It was clear by her demeanor that she regarded this matter as very serious.

When we are young, what appears unacceptable to our parents, authority figures and society becomes unacceptable to us. We become socialized according to the values of the particular family and society we live in. This socialization is aimed at producing harmonious community living.

Our society holds honesty as a supreme value. Dishonesty is seen as something bad and potentially dangerous. Whenever we are *found out* to be dishonest our need for connection, belonging, love and approval is threatened. This leaves us three options: 1) deny being dishonest and claim *only* to be honest, or 2) admit the dishonesty and identify with being *bad and a liar*, or 3) recognize the lie as a mistake, correct it and learn from it.

When we judge, we lose our ability to be kind.

We feel righteous. We attack, or flee, or deny. Human faults become more than a human shortcoming. They become a *sin* and now deserve punishment. We begin to withhold energetically from people. They are not to be trusted and they are not loveable. This process is for the most part unconscious. We are only aware of our surface feelings of upset with others.

We may find ourselves (for example) lying about the most insignificant things. We may have others in our life that we discover as liars. Others now are the mirrors of what we believe but have denied. This may be very upsetting and puzzling. We may feel bewildered by the repetition of the same patterns in our life. *"Why does this always happen to me? Why do I end up with people who don't stand up for me; lie to me; are not there when I need them the most; etc.?"*

It is hard for us to recognize that there is a *blueprint* underlying what we experience today. We do not readily recognize that we are caught in the interplay of opposites.

Our inner life is very preservation minded. It will recycle experiences until we have learned to eliminate the *useless* and assimilate the *useful.* The answer only appears to be in the others' change. *In truth, we hold the key in our own hands.*

Children need to hear that they are worthy of love.

Children need to be taught about values and what is socially appropriate. But most of all, they need to learn that their *essential goodness* is never in question! When we overreact to young children's unacceptable social behavior we, in effect, inadvertently intensify what we don't want.

Different then the kindergarten teacher, the mother didn't doubt her son's "goodness". Once they arrived home, she took him into her arms and gently inquired into what had happened. Tearfully her son admitted that he had taken his friend's toy. He had wanted a toy like his friend's for a long time, he sobbed. The mother went over the right and wrong of his behavior. She laid out ways how he could get the toy he wanted. She maintained a caring attitude and asked him what he thought he could do to correct his mistake.

"I could say 'I am sorry' and let my friend play with one of my action figures tomorrow," he said. "I know he has wanted to play with them for a while," he added eagerly. "And, what about your teacher?," the mother inquired. "I will tell her that I am sorry that I lied to her," came the quick and resolute response. The mother smiled.

Disowning our bad so as to be loved, leads to becoming rigid, fundamental and closed-minded.

Obviously, to be totally truthful in every situation is an improbability, especially at a young age. Our degree of honesty always rests on our degree of awareness and maturity. Young children tend to take on their families' (and authorities') values and morals unexamined.

What is denied isn't any longer available to our conscious mind to mediate and therefore is outside our conscious control. We now meet our own denied self in our experience of other people and their dishonesty (their lack of support; their betrayal; etc.). Total honesty and total dishonesty (supportive-unsupportive; loyalty-betrayal; being there-unreliable; etc.) are the two extremes of a spectrum of possible human experience that has become limited, not by choice, but by hurt, fear and judgment. With it we disconnect from others and ourselves in subtle and not so subtle ways, feeling righteous.

We have lost sight of our essence and confused innocence with being good. Innocence becomes attached to the human experience of total honesty (etc.), instead of remaining independent of it. The very thing we hoped to avoid, lack of acceptance and alienation by dis-identifying with being dishonest (etc.), has come true in reverse. We now feel disconnected and alienated from a part of ourselves and from that part in others. *"I am never dishonest (unsupportive, disloyal, unreliable)," we claim.*

All families communicate with unspoken rules.

"You hurt my feelings," the girl accused her classmate. Her classmate had countered the girl's exaggerated account of her recent horseback-riding lesson. The girl, who took riding lessons at the same barn as her classmate, had attempted to impress her friends. They stood surrounded by a group of youngsters. She had felt a bit jealous of her classmate's more advanced skills. Having her classmate counter her claims made her feel unmasked and competitive. Accusing her classmate of hurting her feelings was a way of leveling the playing field.

One (unspoken) rule in many families is: *don't talk about what you truly think and feel.* Developing the awareness of what we feel and learning to voice one's feelings are essential skills. Yet, at times, we are taught that others can hurt our feelings without discrimination as to where our responsibility for our feelings lies. *"You hurt my feelings,"* becomes a weapon. It is used to manipulate and control. It communicates: *"You are bad!"*

We unabashedly put the blame on someone else.

Due to our tendency to look for solutions to our emotional life outside (in others' change), this tool (voicing when we feel hurt) can become misused to shirk responsibility for us. Now our feelings are seen as dependent on and at the mercy of others' actions and intentions. We can learn to hide behind, *"You hurt my feelings!"* Others now carry the responsibility for our upset.

It becomes their *job* to act in a way so that we don't have to feel what makes us uncomfortable: *feelings of unimportant, not special, or inferior.* This gives a power and responsibility to others that they do not have. It supports us in hiding from what is really going on. It allows us to feel righteous about blaming them for the uncomfortable feelings we have.

Yet, it is a knife that cuts both ways. We too, now become responsible for others' emotional experience. This may move us to be overly careful and instead of hurting others, we begin to hurt ourselves. We sacrifice and deny what we truly want. We may enter a prison of self-denial that is self-created and unnecessary!

Our actions become based in a strange sense of love entwined with sacrifice. Our intention is to love and to not hurt others. It becomes hard for us to see that our actions aren't truly based in love. Love, by it's very nature, is always inclusive and therefore by definition can't leave anyone out, *not even us.* No one truly has the power of hurting another's feelings once they have passed their formative years.

We may carry the salt for their old wound. The original wound was put there long before we ever had a chance to rub some salt in it. Preexisting wounds are an outcome of our past experiences mostly during our formative years. All of us carry these preexisting wounds, which ideally would make us compassionate and kind. The golden rule: *"Do onto others as you would want to have done onto you,"* advises us to be caring with these preexisting wounds, not careful and overly responsible.

Others don't truly have the power to hurt us emotionally.

Initially we may find it difficult to accept this fact. As in most things, it is not what we say, it is our motivation behind our words that tells us what our true intention is. If our intention is to hurt, no matter what words we use, we are responsible. As adults, we are quite invulnerable to being hurt emotionally if we don't carry any pre-existing wounds.

Take yourself through the following mental exercise.

- Think of something that you feel very sure of as being good at...(cooking, teaching, being a kind person, having beautiful hair, etc.).
- Notice your feelings about this something, your body sense and past experiences.
- Now think of something that you don't feel so sure about or actually feel that you surely need improvement on, or that you lack in...?
- Again notice your feelings, body sense and past experiences.
- Now imagine that your spouse/partner or best friend accuses you of not being good at what you feel certain about (your first attribute or skill). What is your inner reaction? You may enlist the help of a friend if *imagining* doesn't work for you.
- Next, imagine this same person accusing you of what you already feel doubtful about (your second attribute or skill). What is your reaction?

Typically, your reaction to the first situation will be one of disbelief, laughing it off...like water off a duck's back. In contrast, your second reaction will be one of defense or guilty acknowledgment, feeling hurt, etc.

This simple exercise demonstrates that we are vulnerable on issues where we already carry wounds...on issues where we hold judgment, shame and guilt towards ourselves. We are rather unaffected by accusations that we clearly recognize as unsubstantiated. (If you find you have a reaction to your first attribute that is akin to your second reaction, you may not be as sure of yourself on this topic as you thought! Try again with a different attribute!).

Our body is subject to physical laws. Its needs must be taken care of from the outside. It is subject to the environment. Our emotional life is much more self-sufficient. We can survive and flourish without others' approval and love as adults. What makes us vulnerable emotionally are *our self-accusations.*

This is in stark contradiction to what we may have been taught, believe and our society and mass media reflect back to us constantly. We are told that our happiness is dependent on and comes from someone or something other then ourselves. What is true for our physical well-being becomes assumed as true for our emotional happiness.

We haven't been taught that our innermost state of worth and innocence is untouchable.

The experience of innocence and essential worth belongs to a different level of our being that remains unaffected by our human errors. Here is where the problem arises. Well indoctrinated, we believe that we have the power to annul our inner state of innocence and worth with our human wrongdoing.

Being good and doing good has become an entry fee into heaven! We have missed the point that being good and doing good leads to amicable human relationships and as such have value and consequences for our human lives.

As adults the choice is ours: get lost in the world of duality of good and bad or listen to the voice of innocence, undisturbed by what we (or others) did or didn't do. The human world of duality is the world of good and evil, reward and punishment, a world ruled by physical laws. Internalized, our own psyche complies. Therefore we might feel bewildered when life doesn't punish the bad people we come across or when bad things happen to good people.

Admitting to our mistakes allows for the possibility of change. The duality dynamic of reward and punishment leads us into the maze of justification, righteousness, projection, denial and a multitude of other defenses. These are all geared towards maintaining that we are innocent and good as human beings.

Instead, we could claim our innocence and worth as a pre-existing and unalterable inner state of being. This would allow us to acknowledge and correct the faults and wrongdoing of our human existence.

Like an ocean, it may be storming at the surface, but the water at the bottom remains calm. This calm is equal to the state of our inner innocence. No matter what storm is blowing through on the surface, no matter what our wrongdoings, this state is unalterable. Admitting to our mistakes makes us *human and fallible*. As such, it makes us more approachable. It can be done with humor!

We Become Defensive When Others Challenge the Good Picture We Hold About Ourselves

Our defenses buy us time.

Have you ever noticed that the very moment that you find yourself losing your compassionate view of others, you become what you just saw them as and accused them of?

You see them as rejecting and instinctively move to emotionally withdraw from them. You see them as controlling and instinctively begin to control their controlling ways. You see them as judgmental and find yourself judging them for judging, etc.

If we truly would let ourselves see this dynamic, of course, there go any illusions about ourselves being *above* their ways. We blame, criticize, defend, attack, avoid, deny, procrastinate, minimize, exaggerate, justify, rationalize, etc. As human beings, we have a profound need to be seen as innocent and good.

We constantly strive to achieve this in our human relationships. To be liked and approved of, if not by others, then definitely by ourselves is very important to us.

The weaker our sense of self-worth, the more defenses we need and the less aware we are when we are employing them. These defense mechanisms are predictable. They are set on automatic. It is their job to respond instinctively to anything that presents a threat to our sense of self-worth. This is not altogether bad. It is our most comfortable way of dealing with what we experience as threatening in the best way we know how. We all do this to some degree or another.

Defenses allow us to maintain a positive opinion of ourselves.

"I am going to mop the kitchen floors, she announced." "Why don't you just sit down and relax," her husband voiced, "...the floors can wait!" "Do them tomorrow," looking up from reading his sailing magazine. She felt annoyed.

They had arguments about similar incidents before. It was difficult for her to make her point since his comment looked like kindness. "He is obviously uncomfortable to watch me work while he is relaxing," she concluded, "but why was his behavior so annoying to her?"

Our psyche has developed countless ways of screening out those things we cannot comfortably tolerate or handle at the moment. Defenses allow us to maintain a positive opinion of ourselves and fend off a threat temporarily. Everyone, no matter how mature will, at times, resort to using defenses.

The trick lies in not feeling right about them but learning to question the need for them. This requires recognizing and admitting personal shortcomings and failure. To do so goes against our human need to be seen as or see ourselves as *good.*

For most people seeing their wrongdoing triggers a deluge of self-reproach and fear. We each tend to develop our own unique set of defenses, to be counted on in all emergencies. Like an operator in a 911 call, they always answer. They are functioning seemingly beyond our conscious control.

The defenses we use are our old way of dealing with our inner, as well as, our interpersonal conflicts. They were put in place to protect us from an originally existing threat to our need to be loved, loving and loveable. The threat has long gone but the protection mechanism is still in operation.

This protection mechanism is now being triggered by circumstances that have the slightest familiarity to the original threat. We continue to fight an old battle with new people.

We find explanations that are socially and personally acceptable to us.

When we explain, justify and rationalize, we attempt to convince others and ourselves. Our body may give us signals that *all is not in order.* We may notice our voice shake ever so slightly, a sinking feeling or *butterflies* in our stomach, our heart beating heavily, or a very subtle *zing* inside our chest.

People who become skilled at reading their own and others' body language are able to unmask themselves. Unmasking ourselves is safe to the degree that we are capable of abstaining from self-loathing. *Who would want to become more aware if the consequence is more self-judgment?*

Unmasking others, besides never truly being our right or responsibility, remains difficult. *They do not know what they do not know* which is the very essence of denial. As such, we won't be able to convince someone else of something they won't be convinced of even if it would be in everyone's best interest.

We typically only see what is right in front of our nose and are quite unaware of any deeper connections to our behavior. This lack of awareness keeps us oblivious about the true motivation or deeper connection for our feelings and actions. It leads us towards finding a socially and personally acceptable explanation for our behavior.

Justifications allow us to avoid.

We avoid having to stand in the fire of someone else's expectations, or anger, or disappointment. Having to make the choice of risking what is known and safe for what is uncertain or scary seldom seems an exciting choice. Informing others of our intentions and then facing the possible repercussions is rather uninviting as well. Facing our limits and failures can be disheartening. Drawing conclusions and consequences that may bring an initial form of loss is scary.

The problem with the unconscious or half-conscious use of defense mechanisms is that they set up a whole new set of problems and uncomfortable situations. Instead of having to deal with version "A", we now have to deal with version "B". The avoidance doesn't really work.

To salvage the relationship or follow what is true for us, we now have to either take responsibility or indulge in further and further justifications and possibly lies. Justifications and rationalizations are very common. They also are commonly accepted. It is often difficult to know if we are justifying and rationalizing or simply stating a fact about our thoughts and feelings.

People always find a reason to support their actions.

They feel right and justified by their reasoning. We may or may not agree with them. If we look deep enough, we can identify with their underlying motivating sense of vulnerability. Finding this identification, or sameness, allows for saying *"Me too! I have felt like that at one time, or done like that, or wanted to do like that."*

We tend to think that not acting on our angry, selfish, or hurtful thoughts makes us innocent in comparison to someone who did. A long time ago Christ challenged the villagers who were about to stone the prostitute for her wrongdoing. He challenged them on their thoughts, their hidden desires and intentions. An imperfect human isn't truly qualified to judge imperfection. As human beings we will fail no matter how high our aspirations and good intentions.

Next time you find yourself incredulous with another, ask yourself:

- Have I ever…(accusation you hold)?
- If I knew, what this other person is afraid of underneath their behavior it would be…?
- Have I ever been afraid like that?
- What do I get out of seeing them as wrong and myself as right?

Maturity is a process that unifies our inner ideal with the reality of the very human being we are.

Self-acceptance, the acceptance of our good and bad, is the foundation of maturity. The moment we accept what was until now rejected, we move beyond resistance. What we resist persists but what we accept can change.

In reality, any divisions mentally injected are artificial. Night comes with day and what we might regard as a positive attribute comes with its counterpart. This counterpart tends to stare back at us wearing the faces of people close to us. Let's look at the energy of giving and receiving for a moment. In reality, whenever we give we as well receive. This is best seen in very young children. When they receive a present, their very act of receiving is so genuine and exuberant that the giver receives simultaneously.

She continued mopping the floors. He sat there for a moment holding his magazine. He could sense that she felt irritated. His first reaction was one of defense. It took him a moment to inquire into why he felt the way he did and not focus on her reaction. He had been raised to be courteous, helpful and demonstrate good manners...To read his magazine while she was working made him feel selfish.

It is not our failure that becomes our prison but the judgment that we place on ourselves because of our failure.

As a result, we employ defenses to hide our failure. These defenses now become our biggest limitation. This self-judging attitude is that much more insidious if we were raised with it. After all, failure is part of an on-going learning process ultimately leading to success. *Only when failure and success are seen as separate from each other and in opposition, do we become afraid of failure.*

Maturity is an outcome of growing in our sense of love and approval for us. Self-approval would be ironic if it could only hold our positive character traits. By definition, it is the aspects of self that we have judged and attempt to hide that need our acceptance the most. This prepares us to deal with disapproval from important others. Accepting ourselves the way we are, *human*, with all our failings without turning away in disgust or on ourselves with criticism is a big task. Once we accept what we regard as negative, we acquire the power to moderate and choose.

Our fear is that accepting the bad will mean we will become the bad. In actuality, it helps us to find the balance point between the extremes that hereto existed, for example: selfish and selfless, leading to a *clear sense of self.*

Painful experiences stay unresolved as long as they are seen as isolated.

When the concept that we can, for example, give without receiving is accepted as true, we might experience ourselves as deprived. We might experience other people as taking and/or giving becomes conditional. If we become afraid of being selfish we get caught in needing to be selfless.

Experiences that are in essence connected are seen and dealt with as separate. Whenever underlying essence energy becomes split or crystallizes into opposites, we experience strain and struggle. We employ defenses to ward off the pain. We can choose to step away from the *tango* with these opposites.

Let me illustrate the above by using an example that carries a double negative: Let's say that you have felt betrayed by a friend. You feel victimized and right in your feelings of having been unjustly treated.

Let's say as well, that you very vaguely remember betraying your sister when you were young. At the time, you felt a deep sense of guilt and equally right in your feelings of being bad.

As long as we stay with the feeling of being a victim in the present, we swirl around in never-ending circles of pain. As long as we remember and stay with the feelings of being a victimizer, we swirl around (as well) in never-ending circles of self-reproach. Both experiences by themselves may seem irresolvable, as long as they are seen as isolated from each other. When we finally recognize that both experiences are at the opposite ends of the core experience of *betrayal and that we are capable of both or have experienced both* something new can happen.

Once we recognize that if there is one there is the other and learn to hold ourselves without judgment (feeling what both experiences inside of us feel like), forgiveness of our and others' humanity becomes easy. In a way, we step beyond forgiveness. When we emotionally hold both experiences simultaneously something inside begins to heal and *whole.* We grow in understanding, compassion and maturity.

In others' love we find reassurance of our own worth.

We turn to our parents not just for our physical survival but also for our emotional needs, our emotional survival. This search for approval and love becomes transferred to extended family, friends and the outer world in general and eventually to ourselves. This leads to us being heavily invested in presenting a picture of ourselves as innocent, good and likeable. We move to defend and ascertain this picture constantly. The investment into this picture for some of us runs so deep that we feel very threatened by anyone or anything that appears to question or challenge it. It is time to grow thicker skin. It is time to question the underlying assumption of vulnerability we carry and let go of our investment that others will see us favorably. What they think of us truly is none of our business. Others will see us through their hang-ups, fears and needs. Those who can see will see.

Learning to become less defensive:

- Learn to not personalize (take on) what others are saying. Once you have made this space you can take a look at what connections exist. How are you accusing (judging, etc.) yourself in the same fashion? What vulnerabilities do you carry?
- Learn to set your own thoughts and feelings aside for the moment and listen. Inquire into what the other is attempting to say…"You feel that…" or "You think that…" "Tell me more…" What they are saying (no matter how it is voiced) is about them, first.
- Learn to ask questions and take a break. "Are you saying that I am…"? "Let me think on that!"
- Learn to agree and make it funny. "You are right, I am such a…runs in the family, etc."

To say it with Goethe, "*Once your reputation is ruined, life becomes very easy.*"

When We See Ourselves as Wrong and the Other as Right

Low self-esteem and false humility often dictates a distorted view of us as wrong and others as right and superior. When our upbringing was filled with shame and guilt, we can never be quite *good enough.* In a way, we become righteous about being wrong and less.

Jesus challenged his followers to put their light not under the chair but on top of it. Our upbringing or experiences may have taught us otherwise and deprived us of a healthy sense of pride in ourselves. Healthy pride, sometimes, is confused with selfishness. Self-depreciation is held up as the right way to be. It is confused with a true understanding and experience of humility. It lacks the recognition of the inherent equality between all people. This is recognition of our place in the wheel of life. We may be a spoke but we are not the wheel. It in turn leads to being humble. This is different from minimizing our talents and actions.

In our midst you may find some of the most loving and good and giving and educated and successful people you have ever met. The problem is, when "*bound by shame*" (Bradshaw, 1988), our own *self-esteem bucket won't have a bottom.* No matter how much is poured into it by others or us, it never fills. Families and communities who value and promote self-worth set the stage for healthy actions and relationships.

Virginia Satir writes: *"...appropriate and loving behavior stem from persons who have strong feelings of self-worth...persons who love and value themselves are able to love and value others."*

When we lack self-worth due to how we were raised or the experiences we had, we lack the power to believe in ourselves. We become prone to compensations. We both *act it out* and *project it out.* We act in the same hurtful fashion towards others as we received, or end up in endless repetitions of victimizing ourselves.

Shame leads to hiding.

"Shame is a sickness of the soul. It is the most poignant experience of the self by the self, whether felt in humiliation or cowardice, or in a sense of failure to cope successfully with a challenge. Shame is a wound felt from the inside, dividing us both from ourselves and from one another." Kaufman, 1996

One of the causes of low self-esteem is unresolved shame. This shame goes beyond a temporary intervention by our psyche encouraging us to ethical living. It corrupts our sense of ourselves as deserving. We begin to hide who we think we are. We struggle with valuing our talents and contributions.

There are times when it is wise to temporarily hide our inner feelings. There are times when we need to delay making our thoughts and feelings public. And, there are times when we need to carefully choose the public we express and show our true thoughts and feelings to. When hiding goes beyond an appropriate response in the moment, it loses its function as a temporary protection and a deliberate choice.

If children are shamed for whom they are, what they feel and think, their body functions or what they have done, they are left with feeling *flawed, defective and unworthy of love*. If we, as children, are left to our own devices when dealing with sexual abuse, discrimination and a perception of ourselves as *odd, different and stupid* we learn to hide.

Being ashamed of *"who we think we are", we* attempt to become *"who we think we should be*" (Foster, 1993). When guidance, understanding and acceptance of age-appropriate and developmentally appropriate behavior is lacking, we learn to *cry silently and by ourselves.*

We feel weak and confused because we don't understand why we feel the way we do. We don't understand our feelings because we haven't learned to name the feelings we are experiencing and put our actions into perspective. From parental acceptance flows self-acceptance. Self-acceptance is an all-important building block for high self-esteem.

There is another choice.

We can talk it out and feel it out resolving our inner pain. Otherwise, consciously or unconsciously, we will fight to protect our own self-image. In this struggle things can get very weird.

People who seem to look through our defenses scare us. And, at the same time, to expose what we are so desperate to hide is exactly what will set us free. To be loved and approved of for who we truly are, faults and all, is what we crave deep inside. Someone who will look with love at what we feel we have to hide so desperately becomes a stepping-stone to finding inner acceptance, approval, forgiveness and love.

Self-exposure in a safe environment is what we need, is what can and will eventually set us free...if only we dared. Until then, we live in a self-imposed prison.

When we lack self-worth:

- We have a low opinion of our abilities or appearance;
- We lack initiative and are unwilling to risk;
- We undercut and sabotage our own efforts and accomplishments;
- We are our own worst critic;
- We find it difficult to feel good about ourselves;
- We find it difficult to decide on our own what is right for us;
- We find it difficult to take action on our own behalf.

Shame generates a deep sense of sadness.

It happened at a neighbor's party. He was five years old. His parents like many others of the neighbors had gathered at the party to celebrate the 4th of July. His best friend's dad had asked him to sit on his lap. Everyone was gathered around, chatting, laughing and toasting the occasion. His friend's father secretly began to fondle him. He just sat there, frozen, not knowing what to do. He looked for his mom and dad who were oblivious to what was going on.

Eventually he struggled to free himself. Everyone around laughed and his mother scolded him for being so unfriendly. He felt strangely alienated from his parents after that experience and terribly confused about his feelings.

Shame cries, *"It must be my fault!"* It cuts us off from the love around us but most importantly it cuts us off from our love for ourselves. It throws us into a vicious cycle of self-blame justified and reasonable or not. *"There is something wrong with me,"* the refrain in our head goes. We live with an ocean of sadness inside. No matter what we achieve, we feel right in our low opinion of ourselves.

We feel bad, worthless and stupid.

No one likes to admit to feeling this way. Besides, it would feel like emotional suicide to admit to doing so publicly. In our society to be strong, efficient and smart are held as prime attributes. *So we don't talk about it, we hide, pretend and fake it.* Actors sometimes wear masks to hide their real identities and show the audience only what the actor wants them to see. Like players on stage, we are all actors with *our own special masks* pretending to be someone we are not, except, we can't fool ourselves.

Deep inside we know all of this is false. And since we can't trust ourselves, we don't trust others overtures of kindness or our own accomplishments. No matter how high our IQ, our intelligence fails us mysteriously. When things go well, we can stand it only for so long. Masters of self-sabotage, we always succeed in making a mess of things somehow. We are compelled to compensate, to become good, smart and worthwhile or drown our inner life in alcohol, drugs, crime and abusiveness.

Denied qualities remain undeveloped.

Our conscious mind will protect us from something that is uncomfortable, scary, or unresolved through denial. *We don't know that we don't know*, such is the function of denial. Truth exists on many levels of the self. When we become afraid that our perceived human failing is all that we are, we shift into denial.

A young child does not have the maturity or resources to recognize the truth existing on the deepest level of self and therefore will use denial as a protection. Denied qualities become arrested without further maturation. Their integration stops at the level of development when the split occurred.

We learn to compensate by shining in one area so as to hide the dark side. The better we become, the more our ego raises its standards. Our expectations on ourselves constantly increase. We try to stay ahead of the feeling of emptiness and phoniness inside. *There is no rest for the wicked!* We become the ones who rescue and help others without asking anything in return. Or is that true? Without words and without a voice we do ask in return. We ask to be seen as good, to be approved of and to be seen as worthwhile.

Just because something has been denied doesn't mean it is truly gone. It simply has been relegated to a different level of our psyche and now works from the *underground*. Our conscious mind has forgotten.

Changing our thinking (different from past conclusions or how our parents thought) means making something truly our own. Resolving old (hurt) feelings sets us free to find a new way of dealing with something in the present. Recognizing old fears and their lack of power over us now leads to realizing that we are capable of handling things differently.

Denied aspects and experiences influence us unknowingly.

They surround and in effect hide the deeper truth of who we are and who others are. These are qualities that are in glaring contrast to our personality ideals, values and wishful efforts. These are the qualities that we find hardest to deal with in others. *Ask yourself what are the things that you find totally unacceptable in a mate?*

Let's assume (as an example) that it is being dishonest. Being in denial about one's dishonesty (obvious or covert) and to be honest at all cost has a cost all itself. Honesty without wisdom and social moderations is a cutting knife. It too will alienate us from others just as dishonesty will.

Our social interactions demand many white lies and niceties to get along. Cultures like Japan, where people live in very close quarters, show a very high degree of social adjustments like omissions, politeness and evasiveness.

Self-awareness becomes misused as a new self-defeating tool.

Maybe when we were little the judges and critics were on the outside but now they live inside our own mind. None is harder on ourselves than we are. The self-judgment and criticism is constant. Being dished out from us to ourselves there is no hiding from it. We seldom doubt the truth of those evaluations. For some reason, we never question the messages we give to ourselves. Following an old habit, we now use our self-insights to belittle ourselves. They turn into a new self-defeating tool.

Self-judgment is an anesthetic that doesn't just numb the bad but also alienates us from the good.

Whom we might find underneath all the hiding and pretenses and avoidance may come as a surprise. Mastery becomes self-exposure for one's own sake. We move beyond any attempts to create an illusion of safety by sharing secrets with selected others.

Emotional safety truly rests on the inside and not with others. And there is only one way to discover if this is true and that is to do it! Then the realization slowly dawns that there is no reason to feel this ashamed and isolated. The world doesn't come to an early end. We stop turning away from parts of ourselves.

We each live the human dilemma of good and bad, right and wrong in our individual versions.

To develop self-awareness and eventually find a new level of connection to all of life and existence is our human story. Along the way we encounter experiences of shame, guilt, abandonment, betrayal, abuse and a multitude of other human experiences. These experiences prompt us to interpret who we are in relation to them. The conclusions we draw and the emotional experiences we have are our *personal ground zero.* They determine our individual *contraction, our individual distortion of reality.*

Self-awareness then is a double-edged knife, it brings us consciousness of our individuality and it can be used to create separation within and without. As we doubt our deeper innocence and connection, we lose our awareness of both. We become *survivors* attempting to cope the best we know how.

As we step beyond instinct we become governed by conscious choice. A curse and a blessing, choice brings us freedom and it brings consequences that we often do not like. We can take responsibility or we can feel righteous and blame others or life. We have become subject to the duality of life. Some of us cope better than others.

Rebuilding our connections and regaining our underlying innocence while overcoming our human shortcomings consciously is our human story.

We expect others to think, feel and do as we would.

Fooled, Tricked and Otherwise Blind

It profoundly unsettles us when others don't think, feel, want or do as we would.

"If you loved (valued, respected, etc.) me, you would want what I want or do what I do," we accuse. What brought us together was the assumption that they shared our world. We assumed that they looked at life the way we did and valued what was important to us. This assumption triggered a deep feeling of connection, belonging and security. Somewhere deep inside the recesses of our psyche, we remember a world without differences and separation. The memory of this world of *oneness* and *sameness* is triggered for most people in their intimate relationships. When we eventually get rudely awoken to the fact that *they* think, feel, do and want differently,

we feel disillusioned, hurt, profoundly unsettled, even tricked and betrayed.

"Why is this so?" An infant is born in a state of preconscious *at-oneness* with all of life. As we grow into adults, we go through necessary (and unnecessary) individuation steps. Yet, we still vaguely sense this original *at-oneness,* which is experienced as connection, security and love. The problems begin when we attempt to re-create an experience that is a natural part of infancy in our adult relationships. We neglect to find its adult version.

Being different and in opposition sends shivers down our spine.

When differences begin to surface we experience them as a threat. Something very essential is being challenged. It just feels wrong. Something inside says, it is supposed to be otherwise. We experience *different and separate* as painful and foreign. We feel sad and mad. *"How and why did this happen?"* Unknowingly, our emotional equilibrium has become dependent on *the emotional home* we thought we had found. We ignore the fact that connection, love and security are part of our deeper inner state of being. They only fleetingly enter our human state of affairs. We cannot permanently find them *in another* but only by *relating to another.* They are an inner quest once we have become adults.

The adult version of at-oneness is an experience of oneness. Our deepest reality is a state of oneness with all of existence as we have been told over and over again by wise men and women through the ages. Everyday life becomes magical when it briefly provides us with the experience of *oneness.* These experiences are a reminder of what is our birthright. We can learn to cherish the moments and begin to string more and more of them together by living a more conscious life.

Falling in love gives us the feeling of having found the meaning of life.

When we fall in love, we catch a glimpse of our possible future state of oneness. However, we are equally tempted to confuse our experience with our original state of at-oneness. This confusion prompts us to lose our separate sense of self, assuming sameness instead of finding unity.

The experience of falling in love can be truly profound. It often stands in stark contrast to our every-day life with all its struggles, obligations and drudgery. For moments, days, months and (for a lucky few) years, we experience a new sense of completion with this other person. Falling in love catapults us high above the ordinariness and meaninglessness of the life we may have lived. We may feel as if we have finally found what gives our life purpose when we are with this other person. We glimpse a sense of wholeness unknown before.

Once again we are everything in potential...in their presence we feel unlimited and touched by the eternal. *"I will feel like this forever,"* we assume. We have found an emotional home that now is ours. Many myths, fairy tales and religions describe a similar state of paradise. They speak of a state of bliss and unconditional love that is our birthright. One day, it will be ours again, we are promised.

Her husband and two teenage children had left for a trip a day ago. She was looking forward to the free time...when he came knocking on her door. He was handsome, world-traveled, kind and helpful. He represented the dreams she once had but hadn't lived. What happened next neither planned...they fell in love.

We, as a society, are thoroughly confused between falling in love and "true love".

Writes Robert Johnson in his book *WE, Understanding the Psychology of Romantic Love:*

"Romantic love is the single greatest energy system in the Western psyche. In our culture it has supplanted religion as the arena in which men and women seek meaning, transcendence, wholeness and ecstasy.

As a mass phenomenon, romantic love is peculiar to the West. We are so accustomed to living with the beliefs and assumptions of romantic love that we think it is the only form of "love" on which marriage or love relation can be based. We think it is the only "true love".

When we listen to songs on the radio or watch the latest popular movie, it becomes obvious how our society idealizes *falling in love*. This leaves us ill prepared for the challenges and reality of our present day human relationships...the differences and struggles we are going to inevitably encounter. It neglects to warn us of the temptation to confuse the intensity and loss of separation we experience with our yearning for psychic wholeness.

Every day human relationships challenge us to become *something in reality* versus being *everything in potential.* We are forced to surrender some of the dreams of childhood and adolescence.

Falling in love lives on ideals.

The intensity of the experience adds to our confusion. It is so profound and feels so real. It therefore is often used as a justification to abandon our every day obligations, commitments and, at times, ethics. It can create havoc for our families and often causes much hurt. We are blind to the knowledge that falling in love triggers a deeply felt memory giving it its profoundness and depth. This confusion makes us believe that falling in love is the real foundation for relationships. In reality, it is the hormonal initiator of relationships (Johnson, 1985). It reminds us of a blissful state of original at-oneness. It can provide us with a glimpse into our spiritual capabilities touching unity.

"When we fall in love, we project our own inner vision of the ideal inner female or male onto our partner; a prince or princess, a soul mate, that we carry around in a little silver box inside our hearts" (Spezzano, 1984).

We use this prince or princess as a standard against which our mate, this so very fallible human being, is held up against. *When we fall in love, we don't see others for whom they are, we see them for who we want them to be*. They now carry our unrealized dreams and become a reflection of our own inner ideal. We project assumptions that they think, feel and want to do the same as we do, or would if they only could. It is probably redundant to say that, in the long run, most, if not all mates fail our unrealistic expectations of them miserably.

Carl Jung has referred to "*animus*" as the male soul in women and *"anima"* as the female soul in men and warned of confusing this inner ideal with the outer reality of our human mate. When we do not heed this warning, this prince or princess appears to *feel and want the same as we do.* A promise assumed but not usually communicated. It is an unwritten subconscious contract entered into unknowingly. To make matters worse, both partners will assume this about each other. He will assume that this goddess will always make him feel *appreciated*. She will assume that this god will always *adore* her the way he does now. It becomes our mate's *job* to provide us with a feeling of ecstatic completion and easy love. We are in misery, agony and despair when our *in love feelings* are not reciprocated.

We lose our sense of separation when we fall in love.

The collapse of self it produces and the illusion of sameness it leads us into, are seldom addressed. When we are in love, we are tempted to lose our separate wants, our opinions and ourselves. We are tempted to assume that the *other wants the same, feels the same, thinks the same and does the same* (or would if they only could).

Her husband and children were returning the next day and she had a choice to make. He wanted her to come with him and she wanted to leave with him...the feelings they shared were intense, profound and all consuming. Yet, a small voice inside of her, told her, that everyone would lose if she left. Her husband was a good man, he didn't deserve this and her children still needed her. How would they be able to understand or deal with the break-up of their family? She was in agony but she knew her place was with her family.

What she had experienced was a glimpse of another life, one not to be lived now. It was a decision made not due to outer convention but inner conviction and commitment. "We are the choices we have made," she said.

The ecstasy we can experience when we fall in love, blinds us to the hurt it can cause to others...its potential destructiveness. This especially holds true if we are already in a committed relationship and particularly, if children are involved. We do have the choice of either fueling the hormonal fire or corralling and redirecting our energies.

Falling in love is a form of personal love.

It is like a flashlight. It only shines on one person at a time to the exclusion of all others. Its drawbacks are its exclusivity and loss of individuality it produces.

Falling in love appears to be by its nature beyond conscious choice. We are literally hijacked by our hormones. We fall in love with the most inappropriate people and, at times, with people we don't even like. It ignores suitability, age, ethics, prior commitments, or appropriate timing. It often catches us by surprise. It may be a wake-up call from the routines, boredom and emptiness we neglected to address. It may challenge us to truly commit or re-commit to the relationship we are in already and re-kindle the tender feelings we once new.

At its best, falling in love happens between two available and willing individuals. It makes life fresh and new. We suddenly know boundless energy. We feel attractive, interesting and tolerant. We discover a newly found depth and meaning. Then falling in love generates the investment necessary to continue relationships when they become challenging. It gives us the good memories we fall back on during hard and trying times later on.

It is easy to be in love with falling in love.

Falling in love makes things easy because it is just that, easy. When we think the same, feel the same and do the same relationships are easy. Because of this ease, we think that "*true love*" is easy. Since we tend to confuse falling in love with "*true love*", we assume that relationships, if they are based on "*true love*", *should not* contain conflict. The hard work of establishing and re-establishing common ground won't be necessary, we think. There won't be a need to spend energy and time to overcome boredom and ordinariness and rekindle the tender feelings and passion once experienced. When passion dies back to a flicker, we yearn for the ease we used to know.

"I have been married for more than twelve years and our sex life is barely existent any more. I don't really know how to talk about it...how am I supposed to tell my mate to be more exciting and passionate? Doesn't the fact that you have to say something already kill things?" I used to try and initiate, but it seems that my mate never reciprocates. When it does happen it feels so routine."

"Now things have become a no-win. If my mate does show interest I feel it is not real. I think he is doing it only because I asked. Things are so complicated and difficult. Most of the time I feel as if we are brother and sister. Is there any way to jump-start what we once had?"

The exclusivity of falling in love is in direct opposition with our need for individuality, familiarity and community. We will eventually fall out of love. Passion will fade. This holds true no matter how deeply or whom we fell in love with. This is natural and doesn't mean that we stop loving the person we fell in love with. Our deeper need for self-realization will assert itself.

Every day human love lacks some of the sparkle.

The ecstatic, invigorating, passionate and blinding qualities of falling in love fool us. They lead us to believe that what we feel today, we will feel *forever.* Everyday life and routines do have a dampening impact and do take their toll on passion. We will have to work at staying connected in a meaningful way.

Others can't read our mind, are preoccupied with their own daily tasks and struggles and rely on a caffeine shot just to wake up and function. All of us are tempted to become lazy and give into familiarity. To keep things exciting takes energy. We will have to figure out *how* the other wants to be shown that we care. Our expectations need to be adjusted to what is achievable. It takes effort to keep our loving feelings alive while finding our own perspective on things, at times, so different from our mate. We can fall in love again with the same person in the same long-term relationship, this time by conscious choice.

What is our definition for romance? The mysterious, unknown and unexpected is part of falling in love and is experienced as sexy, yet not truly dependent on hormonal fire. Hormonal in-love comes with an expiration date and the pitfall of forgetting who we are. We can redefine our idea of romance. It can be equally romantic to know that our partner makes a conscious effort because they know something is important to us. The love that lasts is fed by intention. Conscious gestures may be the only kindling for everyday human romance there is. It may be transparent, but who is to say that makes it less profound. Our mind decides what we experience as exciting.

Human love and human relatedness bring quietude. It is like a warm glow that embraces. We can love more then one person at a time; so, each love we experience is unique. Human love needs constant care and attention, like a fire it needs to be fed.

We wouldn't think of attempting to drive a car with its gas tank on empty. When it comes to our love relationships, we often expect the impossible. Without putting gasoline (effort, time, care, respect and attention) into the tank, we assume that the car (relationship) should function.

Didn't the princess have to kiss the frog to turn him back into a prince?

She didn't feel particularly loving when she kissed him initially. She made a conscious choice. Love can become rekindled when we decide to extend ourselves. When we hit our first relationship wall and feel like we are falling out of love is when we reach a junction. This is when we begin to dismantle our relationship or build a truly meaningful one.

Often we confuse an opportunity of *break through* with *break up* (reaching for our parachute). This is the testing ground where it will be decided if this relationship will be short-term or long-term.

Much depends on a clear understanding of what real relationships are all about, on the *willingness to confront and stretch*, *to grow and overcome.* It rests on our ability to know what we are feeling, thinking and to communicate in a non-combative way. We have to let go of our pre-school assumptions that those we love should think, feel and do as we would.

How to fall in love again:

1. Start with a blank slate daily;
2. Look at your mate like you just met them and are interested in finding out who they are, instead of assuming that you know them;
3. Find the beauty they have today;
4. Be playful and adventurous.

A relationship is like a butterfly. It doesn't fly very well on one wing.

All relationships need food for the fire to burn or get restarted. They require some ongoing TLC to flourish. People need to be touched, listened to, appreciated, respected and valued to feel loved. Even good people are hurtful sometimes. Routines and assuming that we know everything there is to know about our mate is the same as not adding wood to the fire. It will be a slow death. Differences are not a sign of true love misplaced but a fertile soil for a truly caring and profound human-to-human relationship.

The quality and progress of the relationship rests on both partners doing their work. Limitations not addressed in one partner will limit the other. The relationship is a product of both partners relating to each other. A relationship can only go so far on one wing and can only get so good with mainly one partner striving to improve. Having said this let us not be too hasty in jumping to the conclusion that it is our mate who is not doing his/her work.

Our mind will always tempt us to first find something to blame in the other when we feel upset. Doing our work starts with stepping back and asking ourselves: *how we are limiting ourselves when we feel limited; how we are attacking when we feel attacked; how we are lacking a self-loving attitude when we feel hurt; what we are critical of (in ourselves or others) when we feel criticized; etc.* Present pain usually relates to an old pain we carry inside. *When our feathers become ruffled it is our responsibility.* It is this pain that makes the present pain overwhelming and gives it its intensity.

Relationships are in a constant energetic flux where one partner's change will affect the other. As such there is much we can do to improve our relationship. It is our change in behavior that will show if the other is willing to change with us. *"Genius is one percent inspiration and ninety-nine percent perspiration,"* said Thomas Edison. What if the same holds true for happy relationships?

Relationships will always challenge us to face our and others unhealed or under-developed and denied parts.

When we fall in love, we assume once again that our mates will be the bringers of a dream. The betrayal of this original state of connection by our mates is the breaking of an unspoken contract: *"If you truly loved me, you would know what I want, need, think, feel, etc., and/or you would want, need, think, feel, etc. the same as I do."*

Sooner or later our partners will show themselves for the uniquely different and fallible human beings they are. They and we have to...nature programmed us that way. Our assumptions of *sameness* will be disillusioned to open the door to higher levels of self-awareness.

For the most part, we walk into these challenges unprepared. Our society is silent about the growing pains that we will experience if we are truly related to another. The only reference that we may have is the picture presented to us by our parents. Once we come to this junction in our own relationship, we feel bewildered. How could this happen to me?

Successful relationships are measured by how much we are willing to give and receive, how many unrealistic dreams we are willing to surrender, how willing we are to learn to accept the other for their differences, how willing we are to make a new start today by forgiving yesterday and, most of all, how willing we are to find common ground.

It is easy to resort to closing off our hearts.

It is a giving up of the impossible expectation of finding an ideal mate who will think, feel and do the same; a mate who will be that prince or princess of our dreams forever. It is taking what we have and coming to love, respect and value the other and us for who we truly are, human faults and all. It is being willing to confront the other and hold them and us accountable when their or our actions aren't relationship building.

It is easy to withdraw emotionally because they rocked our emotional boat. They will put us in touch with our own deepest fears, hurts, or unrealistic expectations eventually. True human relatedness asks us to give more of ourselves than we ever thought was possible. It definitely is not easy!

Ask yourself:

- Am I upset because I expect the other to think, feel, want, or do as I would?
- Am I willing to work at finding common ground? (If not, I am choosing to not be in this relationship, no matter what the appearances). A mini step is better then no step: affirm your willingness to become willing..."I am willing to become willing to work this out!"
- Am I respectful of who they are? (Or do I want them to be what I think they should be?)
- Am I looking to find in them what I have not realized in myself?

True relatedness asks us to find inside what cannot and will not be found in our mate.

If we confuse the passionate and profound feelings of falling in love with "*true love*", we might end the relationship we are in, or we might resign ourselves to roommate life.

We can chuck our twelve-year marriage and all we have built together and seek to fall in love again with a new person. We move from relationship to relationship chasing our own inner ideal in another person. The call for growth has been ignored. True relationship building and true relatedness never happen.

Human love and true human relatedness are consistent, falling in love changes. Human love and true human relatedness give us joy, compassion, peace and contentment. Our focus and energy are inclusive. We are looking outward towards the world together while holding hands. Falling in love gives us excitement, passion, vigor and a glimpse of the eternal. Our focus and energy is exclusive, we are looking at each other and there is no room for anyone else. The outside world is non-existent.

They both have their place. They both bring their gifts. We can have them both! But we cannot confuse them with each other without paying a high emotional price.

When the Apple Falls Far from the Apple Tree

As parents we think we know best for our children.

Infants start life with a high degree of dependency on us. The identification with the infant as an extension of the parent is part of nature's bonding and survival guarantee. This makes it easy to project *sameness* onto our children. Parental love is an unique experience. It is quite different from any other form of human love. As with romantic love, parental love triggers a deep innermost memory of connection and belonging. We discover a depth of love we never knew existed. We want our children to think, feel and do the way we think we know is best for them.

Children are programmed (by nature) to become individuals. They will challenge what we have accepted as good and right. They have thoughts and feelings of their own. Wise parenting choices made now prevent regrets from arriving later. Poor parenting can discolor our relationships with our children for a long time to come. It can send them into adulthood ill prepared. Our *lack of awareness* will deny them the solid foundation they need and instead provide them with *quicksand* to stand on.

Alice Miller, like many others, comments on how children need a great deal of emotional and physical support to grow into healthy adults. They cannot reach their full potential without: *"...respect for the child; respect for his rights; tolerance for his feelings; willingness to learn from his behavior."* (Alice Miller, 1981)

We want our children to share our aspirations and values.

It can be very difficult to accept certain personality tendencies in our children, especially if we love them. Admitting this may be scary. We want *the best* for them. Really, we want what we perceive and judge to be the best. This may not necessarily be what they may want to choose for themselves. As parents, we project sameness onto our children. Because they are ours, they should think, feel and do as we would, we are tempted to expect.

It is easier to assume that we know better because of our life experience. It is hard work to accept and reinforce the consequences that come with *their* choices.

Her mother asked her to sweep the front deck. "I don't feel like it," her 10-year-old daughter quipped. "We are all doing our household chores now and then we are going out to have a treat, as we always do," her mother calmly replied. "I don't want a treat," her daughter cheekily countered.

Mom and Dad exchanged a knowing glance. Their daughter's most favorite thing in the whole wide world was ice cream on a cone. They knew just the place to get it. Without further ado they finished the household chores and were ready. Mom gave her daughter one more chance; spelling out the consequences but received the same reply.

At the ice cream store Mom and Dad ordered a large assortment of ice cream balls with all the trimmings while their daughter was watching. They piled into their car to enjoy their ice cream. A little voice from the back seat asked "I guess I can't have an ice cream, can I?"

Consequences are the best teachers in life.

Allowing others, in particularly our children, to make their choices and act according to what they think is good for them can be challenging. As parents, we have to get out of the way and surrender the idea that our children should think, feel, want and do as we would or even as we know is best. Our intentions are genuine. We want to spare them the pain we have known. Life is all about consequences. It is our task as parents to prepare our children for life. As parents we invent some of these consequences to teach social skills, morals and values. Consequences don't require emotional value judgments or put downs *"You are so lazy, bossy, bad, selfish, etc."*. They speak for themselves. Consequences teach that cooperation is to one's own benefit and not solely for others' benefit. It becomes a win-win.

If your young child answers NO to when you make a request for help, etc., simply wait a few minutes instead of getting into a power struggle. Respect their NO. After all, you would want your NO respected as well. It won't take long for a young child to ask you for something. This is your chance to teach healthy cooperation. Answer NO and point out why you did. Explain that good relationships are about willingness to find common ground and about working together cooperatively. This is separate from having very different thoughts and feelings on a topic. That is not the true limitation. Give your child another chance. What we teach our children when they are young becomes a non-issue as they grow into teenagers.

Usually we are not upset for the reason that we think.

Often we want others to change or make certain choices so that we don't have to feel the uncomfortable feelings we associate with when they don't. *For example: we want them to stay, so we won't have to feel abandoned; we want them to let go of their plans so we can feel important, we want our children to cooperate so we won't feel challenged in our parental authority.*

Being a good-enough parent is time consuming. Time is a rare commodity in our day and age. There are routines, obligations and the stress of everyday living. We often are preoccupied with our financial obligations, anxiety about work and worries about a mate. Not to mention the doubt and questions *"If we are doing it right?"* When we have a clear mental picture of who we are, we are naturally inclined to support our children to become who they are called to be. Our unfulfilled dreams and failures are ours not theirs!

Parents are there to give us a road map into life.

The values, ethics and expectations that we hold for our children will be their springboard into life. Parents are there to teach their children how to accept themselves and figure out life. Parents are there to give guidance on how to express or deal with thoughts and feelings. Not to either, impose their own thoughts and feelings on the child, or to leave the child without guidance. *No small order!* Children often take on their parent's hopes of who they *ought to be.* They will discover over time that it is impossible to live up to an image, no matter how well intended. Some parents find it very difficult to recognize and accept that it is a child's task to use the parent as it's *pushing off point* so as to form a separate identity from its parent. This pushing off to find his/her own viewpoint and with it own sense of *me* begins very early on.

Dad was reading a book with his 18-month-old daughter. They had read this particular book together many times before. Suddenly one day his daughter asked which of the little rabbits in the book dad liked the best. The toddler looked at her father sheepishly. Sensing that she was anxious about her father's reaction if she liked a different rabbit from her dad, the father stated how great it was when people liked different rabbits.

All healthy children will eventually push, test and, at times, outright revolt.

They must build upon and often completely reject some of their parents' values, rules and expectations, so as to become fully adult themselves. Childhood and particularly adolescence is filled with it. This is, as it ought to be.

When parents overreact to their children's misbehavior, children take on the responsibility for making their parents disappointed, hurt, or angry, etc. This leads to shame and guilt for their lack of cooperation. Labels of being selfish, etc. become attached to their misguided attempts of assertiveness. The true lesson becomes lost.

Consequences teach that participating in household chores, even so a drag, is in their best interest and ultimately in everyone's best interest. Children then are able to maintain their sense of…I am loved, loveable and loving. They learn to use their behavior and communications to bring about what they want. Their essential self-worth is never questioned.

If, as parents, we feel insecure in our sense of authority, we will experience their developmentally appropriate searching as threatening. We become tempted to immediately move to squash any signs of opposition. We will correct too much or too little. We will tend to be too harsh or too lenient. The problems begin when our children start to flex their muscles and find their voices, around the age of eighteen months. As parents we are tempted to expect them to be carbon copies of ourselves. If we give into this temptation, we will experience their searching as a rejection of everything we gave them or hoped to give them.

Parents parent their children the way they have been parented.

If we weren't able to overcome the limitations of our own upbringing, we are vulnerable to passing on our shortcomings to our offspring. We repeat the parenting style of our parents or we compensate by parenting in opposition to it. If we have learned to stay present with our own pain and handle it, we teach children by example that they are capable of handling theirs. If we have strong self-esteem and are able to accept our strength and weaknesses, we will minimize their failures and cheer their successes. If we believe ourselves to be able to handle life, we will let them go out into the world to experiment and explore. If we are secure in ourselves, we will allow them to express their thoughts and feelings without feeling threatened. If we are clear about who we are, we give them the limits and freedom they need without confusing freedom with a lack of boundaries.

Most parents are sincere in trying to do what's best for their children. They are not out to selfishly crush the child's spirit. They act out of ignorance and misguided beliefs. It is much more constructive to focus on how we can do better by our own children then on *"what my parents did wrong".*

Writes Alice Miller, *"...any parent who abuses a child [knowingly or unknowingly] has himself been severely traumatized in his childhood in some form or another...an abused child, (emotionally), does not know it is being abused..."*

It is tragic when *well-intended* people become unaware parents. Filled with good intentions but lacking the necessary awareness, these parents now do to their children what was done to them. Coercion and manipulation take the place of guidance. Love becomes confused with sacrifice. Freedom becomes confused with a lack of behavioral guidance. It is every parent's challenge to not engage in power struggles with their children. One's abuse of power over others truly is an attempt at holding one's own deeply seated sense of helplessness in check.

Ask yourself:

- When my child is disobedient, why do I get upset instead of smile and set out clear expectations?
- When my child challenges one of my values and beliefs, why do I dismiss what they have to say instead of consider their point?
- When my child doesn't listen, why do I threaten and argue instead of calmly give choices that have consequences attached?
- When my child fails, do I minimize their failure and reassure them that success is just around the corner? Do I point out my own failures (past or present)? When they succeed, am I there to cheer them on?
- If my child needs help, am I there to back them up? Or, do I shrug my shoulders and rationalize my lack of support and involvement.
- Am I there to listen to their thoughts and feelings about things that are important to them? Or, do I give my opinion right away.
- Am I saying YES to them whenever possible instead of taking the easy and habitual way out of saying NO?

Slowly surrendering our children into life's care is every parent's challenge.

Our parents weren't saints capable of guiding us perfectly to walk the tightrope of connection and individuality and neither will we! All of us fail along the way to some degree. It is up to us to pick up after ourselves.

Too often as parents, we are tempted to confuse the apple with the apple tree. We expect our children to think, feel and do the way we did or would have done. We provide them with the opportunities that we never had and expect them to cease them because we would have. We overcompensate by showering onto them what we lacked or felt deprived of. We project our own unmet needs onto them expecting their gratitude. They are supposed to step into our footprints so our culture implies.

We too often ignore that they may have footprints of their own and a calling of their own...maybe one very different from ours. We find it hard to accept when *they walk to the music of a different drummer so foreign to our ears.*

It is in our earliest childhood experiences that the assumption of sameness is a natural developmental step. Children are born with it and parents discover it. As adults, it is our responsibility to not expect to find sameness outside, not even in our children.

As an adult child communicating with his/her parents remember to acknowledge:

- What your parents have given you. The sacrifices they may have made for you.
- The dreams they may have (had) for you. The unfulfilled dreams they never were able to live themselves.
- The strength, care, etc. they have given you which now allows you to venture out to find your own path (if they are capable of supporting you in it or not).

How "Being There" Affects Who We Become

Our parents were like gods to us when we were very young.

Infantile preconscious at-oneness is filled with the assumption of godly powers. Our parents seemingly were *always there* when we needed or wanted them (omnipresent). They were able to *make all things right* (omnipotent). They *knew* what was going on with us before, it seemed, we knew (omniscient). We felt safe, identified with them and experienced ourselves as loved, connected and the same.

These godly qualities, *omnipresent, omnipotent and omniscient* are now at the bottom of our struggles. We experience them with our mates and others close to us. If we take the time to follow the ant trail of our surface level frustrations and disappointments this is what we find. These early childhood assumptions are underlying our present day hurt and anger. With our loved ones the prefix may be: *"If you loved me…"* with others it is: *"What the…is wrong with you!?"* We either expect others to be these *gods* to us or we hold these superhuman expectations over our own heads.

Mother is always there, the child assumes.

"…once an hour was a day and a day was a month and a month was surely an eternity. Small wonder then that as children we may grieve our missing mother [and father] the way that as adults we grieve our dead. …[For the young child] Absence makes the heart grow frantic, not fonder." Judith Viorst, 1986.

Children of mothers and fathers who *are not there* suffer from unsatisfied longings. It is in our interaction with mother, father and family that we learn or fail to learn the very basics for successful relationships: that we are loveable, how to be loving, and that it is safe to be loved. We internalize that we are worthy, capable and loved if we experience continuity, consistency and predictability. To be separated from mother before the child is emotionally ready to leave her or be left by her is like a burn wound on the psyche. It leaves a deep emotional scar. Her presence equals being safe and being loved. Her presence is the first form of love we know.

The world of the infant is a state of unconscious at-oneness, a state of sameness, that doesn't contain the possibility of separation, conflicting wishes, oppositional thought, or loss. For the infant there is no distinction or any sense of separation between itself and its mother or its surroundings. As a result, mother is *always there.* Only by age three do we become emotionally ready to tolerate her absence in varying degrees.

This state of unconscious at-oneness with all extends itself into the first few months of life as a physical assumption and into the first few years of life as an emotional assumption. Every young child assumes beyond a shadow of a doubt that mother will always be there and is shocked and often severely distraught if she is not. The awareness that mother is not a part of the infant and could go away, yet still be alive and eventually return, only slowly develops. How the people who raised us were able to meet our needs during the first two, three years of life laid the foundation for our sense of self and later relationships. Trustworthy care produces a strong sense of self. We learn to either view the world and the people in it as *safe or unsafe.*

You may find yourself saying the following:

- "Nobody is ever really there for me when I need them!"
- "I don't like it when things change!"
- "If you loved me, you would be there."
- "I feel as if I am not deserving of the good in life!"

The infant's lack of time appreciation makes separation traumatic.

Birth represents the first physical separation between mother and child. An infant does not appreciate the passage of time as adults or older children do. The appreciation for minutes, hours and days is an awareness that only slowly develops over the following months and years. Infants and young toddlers do not attempt to manipulate their parents by crying when separated from them as parents often wrongly assume or are told. Their experiencing is basic: mother is always there when I need her (omnipresent). If she is not there, she is gone forever. The child is thrown into an experience of a too advanced developmental step with only an infant's resources to cope.

As a society, we impose artificial expectations of needing to make our children independent and self-reliant before they are developmentally ready. Every healthy child will seek independence when they are physically and emotionally ready for it. Nature programmed us that way. Writes renowned early childhood psychoanalyst Margaret S. Mahler:

"Quite late in our study, we came to realize that it is the rule rather than the exception that the first unaided steps taken by the infant are in a direction away from the mother or during her absence; this contradicts the popular belief that the first steps are taken towards mother."

For the young child love and safety are an intertwined physical and emotional experience. A child that knows that the parent will be there is free to venture out into the world. Nature programmed us to strive for independence, not just physical but emotional independence as well. Emotional independence is ultimately recognition of our vulnerability. It generally is scary and at best taken in mini-steps. A sudden drastic introduction to this awareness of vulnerability is traumatizing. Healthy development requires an environment of adults who are consistently there to grow that independence. No one (with rare exceptions to the rule) will view our obnoxious, runny-nosed and whiny child as lovingly and patiently as the parent can. It's called parent-child bonding. It makes us tolerate or simply overlook what we would find impossible in other people's children. It enables us to be patient with our toddler's vacillations between independence and neediness.

What is not given when it should have been leaves us wanting.

For mother or father to be there is essential to the young child's emotional equilibrium. Infants and children, who were separated from their mothers too early before they were developmentally ready for it, often show severe signs of dependency and anxiety as adults. Their development becomes stuck. And, sadly later relationships become affected.

"If you loved me, you would be there...you would want to be there!" Presence and love stay intertwined. They develop a strong need to control, fear that they will be left or not loved, feel apprehension about venturing out into the world and have a keen sense of isolation. They have a tendency to look for nurturing in relationships with partners who can't possibly meet their needs or will leave the ones who can.

Very few teenagers still hold on to their mothers' skirts when going to school. Yet, we feel we have to force our one, two, three and four year olds to become independent. Spending the time early on often is inconvenient in our fast-paced modern lives. Children's' needs often are still relegated to second place after our adult needs instead of regarded as equal.

"Being there" takes on an extraordinary importance.

These children become adults who relive over and over that the person they love and feel dependent on is not there (physically or emotionally) when needed. These adults are essentially stuck in a need, of having others or themselves, be omnipresent. Their mind fears and therefore perceives abandonment where it is not. They choose physically or emotionally absent partners who are not capable of being there the way they need them to. Sometimes, they become physically and emotionally absent themselves.

These adults are governed by fears of not being there for others. They end up staying in relationships too long, staying when they should leave and leaving when they should have stayed. Much valuable time and energy is wasted in dead-end relationships and work positions. They tend to overprotect their children and end up smothering the people they love.

As parents and mates, they are prone to overcompensate by attempting to always be there. As a result, they may keep their loved ones *babies*, stifling their drive and need for independence. They foster dependencies in their husbands, children, friends and neighbors.

Or, like their own parents, they lack the awareness of how and when to be there for their own children. They lack the sensitivity to give comfort when needed, denying their children what was denied them. Unaware of what moves them, they control and overpower and put their own needs first. *"You haven't been there!,"* their children now will accuse. At times, they may avoid relationships or having a family altogether. They may never allow themselves to become truly committed, intimate and loved. In hidden and obvious ways, they are *not there for themselves.*

There are times when it isn't humanly possible to be there when someone needs us.

To be omnipresent is a domain of the gods. We are not the only outlet for help and comfort. It isn't our job (unlike mother's or father's) but our choice to be there when someone else needs us. And, even mom and dad won't be able to always be there even if they wanted to and try to be. It is possible to love someone and not want to physically be in the same place. Physical presence and emotional connection are two different states of experience for us as adults. *Not there* doesn't have to equal *not loved.* As a matter of fact, it may be a necessary experience to direct our focus to our inner resources and connections.

For a moment think of the electrical system in a house. The electricity that runs through the wires is independent of the outlets in each room. If one outlet isn't available for whatever reason, there are many more that are. Think of yourself as one of these outlets. The electricity is life force that is available all the time and is independent of you. There are other outlets available to those who are willing to find help. The hand of life holds all of us.

"I should be there," can become a stifling expectation and obligation instead of a choice when we forget our place in the house of life. We take on the feeling as if we are the *one and only source* for others' happiness.

The super-human unrealistic expectation that I (you) should be there dictates our behavior and becomes an underlying psycho-emotional block in our relationships. The only way out is to resolve our past hurt, take a risk by trusting in others' capabilities and ultimately, to trust the hand of life.

Why Some of Us Have to "Fix It"

Just listen to five-year-olds, bragging to each other how their dads can do anything! They see their parents as gods who can do anything and make anything better or right.

NO is one of the very first words a child learns!

Every child is programmed by nature to learn about *"Who am I"*. The focus is on his/her sense of personal power. The child begins to flex his/her *independence muscles* and learns to say NO! For parents it is tempting to overuse NO with their toddlers. The once compliant infant has transformed itself into a walking and talking two-legged terror. It is tempting to overpower. It may not be our intention to make them feel helpless when we act guided by our own needs.

It takes time, effort, patience and ingenuity to teach children that all actions have consequences and rewards. There is always a choice that can be given to the child, no matter what the circumstances or how young. It may be as basic as: *"You can put your toys away now the way mommy asked and then go see Winnie the Pooh (have a cookie, etc.), or you can put your toys away after dinner and then go straight to bed"*. In other words, not putting the toys away is not an option. What is optional is the *when* and the consequence or reward. This teaching is best delivered with a calm light-hearted demeanor.

Giving choices maintains their sense of being able to affect their life and environment. It builds capability. It teaches them young where the impact they can have begins and where it should end. This way, children have a chance to slowly wake up to the true scope of personal power. It allows them to eventually grasp the idea of a higher power.

Children feel all-powerful (omnipotent).

They see their parents as all-powerful as well. The challenge for a parent lies in displaying the patience necessary to wait the child's rebellion and oscillations between self-assertion and neediness out. As adults, we have so many more options open to us than the child who is dependent on us.

Children at this stage often take on the responsibility for the unhappiness of certain family members or the family as a whole. Their experiencing is: *"I am all-powerful and therefore it is my responsibility to make those I love happy". "If I love them, I have to do something". "If they loved me, they would do something." Our parents did for us what we couldn't do for ourselves yet when we were very young. We experienced their doing as love.*

The impact becomes intensified if the family undergoes an experience of loss (divorce, illness, death, etc.). The sudden realization of helplessness on our or our parents' part can be bewildering. The energy of *"I have to do something..."* may become reversed to: *"I can't do anything!"* An *"I can't do" attitude* is often demonstrated in our society. We hide behind rules and regulations instead of risking making moral judgments.

Underlying the taking on of omnipotent responsibility often hides the hope that then the child will get the love, attention, recognition, or happy family it craves.

Love and *doing something* are intricately intertwined for the young child. To *not do something* becomes equated with *not loved.* The confusion creates disconnection. Connection was our very first from of love. It equals survival and love.

Helplessness is terrifying. It rests at the bottom of every unresolved trauma. *"...a too sudden and too painful realization of their [children] helplessness has resulted in a too sudden deflation of their previous sense of their omnipotence, as well as of the shared magical omnipotence of the parents..."* (Mahler, Pine, Bergman, 1975)

Parents often are tempted to squash their children's assertion of independence or just throw up their hands.

It is much easier to say NO than to say YES. NO generates a feeling of power, control and safety and is often much more convenient. YES leaves things more open and vague and therefore may take more involvement, time and energy. It gives us less control.

Raising children well takes a lot of energy early on. If the foundation is laid well, we reap the rewards later.

Parents' initial reaction is to demand compliance by threatening punishment *"You start doing what I asked right now, young lady, or you will be grounded for the rest of the week!"* At other times they might throw up their hands and do the task themselves. However, their tone of voice and body language will communicate how disappointed they feel about their children's non-compliance. Children need to learn that they have a healthy ability to affect their environment. Insecure and immature parents and authority figures will overpower instead of stay calm and give appropriate guidelines. They will feel threatened in their own sense of power.

Parents are there to guide and mediate the energy of early assertiveness and the temper tantrums it sometimes produces. To overreact to or allow children's aggression and willfulness arrests the child's ability to develop and slowly mature the energy of all-powerful. As adults these children struggle with finding a balanced sense of personal power in their later relationships. Their natural will power has been distorted, stifled or left to run wild. As such, it is either not used when it should be or overly applied.

It's my fault the child will assume.

To a child a parent appears like a god that has all the power and *can always fix or do* what is necessary. At the same time the child, still living in magical identification, assumes itself to have this same power. He/she will take on the responsibility for things that go wrong in the family. *"It's my fault or it's my job!"*

The world of the young child is as yet very egocentric. The child (that lacks secure bonding) may get caught in a place of competition attempting to show that he/she can fix things better than a parent or sibling.

It is absolutely crucial that parents clarify what the child may be responsible for and what he/she is not responsible for. It is a parent's task to outline what is reasonable taking into account age and developmental readiness.

The three-year-old boy was proud and intently focusing on his writing. His aunt had given him a pen and ink jar to teach him how to write his name. Suddenly the ink spilled across the kitchen table. His aunt flared at him "You go get a towel to clean this up and then you go to your room!" Later as an adult, he still remembered the incident...he had been so proud and then so devastated. "When I make a special effort to do something special it turns into a disaster," "It's my fault, I can't do it right," he concluded.

A three-year-old as well as older children will sometimes spill things. Their motor skills are not yet fully developed. They don't have the attention span or foresight of adults.

Young children easily become confused between *omnipotent responsibility* and everyday personal responsibility. They are prone to take on responsibilities that are not theirs to carry. They will see themselves as the cause for hurtful and neglectful actions of others.

Children will instinctively take on the responsibility as *"It's my fault,"* when parents are neglectful, critical, uncaring, or consumed with their own problems. They will attempt to fill a love or responsibility vacuum that exists in the family or marriage. They will blame themselves for the unhappiness in the family "*I should fix it...I am the cause...it's my job to make this better!*"

We are tempted to misuse our power when we feel insecure.

When we lack a clear sense of self-worth and personal power, we might attempt to balance things by criticizing others. We put people down so as to elevate ourselves. Only those who are unsure and insecure will have bad things to say about others. It is an attempt at equalizing what is sensed as lacking.

The coach looked like a jar of tomato sauce ready to explode. The teenage paddlers he was instructing had been doing sprints in preparation for the upcoming race. He had told them that they had to do one more lap before they were finished for the day.

To be finished usually entailed going for a fun swim jumping off the boat into the ocean. Finishing what they had been told was their last lap the teens turned the boat heading off shore as they had routinely done in the past. At that very moment some other coaches walked up. The coach hollered at the teenagers "What do you think you are doing??? Who do you think is the coach around here!!! I didn't tell you, you guys could go for a swim!!!"

When we lack a clear sense of personal power, we are plagued by feelings of *unimportant and unable.* This prompts us to having to proof to the world that we are in charge.

The more unimportant I feel the more important will I attempt to make myself. I will become a show-off or give up and turn into a wallflower. If I know that I am important I have nothing to prove. The deeper my feelings of "I can't do it", the more desperate become my attempts of proofing that "I can". I will throw caution to the wind and attempt the foolish or neglect to even try "Why risk, I know I am going to fail!"

We all have to learn to come to terms with feeling helpless at one point or another.

We are not able *to fix everything* for those we love or for ourselves, no matter how hard we try. If our childhood experiences have left us feeling unsure and powerless, we will act out. Some will become righteous, dominant and controlling so as to be safe from their deeper feelings. Yet others will become submissive, wishy-washy and not take a stand when it is essential to do so.

Either approach lacks a clear sense of their own and others rights and responsibilities. This opens their relationships up to becoming marked by their own or their mate's dependencies and confusion about what their rights or responsibilities are.

When a child assumes too much responsibility for things he/she truly has no power over it learns to excessively blame him/herself. If he/she is not held responsible and therefore taught to make excuses it learns to find someone else to blame. "*I should fix it,"* or *"If you loved me, you would fix it"* becomes the demand in their later adult relationships.

Rushing in to fix it becomes a habit and avoidance.

Boys often hear that it is their job to be *the man* in the family or will step into this role if their father leaves a vacuum by his physical or emotional absence. Later in their adult relationships they will feel ill prepared to deal with a woman's expression of emotions. Instead of being an active listener, there with a loving presence, they flee into attempting to fix it/do something. *"I love you, therefore I will do something...I have to do something!"* This behavior often is passed from generation to generation. As future husbands their self-esteem feels shaken when their wives don't understand their offer as a demonstration of how much they care.

We *do* for the people we love. We make a cup of tea for them when they are upset. We cook them some chicken noodle soup when they are sick. We make them breakfast in bed. When our doing becomes separated from our ability to feel our emotions, it loses its effect as a loving gesture. It now becomes avoidance and therefore will not be experienced as love.

"I am tired of having to look after everything in the house, he complained. One would think that at her age she would show a bit more responsibility. The other day the fan in the kitchen broke. My adult daughter seemed undisturbed...she expected me to call the electrician!"

"Isn't it time for her to do something for me now? I just wish that she would become more responsible".

People confront their demons when they have to, due to outer necessity, or inner despair or resolution. As long as we *mop up* after others (do for them), they don't have to face their deeper feelings and take on their responsibilities. And, we don't have to deal with our deeper scary feelings either.

We don't have to express what the other may see unfavorably or what may provoke their anger. We don't have to risk to not be loved. We don't have to deal with the fall-out or simply trust the hand of life. This tempts us to become overly responsible and over-function. It is our *choice,* not our *job,* to be considerate of others.

We need our fangs and claws as much as our ability to mediate and find compromises.

Healthy and thriving relationships with others are built on our being able to step back, take stock, deal with our feelings, take responsibility for ourselves and take action as needed. We need to be able to say NO and let others know when they step on our toes as much as be able to listen. *If we are not willing to deal with conflict in our significant relationships, we are really not willing to be in relationship.*

Seeing ourselves truly is not an easy task. We need the ability to set our feelings aside temporarily from what someone else did or didn't do, or we ought to do, or are going to do. We are going to take action eventually...right now admitting to ourselves what we truly feel is a beginning.

"What is this really all about for me?"
"Why does this bother me the way it does?"
"What do I truly want here?"

Sometimes other people throw their aggressive energy at us and we feel affected. Rejection, abandonment, betrayal and having one's emotional space invaded are big challenges. Other times, it is wise to ignore what doesn't deserve our attention. Yet other times, it is necessary to show our fangs and sharpen our claws. If we won't stand up for ourselves, who will? The trick is to stand up without returning the attack!

People who "Can't say NO" and the ones who "Can't hear NO".

Mysteriously, they seem to be attracted to each other (a dictate of the law of opposites?). Maybe all of us carry more or less mild versions thereof. At the bottom of both versions rests our deeply rooted sense of vulnerability mixed with a lack of balanced personal power. Some people have not outgrown the magical assumption that the world should revolve around them and that they should have things their way. They lack the essential interpersonal skill of establishing common ground in their relationships.

They perpetuate an earlier developmental stage where they assume to know often without personal experience in the matter. They usually can't hear NO, but are very good at saying NO. They don't invite others opinions, since they have plenty of their own and have already made up their mind.

There are exceptions to this rule...there are times in life when it is wise not to hear NO. Those are times when we follow our inner conviction despite outer *closed doors*. Those are times, when we commit to opening every door possible to accomplish what is dear to us. Our actions are guided by the knowledge that injustice is not just unfair to us but to others as well.

And then there are those who *"Can't say NO"*. Their sense of personal worth often is weak and they are tempted to allow others to take too much. They were raised to confuse love with sacrifice. Often they had parents who didn't allow them to feel powerful and have a voice and ideas of their own. At the bottom of their being, they may feel helpless. There is nothing noble in being a doormat.

We habitually put others needs ahead of our own, thinking we are acting from love. In actuality, this is a refusal of being and seeing others and us as equals. Being afraid of hurting others feelings communicates: *"I don't think you can handle this"*.

There are exceptions to this rule as well. When we approach another with compassion, we say YES to embracing them for the human beings they are.

We are tempted to take what isn't truly ours or give up too much.

We are tempted to control what we think we can. We rustle our sabers, threaten and deny others what would be easy to grant or we never can give enough. Everyone is tempted no matter how *mature* they may be. It is part of our human condition.

Learning to say NO:

- Start with small unimportant things. "No thank you, I would rather..."
- Learn to acknowledge others good intentions (or ideas) while declining their involvement, help, or opinion, etc. "I appreciate...I would rather...(what is important to me is...)"
- Learn to ask for your needs. "I really would like it, if you would..." or "I would like to ask you for a favor..."
- Resist justifying and explaining why you want what you want.

Learning to hear NO:

- Start with not responding immediately…take a breath and try to truly listen to what is being said.
- Before commenting and giving your opinion, delay. "Let me think about this…"
- Learn to ask others for what they want, need, or think. "Would it be helpful if I would…?" (Instead of "How can I help?" which requires the other to think of how you could help, since they are most likely already upset, this is difficult to do. Coming up with an idea on how to help demonstrates involvement.)
- Learn to state your opinion ending in "This is what I think, what do you think?" and then pause, giving your response later.

If we shirk responsibility for ourselves, we will blame others.

They now become responsible for how we feel, for what happens to us, for why we do (or not do) what we do and for what we have or don't have. We will feel victimized and are tempted to become martyrs. We refuse to own the personal power we do have.

Taking responsibility means admitting our wrongdoing. It challenges us to find out what we can do and what we can't do. It challenges us to stand face to face with our deepest sense of hurt and helplessness.

On the other hand, it widens our capacity for compassion and restores our sense of personal power. It allows us to take constructive action. This always moves us beyond blame. Once we are willing to take responsibility for our part in what happened, we are ready to resolve our sad, angry, or guilty feelings. We reconnect with the positive feelings inside of us. The world doesn't revolve around us and everything isn't about us or our fault and job.

Responsibility understood rightly is the realization that the quality of my present day life is the result of the choices I made and make.

Our responsibility now is not to be overly *"careful[3]"*, nor reckless or *"careless"*, but to be *carefree*...doing what can be done, being aware of our deeper connections...and then letting go and trusting.

Our relationships depend on knowing where we end and where others begin.

Every child will attempt to impose his/her wishes onto others for children live in an egocentric world that must slowly and carefully be outgrown. We are (or are not) taught to outgrow egocentricity. We have to be taught to respect others belongings. We have to be taught when to respect others' thoughts, feelings and wishes to lead successful relationships. We have to be taught the rightful limits of our human power, our rights and obligations. We have to be taught to be valuing of and caring towards others. If our parents weren't able to teach us and we haven't taught ourselves as adults, we will attempt to manage our present day relationships the way we behaved as children.

It is a natural part of childhood to want to deny responsibility. *"Not me"* comes with runny noses and scraped knees. Successful adult relationships depend on our being able to take responsibility for us. They rest on our ability to find common ground. None of us will be able to do all the right things all the time. As parents it is our task to give our children a core feeling of being loved, important, capable and valued. It allows them to walk into adulthood prepared.
To feel loved as a child, I must have experienced others actions as loving towards me;
To feel approved of as a child, I must have heard others speaking to me with respect and support;
To feel important as a child, I must have observed others putting my needs equal to theirs;
To feel understood as a child, I must have heard others acknowledge my thoughts and feelings.

[3] Foundation for Inner Peace, *A Course in Miracles*

Why We Can't Always Know What Someone Wants

All young children are little *"know-it-alls"* and equally they assume their parents to know-it-all. *Do you recall the feeling that mom would know when you had done something wrong when you were little?*

Her toddler daughter was playing at the neighbors. When dinnertime approached and she was asked to clean up and go home, she refused. After being asked several times (and being physically guided towards the door), she hit her friend's mother and turned to run home. Running past her mom on her way, she hit her as well and slammed the door on the way to her bedroom. A few moments later the neighbor, a very kind woman, appeared telling the mother what had happened.

Obviously the mother had been surprised when her daughter had run past her, hitting her as she passed. To the child's mind, however, *mom knew what she had done*. Her guilt made her lash out.

All children have to learn the limits of their and others actual knowledge. Young children have a right to be *little know-it-alls,* they live in a magical world governed by different rules than our adult world. Children at a young age will tend to repeat word for word with the seriousness of a death sentence, something that they may have overheard their parents discussing. People are good or bad, villains or heroes and parents are the gods that *know everything.*

"If you really loved me you would know".

A young child assumes that his/her parents are *omniscient*. It will assume that mom and dad know what it wants, thinks, feels and has done. It will by the same token assume having this ability his/herself. "*If someone loves me or I love them then they or I will know what the other thinks and wants*. If these assumptions stay unexamined as the individual grows, they are taken into adulthood and manifest as: *"If you really loved me, you would know" "I know what is good for you" "I know what you really want and think".*

In later relationships the individual insists that true love is based on this omniscient knowing. If this level of knowing were possible between two individuals words and communication skills would be obsolete.

At times, we may have experiences of intuiting what others think, feel, have done, or will do. The problem arises when this insight is confused with omniscience, the ability to know all things. "*I should have known,*" we then tend to blame ourselves as adults when trouble is on the horizon. "*I know what is best for you,*" we insist as parents or against all rationality in our adult-to-adult relationships. Claiming omniscience we are subject to suffer its dual effect. We (and others) are guilty when we (they) fail and at the same time burdened to live up to an impossible expectation.

Certainty turns into doubt.

Every young child will pipe up and insist that they know things that truly they don't. Being told that we are stupid or being shamed and exposed when found out can be toxic to our self-esteem. If we believe in our children's essential goodness by overlooking an occasional slip or gently correcting what is needed, they will tend to live up to our expectations. Most children at an early developmental stage do not tell the truth, as we adults would define it. The truth is something that seems true or wished for in the moment, always fluid and not necessarily related to facts.

What we focus on, we give attention to and therefore invest with emotional intensity. Owning what we know sorting out what we truly don't know and slowly relinquishing our omniscient identification with the world around us are necessary steps of growing up. All children need to discover and accept the limits of what they know and what others can know about them or them about others. Typically, this is learned by outgrowing it.

The little girl in the above example wasn't developmentally ready to realize that mom couldn't possibly have known what she had done at the neighbors. At age two she is ready to learn that hitting people, no matter what her reason, is not acceptable.

We get to know ourselves and feel understood, if we were listened to.

When parents give us words for what we experience and feel, we instinctively learn to verbalize what is going on inside of us. We are in touch with our truth. We learn to *know ourselves*...our thinking, feeling and motivations that underlie our actions. *"Know thyself"* is written on a temple in Delphi, Greece. It is the non-judgmental attitude of our parents towards our experience that teaches us that the world and the people in it, including ourselves, aren't truly good or bad.

The little girl's mom allowed her to cool off in her room. Once her daughter decided to leave her room and rejoin the rest of the family by appearing in the kitchen, she suggested that the two of them would read a book together. The book provided a prompt for the mom to broach the topic of what had happened earlier. She asked her daughter why she had hit her friend's mom. "She asked me to go home," came the shaky answer, "...and I didn't want to!" "You didn't want to because...?," the mom responded. "I was drawing a picture and I wasn't finished," a little guilty voice said.

The world will eventually take our innocence and our ignorance away from us. It is our parent's task to pick us up when we fall. It is up to parents to re-frame our failures and put them into age-appropriate boxes. It is up to them to minimize our failures while cheering our successes, no matter how incremental.

When parents don't know how to listen in a non-judgmental way to their children, to how much they know, to what their experiences and opinions on things are, children don't feel understood. They don't learn to understand their own thinking, feeling and acting. Failures become isolated from success.

To understand someone is to mentally be there.

In later relationships we repeat this experience and can't grasp why our mates don't understand us or we just can't understand our mates. These children have become adults who do not know how to attentively listen to others or listen to their own inner knowing.

They find it difficult to be in touch with their own deep thoughts, feelings and motivations. They are prone to *living on the surface, hiding in doing.*

First, the mother took the time to acknowledge the importance of what her daughter might have felt and her motivations might have been. Mom then was ready to introduce the concept that no matter what one feels hitting others is never an option. They continued brainstorming what else the daughter could have done to deal with her frustration and what the consequences might be for a future slip-up.

Knowing what we want is essential for finding direction in life.

Parents may consider their children's wants as childish, inconvenient or seemingly ridiculous. A child learns about *who it is* by watching the parent's response to its feelings and actions. If parents communicate that what the child wants is bad, ugly, stupid or harmful, they leave the child unsure and confused. Overruling the child's want, imposing their own better ideas, they impose but do not teach. These children learn to surrender their inner knowing of what is right for them. Taken into adulthood, it potentially interferes with finding direction in life.

Self-doubt is one of the most common blocks to cashing in on opportunities later on in life. Instead of thinking of ways how something could be done we learn to think of all the many reasons for why it can't be done. Instead of learning to have a "can do" attitude towards life, our first response when facing a problem is "can't do". To find purpose and meaning in life we have to be in touch with what we want.

1. Make a list of what you *"don't want"*...usually this is easier to do then identifying what we *"do want"*.
2. Next, come up with the opposite to what you didn't want...this is the closest you might be able to get to what you want for right now.

3. Take small steps towards what you have identified...(you are still in a sorting out phase, you probably will change your mind realizing what you thought you wanted wasn't it after all). Experimentation is a natural learning step.
4. Expect resistance. You may find that most people don't like change. It creates uncertainty and surprises. Instead of ending up with "A" you may end up with "B", realizing "B" is really what you wanted in the first place.
5. Remember change is a process not a final destination. What we want changes as we mature.

Intuition is that little voice inside of us that warns and advises.

Intuition is a form of *omniscient knowing* beyond facts and reason possible for the average human. Our society and culture overvalues analytical thinking and memorizing facts and data. We truly only tap a very small percentage of our mental capabilities in our usual daily lives.

Our preconceived ideas get in the way. They cloud our ability of what may seem as a form of *other-worldly* knowing. To be able to access our intuition and the capabilities that our mind has, we must learn to listen without immediate judgment. We must learn to become still and empty. Intuition is impartial. It is free of value judgments. It is a knowing that arises spontaneously.

His son was watching his father's acquaintance intently. The Lady was relating a recent interaction with one of her co-workers. Suddenly a little voice said, "Why are you so sad Mrs. W.?"

Intuition allows us to grasp the essence of a situation. It goes straight to the core of something. Often the accompanying feeling is that I know without being able to *prove why I know or know why I know.* Young children don't have as yet a storehouse of personal memories, book learning and associations to distort and influence their perception. Intuition, if validated and encouraged when we are children can become a steadfast tool to help us make important decisions in later life.

Our mind plays a major role in our experience of life and ourselves. Our mind, our experiencing and behavior and, to some degree, even our physical responses are governed by our awareness or the lack thereof.

"It is now a accepted fact that one's body spontaneously responds to one's state of awareness..." (Chopra, 1989)

Ill-prepared parents raise ill-prepared children.

Guiding our children to be aware how their thinking relates to their feeling and acting teaches them early about the purposeful use of thought. They naturally grasp the responsibility they have for thoughts, which manifest in emotional experiences and then lead to attitudes and actions.

The mother of the little girl in the above example took the time to teach her daughter to explore why she hit her friend's mother and her own mother. Together they discovered that the little girl's thinking of *"I want to finish my picture now...and she is not allowing me to,"* led to feeling angry and then made her lash out.

There are many things in life we cannot change. However, we do have power over our thinking, our attitudes and actions. Our thinking and attitudes will to a very large degree determine our experience of what occurs. Ill-prepared parents tend to raise ill-prepared children. As adults the task of self-discovery and healing is often arduous. However, it is the only way to not *visit the sins of the fathers onto the sons.* Surrendering the fantasy of being able to know for others and truly coming to know ourselves, breaks the cycle of repetition and opens the door of choice.

Part of accepting our humanity involves relinquishing the child-like omni-powers.

We have to let go of the assumptions that either others or we are capable of always being there when someone we love needs us. That we are capable of being able to always fix and make better what went wrong. That we are able to always know what someone else might need, want, feel, or has experienced. These are super-human qualities. *Not very many members of the human race qualify for that category.*

When we look deeper, we find that much of the sense of obligation and guilt we carry rests on exactly these assumptions. We expected it of our parents and we expect it of ourselves. As we set our fallible parents free, we gain our freedom and enter reality. As we set them and ourselves free, we take on the responsibility for our emotional and physical well-being and give the responsibility for others emotional and physical well-being to where it should be, to others.

One of the deepest longings we carry is the eternal memory of oneness and the closeness, intimacy, sense of connection and love it brought. Relationships can be a means to glimpse a new version of this memory. *We have left paradise, a state of preconscious oneness. There is no going back! What we can have is heaven, a conscious state of unity that incorporates individuality. This state of unity is like the roof of a temple held up by pillars, which have to stand apart to accomplish their task.* (Kahlil Gibran, 1923)

"...Letting go of our vain expectations as parents and children and spouses and friends, we learn to give thanks for even imperfect connections." Judith Viorst, 1986

If We Feel Listened To, We Learn To Communicate

We need our ability to communicate and problem-solve to be able to bridge our different worlds.

As we leave the magical thinking of our pre-school years behind us, we enter the world of duality and opposites. Now we need communication, words, as a bridge between our different, individual worlds.

The clearer we can be about *what we truly want, independent of others wants,* the higher the success rate of achieving it. The clearer we are *why something is important to us*, the clearer we can be in asking for it or saying NO when we need to. It is communication based on personal awareness that will keep our worlds connected, *like an umbrella under which two people find shelter while it rains.* Then we can experience ourselves as liked and loved even so we disagree. Otherwise our communication tends to spin off into separate worlds.

Problem solving and as an outcome communication can only be successful if we are willing (and aware enough) to look for our inner association with what confronts us. Without understanding these connections, we get lost in problem solving the surface manifestations. Results are mixed and successes remain temporary.

When we directly address, in a non-combative way, what we thought we heard the other imply, we put *the onus* back on them. *They now either have to deny what they said, clarify, or take responsibility for it.*

Communication can be the bridge between our individual different perceptions of what is. Questioning allows us to give the other a hearing. This makes their thoughts and feelings equal to what we think. Acknowledging what someone else thinks and says builds mutual respect and acceptance. It fosters valuing of each other's differences.

We take others comments too personal.

We relate to others as if the whole world still revolved around us and personalize what they have to say. We need to learn that others' thoughts and feelings are about others first. They are about their unmet needs, their hurt feelings, and their wants that have been frustrated by whatever we did or didn't do. And, they are about us second. What is being said does not have an *automatic meaning* about us.

People will always put personal interpretations on what is said. Others will and we will. Some of this is outside of our control. Being able to communicate clearly, verbally and non-verbally has the highest chance of success. A perfect sharing of meaning is most likely impossible or extremely rare. At times we hit the zero mark.

The drowning man who signals wildly for help to one of his friends on a sailboat only to have him wave back is obviously not getting his message across. Sometimes this is how we feel in relationships.

We don't know how to listen.

Being listened to as children helps us develop a vocabulary for our thoughts and feelings. We learn naturally how to express ourselves. Children feel loved, approved of, important and open to wanting to listen to their parents, when they are listened to.

To truly listen is no small task. Our lives are busy; we feel distracted and pulled into too many directions at the same time. *Our buttons get pushed* and we feel defensive. Most of all it takes discipline and it takes attention and time, sometimes rare commodities. We have to make an effort to be genuinely interested in what the other is saying. This requires setting our habitual judgments and preconceived ideas on the topic aside.

Genuine listening takes an attitude of assuming that we *don't* know and are willing to find out. We can't fake listen. The other always knows for genuine interest is lacking. They may let us get away with it if they are adults or are truly desperate but children don't. They draw conclusions about their own self-worth.

Our communications are interdependent.

Writes Mark L. Knapp, Professor of Communication at The University of Texas at Austin:

"...many times we talk about relationships with people as if we had no relation or connection to them–as if our behavior had nothing to do with what the other did. In actuality, however, we have a lot more to do with our partner's responses than we may wish to acknowledge. The reason we often fail to acknowledge this interdependence is that it means we have to accept more of the responsibility for our communication problems. It is much easier to describe your partner's behavior as independent of our own... Acknowledging interdependence forces us to ask ourselves what we do to elicit such responses and what we can do to get the response we desire. Communicators who recognize their interdependence also recognize that communication problems are the result of mutual contribution."

We have convinced ourselves that what we say is *independent* of how the other responds to what was said. We need to learn to actually be courageous enough to say what we mean and take responsibility for it. Young children are masters at this. In their innocence they will make the most outrageous and socially taboo comments. The truthfulness of these comments makes us uncomfortable.

We cannot judge our own effectiveness if our intentions are not clear.

This is more likely to happen when g*etting our point across hopes to accomplish several different goals.* We may seek understanding, closeness, to influence someone else's attitude or opinion, motivate ourselves and others to take action, avoid how we truly feel, or simply be right. If we have failed to learn to communicate with awareness the likelihood is that we fail again in our relationships.

Instead of honestly stating what we feel which means our words and feelings match, we:

1. *Placate and appease*...to avoid someone's anger, depression, or rejection and to be liked. We go along with others so as to avoid

conflict. We work to change others mood. “Whatever you say dear!”

2. *Intellectualize and detach*...to avoid what feels threatening, to deal with uncomfortable emotions and to assert control by fact-finding. “Your reaction is not logical! I did such and such...” (stating an obvious fact but ignoring the underlying energy).
3. *Distract*...to avoid what feels uncomfortable and dangerous. We bring up what is irrelevant or comical, or act helpless, suddenly have a problem, or minimize to change the focus. “I don't know how...!”

Communication is filled with subtleties and often hidden implications.

It is not just the words we use but also our voice, its tone and intensity; our body language, our facial expressions and what we don’t say but energetically communicate. Once we have entered the world of duality in our relationships, we have to communicate that we care, verbally and non-verbally. We need to step beyond assuming that the other *thinks, feels and wants the same*. We have to let go of our expectations that they should do, think and feel the way we would.

Everyone wants to be loved (liked), be seen as loveable (likable) and be seen as loving (good). When we tell people otherwise they will get defensive as will we. Everyone wants to win.

We are all masters at jumping to conclusions about other people, especially those we are closest to. We get angry and feel hurt when our picture of what we want conflicts with what is. The needs we typically *demand* to have met originate from a deeper level of our psyche. Without awareness of their origin, we look at other people in terms of what we expect they can and should do for us.

Knowing what is right for us is based in knowing ourselves. Meeting others needs is a choice not an obligation on our part. However, it is a normal part of any relationship to be sensitive to others vulnerabilities.

Successful relationships are about what I can give versus what you can do for me.

Many people don't realize how their personal associations will cloud what is being said and they are trying to say. These associations will actually prevent them from accurately understanding what has been said. When human relationships are clouded by mistrust, past unresolved hurt, self-absorption, a lack of willingness to take responsibility and a lack of openness to be wrong, endless opportunities arise to distort. It becomes easy to discredit even the most skillfully prepared messages. Relationships are like a tango both partners determine the end result.

Did your family teach you to handle conflict by:

- *Attacking before you will be attacked.*
  Offense is the best defense. "You always overcook the steak!" (All the while feeling guilty about not helping with dinner.) We find fault with others when we are afraid of being at fault.
- *Giving double messages.*
  A double message holds two or more contradictory meanings. "I want to hear what you want...(while already having made up one's mind to proceed in a certain way)." Double messages confuse and distract. They allow us to hide.
- *Make fun of others' thoughts, feelings, or actions.*
  This is a subtle attack. "Oh, poor you, life is just so unfair!" It allows us to cover up our own insecurities and appear in control. We deflect attention away from ourselves.
- *Giving others the silent treatment.*
  We make a conscious choice to withdraw and not talk. Our body language communicates: "You have hurt me so deeply I cannot talk," or "What you have to say isn't worth my time." This allows us to retreat from confrontation and to regain power in the relationship.

First, take a moment to step back.

Whenever we feel the need to address something that feels dissatisfying or upsetting, the first thing to do is, to take a moment to step back from our thoughts and feelings. *Our feelings, at this point, will revolve around what we don't want or are afraid will happen. They will revolve around the behavior of the other and around how right we are and how wrong the other is. Most likely, we are going to feel unjustly treated or guilty about treating someone unjustly.* Feeling this is normal. Acting on these feelings will be counterproductive.

Stepping back from being caught in the whirlwind of these thoughts and feelings will allow us to take a moment and identify what it is that we do want. Clarifying and identifying what we do want is most important for constructive problem solving with people around us. It changes the direction and energy of our communication. *It is our goal and our intention that determines the outcome.*

We may have learned to address the problem first or to avoid and not address anything at all.

Without a *clear cut, positive goal,* that also considers the other persons best interests set at the outset, the situation just seems to happen. It typically deteriorates into justifications, defensiveness and more attack. *Whenever we attempt to problem solve a situation beginning with the problem, our focus is the problem not the hoped for outcome.*

A problem exists because two people find themselves temporarily in two different worlds of experience. Focusing on the problem intensifies this. It doesn't alleviate it.

A common or joint goal establishes a meeting ground that both parties can identify as being important to them. When we decide in advance what we want to have happen, the situation becomes an opportunity and a means to *make* it happen. It is then possible to not get caught up in others defenses, attacks, avoidances and misinterpretations but stay focused on the goal and take steps towards it.

Next, identify the common goal.

It is paramount that we take the time to establish this common goal before moving any deeper into the conversation. A common goal is something that we both want and have identified as being in both parties best interest. This goal gives focus to the communication. If we encounter resistance it provides us with a tool. By repeating and restating our goal we will eventually get past our partner's defensiveness. It functions as a bridge leading us to a new, shared ground to stand on.

To identify this common goal we need to ask ourselves some of the following questions:

"If anything was possible what would I hope to achieve in this situation that was in both our best interest?" "If I had been able to achieve this then how would I feel?"

At this point you may have an *"Ah Ha!" experience. You may realize that what the other person or you are afraid of is not receiving this feeling.* It is this feeling, that is unknowingly shared by the other person that represents the common ground we are in search of.

It only takes a moment to ask the other what they feel they need, hope for and want. The trick lies in moving beyond the initial *surface goal to a deeper feeling goal.* Once both parties realize that they share the same goal, half the battle is over. Establishing a joint goal at the outset isn't necessarily time consuming, however, it does take discipline.

Identifying the fears we have.

Next, it may be necessary to first address one's fears or concerns about discussing the problem at hand. Fears exist because of past failures in attempted problem solving about this issue. Fears exist because the problem hits a nerve deep inside of us and we feel very vulnerable talking about it. All humans carry a deeply rooted sense of vulnerability about something, conscious or not. The individual version is what is being addressed here.

Voicing our fear, assuming that we feel that it is safe to do so with this person, will put the other on notice not to act so as to hurt us where we feel most vulnerable. Showing our soft underbelly in intimate relationships will lead to a greater level of intimacy if rightly handled. Having first expressed and agreed on a common goal will make this step possible and productive. In less intimate relationships there is always room to voice our fears as concerns.

Voicing our fear establishes trust between us and the other person. Only someone who is very callous and selfishly motivated and cut off from his or her feelings will not respect our vulnerabilities. It stands to reason that having taken the step into being vulnerable comes with the agreement that this disclosure will not be used against the other at a future time of conflict!

Indeed this may be the fear that needs to be discussed. The consequence of such actions is the undermining of any trust or intimacy that is starting to fledge in the relationship. This breaking of trust repeated is very well capable of dismantling the relationship in the long run. Trust is a key corner stone for any relationship.

As we voice our fear, we *give notice* to the other on how not to act. It gives them some preparation time to ready themselves for discussing the problem we hope to resolve. As such we prepare a space to address the problem at hand with a new focus (common goal). We voice a request for a new behavior (fear) to make the relationship safe (or more productive). We move toward the other in the hope of finding a new outcome (problem resolution).

Talking about what is bothering us.

Finally, we are ready to talk about what has caused us hurt, or discomfort, or has been a hindrance to achieve a desired outcome. The *problem* or issue at hand now can be addressed as an obstacle that stands in the way of reaching our mutual agreed upon goal. It is now nothing more then a *red herring*, attempting to throw us off course, get in the way, or distract us from what we truly want.

Our partner may at first react defensively, justifying their actions or even attack us. We attack and defend when we feel threatened. Depending on the degree of insecurity and vulnerability we carry inside this will be more or less intense. As long as we believe in our sense of insecurity and vulnerability as a fact we are going to feel threatened. We do and they do.

A clearly established goal restated again and again will eventually overcome the others defensiveness. With that goal as our focus, we are not tempted to react to their defensiveness or attack and get side tracked into how we are right and they are wrong. This allows us to stay focused on what we truly want. *We can hear their pain, needs, or fears around the issue. Beyond our individual differences lies a layer of the psyche that holds common human experiences. We identify with their humanity and therefore share in their pain, needs, or fears.*

Our partners have their thoughts and feelings on the subject. From their perspective they are as right as we feel right from our perspective. To acknowledge someone's feelings doesn't automatically mean that we agree with them. We are simply acknowledging what they are feeling and thinking. This avoids battling over who is *right* and who is *wrong*. We can agree to disagree.

It is the impact of another's actions on us that we hope to change.

This change then would lead to us feeling how we want to feel (goal) with and about this person. Often another's intentions are genuine and in alignment with our own but their way of going about it is where we differ. They may want the same but have a completely different plan on how to accomplish the task.

We may value different things. We might be asking our partner to meet an unmet need that we have. In their way, no matter how misguided it may be, they too are asking us to meet a need that they have, reasonable or not.

Of course it isn't our job to meet these needs for each other. It *can be* our choice to do so. Good relationships rest on meeting each other on common ground. Finding a common platform to stand on rests on our willingness to find it. If we are at the end of our rope and just cannot find willingness, *we can always be willing to become willing.*

When we don't *level* with others about what is true for us, we are attempting to adapt and avoid what we experience as unsafe. This is learned behavior and usually habitual. When we *level* with another we tell them respectfully how we truly feel. This has nothing to do with being tactless, attacking, or blaming. To level about how we feel is a conscious choice.

In the final analysis it is not if we use "I" or "you" statements that makes the difference.

When we use "I" statements whenever possible when speaking about our experience in a situation, we indicate that we are taking responsibility for ourselves. It is proof that we know that our needs are ours to meet. We communicate that no matter what it looks like we are the ones responsible for our choices.

"You" statements are not necessarily *bad.* However, they too easily tempt us to fall back on a time when the power to change all things and meet all of our needs did indeed rest outside of us with our parents. They are a leftover from a time when the world appeared to revolve around us and we liked it. When another speaks to us and phrases his/her sentence with "you" indicating that we are to blame it is up to us to stay grounded. It is an opportunity to realize that their hurt has temporarily returned them to that time when the power was on the outside.

In the final analysis it is not if we use "I" or "you" that makes the difference but what our attitude and intention is underlying what we have to say. A sentence starting with "you" may simply be a statement of fact. If someone begins his or her sentence with "you" instead of "I", we don't automatically gain the (arrogant) right to simply dismiss or make wrong what is being said because of the way it was phrased.

Finding a solution that works for both.

"You cannot shake hands with a clenched fist." Golda Meir

The last step that follows is either simple and natural or a tricky one. It is now time to jointly decide what to do. What new action or behavior to follow. Relationships more then anything thrive on willingness to work things out. Finding a joint solution is very important as it implies commitment on both sides. As long as the solution is only one partner's answer it often gets *forgotten or undermined.* The other partner doesn't have any ownership in it. They just went along for the ride.

If underlying unresolved issues are at the base of the problem then this step may be the most difficult communication outcome to produce. Without deeper insight into the underlying connections people tend to revert back to their old way of being despite their best conscious intentions. One can predictably expect setbacks and relapses. It is easier to get someone else to understand our message then to get him or her to agree with it. And it is easier to get someone to agree with us then to motivate them to actually act on it. One partner in the relationship may be the one good at communicating and problem solving. Maybe the other feels rather inept at communication. He/she is the one who generally stays quiet letting the other take the lead. A joint solution is owned by both partners and therefore will work.

"There are risks and costs to a program of action, but they are far less than the long-term costs of comfortable inaction."

John F. Kennedy

- STEPPING BACK/PAUSE;
- CLEAR-CUT POSITIVE GOAL (what is good for both of us);
- FEAR (past failures, reactions or deeper sensitivities);
- PROBLEM (an obstacle to get rid of);
- WE-ACTION (joint solution).

Butterflies need two wings to fly. On one wing they might *hobble* but one can hardly call it flying. Relationships are the same. *Sometimes, despite our best efforts, we will come to the end of our rainbow. New doors will open bringing new opportunities...there are many starfish in the sea.*

We seek happiness from something or someone outside of ourselves.

The Physical is our "First Home"

We carry a deeply seated longing to "go home".

E.T. whispered, "Home Elliot, home!," and moviegoers young and old felt touched.

Our mother's body is our first body. Food and being physically held is our first form of love. Mother earth is the home of humanity. Once we became aware of having a separate body from mother, we had to face our first fears of abandonment, helplessness and alienation. Pleasure and necessity now were outside of our control.

Our surroundings and body become a way of reflecting back to us *who we are.* They become the carrier of our identity as *me.* We know ourselves and are known by how we look, what we have and within the outer demarcations of the people we associate with, the village or town we call home. We are all painfully aware of the finiteness and vulnerability of our physical existence.

The San Diego Union-Tribute, Monday, March 19, 2007; burial held for 5 Bronx fire victims, by Almahady Cisse, *"...Mrs. Soumare and her four children (ages 7, 4, and 7-month-old twins) were among 10 people...killed when a fire tore through their shared row house in New York's Bronx neighborhood...The woman and her four children killed in the fire were immigrants to the US. ...The father of the family, a cab driver...returned to Mali to bury his family. Relatives spoke of the importance of returning the bodies to their homeland, even if none of the children had spent time in Mali..."*

We live a life that is identified with us as a *vulnerable earthling.* Our physical existence seems constantly in jeopardy. We draw borders and build walls, literally and symbolically, to protect ourselves. Our body, possessions, roles and structures are what we identify with. This leads to feeling separate from others, nature and ultimately from our true inner nature. A strange feeling of longing remains. We come to believe that what we want and need is on the outside and with others.

How often do we think: "Once I have that...(job, relationship, money, health, or whatever the goal of the moment) then I can relax and be happy. Then I have made it!"

"...the presence of mother, our mother, stands for safety [and survival]." Judith Viorst

Deep inside we carry a memory of instant gratification. Once there was a time when all of our needs seemed miraculously met. When we were home. *This was paradise!* The world (mother) seemed to know instantly and tended to our needs. What we wanted, the world (mother) wanted for us. *No wonder, so many of us carry this original experience as an unconscious expectation.* The source for all of our needs apparently lies with someone else or something else.

The little girl looked about ten years old. She was desperately trying to comfort the baby she was coddling...to no avail. The infant kept screaming at the top of his lungs. The 10-year old kept walking up and down the hallway ever so often glancing towards the escalator. The infant's cries by now had become filled with desperation and terror. An elderly lady attempted to help...without success. After thirty minutes of pacing up and down the hall the infant finally fell asleep, exhausted and still sobbing.

As a child, the terror of losing our mother can be one of our earliest deep-seated memories engraved on our brain. Our connection with mother stands for safety and fulfillment. Once we become aware that we are separate from mother and that mother can leave us, we enter the world of vulnerability and duality.

Mother earth has sustained and failed us. The volcanoes, tsunami waves, droughts, famine, torrential rains and many other disasters that have deprived or killed our neighbors and ancestors remain a terrifying memory within our psyche. The rituals of primitive tribes which are attempting to please and appease nature speak to us of the age-old terror mankind has known. The helplessness and awe of these distant memories live on in our daily fears.

Our daily life is filled with the stress of achieving something in order to be safer and happier. Accomplishments tempt us to move from one goal to the next and the next. Each promising what the last didn't permanently fill. Satisfaction rests on an understanding that we are safe, capable and resourceful. Life itself is the source for our needs. This stands in stark contrast to expecting significant others or significant events to be our only source. *We can learn that there are many starfish in the sea! The hand of life will hold us. We can learn to trust that good will come our way.*

"When one door of happiness closes, another opens; but often we look so long at the closed door that we do not see the one which has been opened for us." Helen Keller

We are taught from when we are young that the only reality to be trusted is what our senses can perceive.

It is only logical to conclude that then all we are is our physical existence. The many religions and philosophers spanning ages speak to another reality. Modern quantum theory scientists alike have begun to speak of multidimensional reality, offering new insight into what our world is and therefore what we are. Albert Einstein stated:

"A human being is a part of the whole, called by us Universe, a part limited in time and space. He experiences himself, his thoughts and feelings as something separated from the rest--a kind of optical delusion of his consciousness. This delusion is a kind of prison, restricting us to our personal desires and to affection for a few persons nearest to us. Our task must be to free ourselves from this prison by widening our circle of compassion to embrace all living creatures and the whole nature in its beauty."

As long as we continue to live by the principles of traditional science, we are tempted to assume that anything that cannot be measured, tested in a laboratory, or known through our senses is not real. As a result, we are tempted to meet all of our needs through the physical and then feel bewildered and in despair when we fail. Now we have every reason to be afraid.

Somewhere we do sense that there is more to life then what meets our eye...as a result we feel divided. We profess to the values and teachings of a particular religion but keep living life as if it is solely up to us to make ourselves safe and happy. Faith is accepted and chosen minute by minute. There will be times when our certainty will waiver. We will be tempted to allow fear to guide our thoughts, feelings and actions. We have to be willing to *"pick up our cross daily,"* to try again, to choose again and to trust again.

We either learn to trust or mistrust life and others.

The values and attitudes that we internalized from our parents and society and the decisions that we made about our experiences, become our road map into life. When our parents provide us with consistency and continuity we learn to develop a basic sense of trust into life and others. *An infant or toddler crying in vain for his mother learns that those who he loves and are supposed to be there for him are not reliable.*

Basic development of trust:

- developing a basic sense of trust into life and others; ("Others will be there when I need them");
- developing trust into oneself; ("I am good and deserving"), capable ("I can do this") and resourceful ("I can find a way");
- developing trust into a higher power or purpose. ("One day I will understand the purpose and meaning of this.")

When our wants and wishes are in conflict with our parents, we too often simply learn to submit. Wise parental guidance allows us to learn to endure a healthy amount of conflict and separation. The ability to tolerate failure, tension and conflict leads to recognizing our physical and emotional self-sufficiency. Eventually this leads us to finding ourselves as capable individuals. We learn to trust ourselves. Trust becomes a conscious choice.

Our "me-versus-you" focus has been at the root of much misery for humanity.

The physical is limited and finite; there is only so much to go around at any one time. If all things are on the outside then other people are potential enemies. They can take what we have and want. It is this underlying fear of loss and deprivation that lie at the bottom of our hostility and greed. We do not understand and trust that which is truly meaningful cannot be taken from us. Inner abundance is our birthright and cannot be substituted for by outer wealth or accomplishments. The only one that can deprive us of inner abundance and worth is us. As humans, we are physically vulnerable, no matter how safe we attempt to make ourselves. Our invulnerability is of a psycho-emotional nature. Once we identify with this part of our being, physical vulnerability loses its fear.

The assumption that hostility towards others won't affect us is based in our sense of separation. If we would experience another as part of and connected to ourselves, we would not set out to cause them harm. There wouldn't be any: *"You have to lose so that I can win".* Others, instead of being our kin become our enemy. They are capable of taking or denying what we want, *what we must have.* We acquire not so as to *give*, either to others or ourselves. We acquire so as to *have*, accumulating and hording food, possessions and trophies of any kind, just in case. Money and wealth are viewed as buying us freedom. There is no denying that they can buy us comfort. Yet, the freedom our soul desires is of a different nature. Our attempts at protecting our physical well being by insisting on dominating others by force or manipulation eventually backfires.

Developmental stages of finding the Win-Win in a conflict situation[4]:

- Lose-Lose "If I can't have it then I will make sure that you can't have it either."
- Win-Lose: "I want it and there is only enough for one of us."
- Lose-Win: "I will sacrifice what I want (out of kindness) and let you win."
- Win-Win: "I want us both to equally gain from this."

Our families, being part of the society we grow up in, teach us young that "having" is important in life.

Having money, having a nice car, nice clothes, a good education, a nice house, a nice husband (wife), success and fame, etc., will bring us happiness we are taught. *Once we have, we have made it.* The more we have the safer we are going to be we reason. Only much later do some of us realize that happiness doesn't rest on *outer* having but on *inner* having.

There is nothing wrong or non-spiritual about being rich. Wealth and money in itself are simply an expression of the physical world. They can be an outer expression for our inner abundance or a symbol of inner emptiness. It is the meaning we give to having and

---

[4] Adapted from a lecture by Dr. Chuck Spezzano, Hawaii 1984

the wrong identification we place on having (or not having) that makes it what it is to us.

As a society we place too much faith into money, material possessions, the body and science as a source for happiness and safety. We put our faith into what is ultimately outside our control, obviously not learning from past experiences. We forget to take time for the truly meaningful things in life. To say it with Napoleon:

"Graveyards are filled with indispensable people."

"Having" becomes a symbol of love.

When our energy becomes reoriented to *getting to give* (to oneself and to others) instead of *getting to have*, life with all its riches takes on a new meaning and beauty. The physical in all its endless manifestations is given into our care to govern wisely. When we finally surrender the futile race to seek from the physical what only our inner emotional world can provide, we learn to master it. The material becomes a beautiful instrument to assist our experiencing, experimenting and expressing in this world.

If outer wealth is an end by itself, it will never hold us and bring us the fulfillment we seek. If we are rich on the inside emotionally and spiritually then outer abundance becomes a natural expression of our inner state of being. Our essence is independent of any particular outer source for fulfillment. Once we realize and practice that essence power is a state of our inner being, we access the *law of attraction*. Now things and other people come to us, at times in miraculous ways.

Let me compare it to the effect of two magnets on each other. Our essence is by nature positive. If we empower things or people outside with this essence power we make them positive as well. In reality they carry a negative charge with regard to the position they hold in our life. If you put the two positive ends of two magnets up against each other what happens? They will repel each other. It is impossible (depending on the strength of the magnets) to do this. The same is true for things and other people. As long as we empower the outer with positive essence power (by needing and wanting, seeing it or them as the source for our happiness) they will seem to elude us.

We look for validation, purpose and meaning through possessions and accomplishments.

Our body has physical needs and they indeed need to be met from the outside. These are basic needs: food, shelter, clothing, etc. Because these needs are met from the outside, things become even more confusing. We need food to feed our body, clothes to dress ourselves, houses for shelter and medicines for health. We earn money to support our life styles. Our difficulties and struggles in life and most often in relationships begin when we expect to receive all things the way we receive all things physical. A sense of purpose, meaning, connection and emotional safety become entwined with our physical accomplishments. Love, self-worth, equality, recognition, etc. are sought through the physical.

As a society we are obsessed with money, food and the comforts and *looks of the body*. We look to money and physical possessions for status, value and safety. Physical attractiveness becomes the criteria for desirability in relationships. Alcohol, sex and money become the initiators into adulthood. Getting married is supposed to guarantee connection, happiness and belonging.

Happiness in all its many forms is an "inner affair".

When we are very young it is natural for us to look to others for validation, value, success, emotional comfort, purpose and meaning. Parents play a major role in reaffirming that we are loved, loveable, loving, deserving, capable and resourceful. As the product of their upbringing and due to the society within which they were raised and live, our parents often do not know how to provide this very essential reaffirmation.

We become *roundies*, desperate to fit in while feeling like *squaries* inside. This leaves us forever unsure of where we belong, who we are and what we are capable of doing. It leaves us deeply conflicted and alienated. We struggle with claiming our personal power. We become who we think we ought to be. In varying degrees all of us carry this dilemma inside. *The world has what we are in desperate need of...to have worth, be happy and be whole.*

As adults we have a responsibility to grow beyond what our parents were able to give us. Confusing physical and psycho-emotional laws sets us up to expect that all of our needs *are to be and indeed will be* met from the outside. We tell ourselves that if we only try hard enough, find the latest cure for an illness or find our soul mate all will be well. This is not to minimize the powerful possibilities science has opened for us, in particular medically. Part of becoming fully adult is the recognition and acceptance that we are responsible for our happiness.

We constantly confuse cause and effect.

The problem lies not in having needs. The problem lies in looking to others to compensate for what wasn't given and met when it should have been. *It is a bit like insisting to get coconuts off an apple tree. Both are perfectly fine trees providing us with delicious fruits. Both fruits are round and tasty. But our search can never succeed.*

In actuality, it is so simple to identify what we yearn for and find it where it can be found. Use the following questions[5] to start your search (filling in your answers).

"What do you think would make you happier?" Answer the following open-ended question as spontaneously as possible (insert your own words)..."<u>If only</u>...(i.e. my husband wouldn't be so controlling)", <u>then:</u>...(I could do what I want to do, etc.)!

"If you had this (i.e. could do what you want to do)...then how would you feel?...(e.g. like I have worth)", "And if you would feel like this then...(i.e. I would feel more confident)!"

Continue this line of questioning inserting your own words until you feel you have reached a *bottom line feeling.* This feeling is what you ultimately hope to achieve by all your upper level striving and struggling. The interesting thing about this feeling is that in actuality you can begin to feel it now without any outer change at all.

---

[5] Adapted from a lecture by Dr. Chuck Spezzano, Hawaii 1984

It is there inside of you already! Feelings are generated from the inside first and then reinforced or triggered by happenings on the outside. This feeling represents your bliss. Claim it for yourself now! Claim it as your right to have. Don't allow outer circumstances to dictate when you will feel it or to remove you from it. *"Fake it until you make it!"* You may be surprised how the outer world starts to rearrange itself when you begin to claim this feeling as your birthright.

Continue your line of questioning by brainstorming. Write down the first thing that comes to your mind no matter how far fetched it may seem. Continue to write down all answers to each question until you keep going *blank* repeatedly.

"What does having or feeling (more confident)…allow me to do?" "What do I not have to do by not having or feeling…(more confident)?" "If I am more…(confident) then…?

We have in our life what we believe we have a right to have, are familiar with and what we think we can handle. There are reasons, usually dictated by past experiences, for not having in our life what we say we want. The physical world is there to meet our physical needs.

The Body: Torture versus Temple

We have attempted to compartmentalize our health from the rest of our being.

When we think of ourselves, we automatically think of how we look. Our body stands for who we think we are. It is the part of us that differentiates us from the next person. We are often attempted to solve all of our health concerns through science neglecting to consider the role the psyche plays.

Food, a necessary means of survival, has in our society of over-abundance become a source for pleasure and emotional comfort. *Food comforts us where it should simply feed us!*

Listen to the many TV commercials revolving around food. They either advertise food or advertise various forms of diets to undo the effects of our excessive and unhealthy food consumption. The resulting health problems intensify our fear of the body and ultimately death. We misuse the *body of the earth* as we misuse our own body. Our environment is becoming more and more toxic. Again, this intensifies our search for cures to the illnesses that result. We never resolve the issue at the root, our misuse.

Physical symptoms are a "heads up" to what's going on inside of us.

They alarm us to what we might have sensed but weren't willing or ready to fully acknowledge. Unresolved emotions locked deep inside out of shame, fear, or guilt, wreck havoc in ways we typically are completely oblivious about. One of these ways is our health. Illness is influenced by many factors of which our psycho-emotional state is a significant one. When we get angry or sad, notice how our heart starts to beat faster, our chest feels heavy, our stomach tenses and our muscles tighten. Criticism, anger, resentment, loss and guilt are some of the main culprits underlying many illnesses. We feel tired and tense and uneasy.

Emotional trauma and stress can and will weaken our immune system. They set us up to being re-traumatized. When we feel threatened, helpless, overwhelmed, or criticized our heart rate climbs drastically. Our body pumps adrenaline and goes into a hyper-alert state. An emergency sign flashes in our brain and our body attempts to draw on its resources to fend off the threat. The animal part of our brain reacts with fight or flight. If we habitually or for too long live in this heightened state of *emergency* our health will show a toll. There is ample evidence showing that people who can stay truly present with their feelings generally are healthier and happier. When we finally think about it, it becomes obvious that we *feel* in our body and express feelings through our body.

"...Emotions have energy. And this energy does not just disappear when it is repressed or held back. When we cannot or do not express what is happening on an emotional or psychological level, that feeling becomes embodied (we take it deeper within ourselves) until it manifests through the physical body."

Debbie Shapiro, *Your Body Speaks Your Mind*

Illness becomes a way of solving our problems through the physical.

There are times when we fall ill due to physical causes beyond our control. Genetics and the environment take their toll. We are subject to the physical laws of our planet. Yet, our identification with the body as us can turn it into a *silent voice* for our subconscious. Now our physical ailments have a psycho-emotional cause. The body, as that silent voice, will speak to others and us through our aches and pains. Its proper function as a tool of our inner being to experience, experiment and express becomes distorted. It is left to do the *dirty work* for which it was not designed and is very ill equipped.

It would appear to go without saying that a person would rather be well than sick. However, for some people and maybe most of us to varying degrees, being sick is not completely unrewarding. In part it depends on the pay-off. (Shapiro, 1997) *What are the benefits to being sick? What does being sick allow us to do or allow us to avoid or delay?* When we avoid, ignore and deny conflicts and upsets, we give their resolution to our body. *A job it was not designed for!* Then physical symptoms are the body's attempt at resolving what only can be truly resolved through our mind and emotions.

Recalling psycho-emotional conflicts from the body:

- Quiet your mind and turn your attention inside;
- Affirm your willingness to know and deal with the emotions underlying your physical discomfort;
- Look at the natural function of the part of your body that is affected. For example: *"The lower back offers support. How do you feel unsupported or burdened"?*[6]
- Pause and listen inside. If you would know what is going-on on an emotional level it would be...?

Illness is often multi-faceted.

It is definitely too simplistic to say that all illness is psycho-emotional. Genetics and the environment affect our physical well-being. At which point then becomes illness curable simply by raising our awareness?

"The mind can go deep enough to change the very patterns that design the body. It can wipe mistakes off the blueprint, so to speak, and destroy any disease--cancer, diabetes, coronary heart disease–that has disturbed the design."

"...Ayurveda cannot guarantee a cure because sometimes it is not there in nature's scheme."

Deepak Chopra, *Quantum Healing*

There are many different voices on this topic. What is *"nature's scheme"* for each individual? Is the *"blue print"* we carry a fixed design? We clearly do not have and maybe never will have all the answers.

There is no question that the highest regard is due to pioneers in this field. They have brought much needed understanding and help. Questions remain, as they should. Controversy is positive as long as it is not confused with crucifixion. Some mysteries have to be answered through our deep individual spiritual understanding. Only this understanding provides us with answers that are immediately practical.

---

[6] Louise Hay, *Heal Your Body*

What is a mistake?

Is a genetic inclination towards a certain illness a mistake? Is somebody born handicapped a mistake and curable by raised awareness? Is an illness caused by a virus a mistake? Is illness caused by what we eat a mistake? Certainly, one may say an illness due to unresolved psycho-emotional issues is a mistake since the body was not designed to deal with these. Does that mean that we carry responsibility for getting sick? Is our longing for perfection just another version of rejecting the dark side of life?

The confusion, misinterpretation and misunderstandings on this topic have caused many people much sorrow and led to judgment. Is a nine-month-old with cancer responsible for her cancer? What about a forty-year-old with cancer? Since most of us carry an inclination towards self-reproach when we fail, any misunderstanding leading to judgment intensifies the suffering and adds a totally unnecessary new level of suffering. In this manner, we *bedevil* those that need help and understanding and often ourselves in our greatest hour of need.

If illness can at least partially be due to a lack of awareness, we do not necessarily carry responsibility for having gotten sick. Denial, avoidance, etc. are defense mechanisms that we will employ for as long as we think we have need of them. We will assume that we have need of them as long as we lack the awareness that we don't need them anymore. Do we carry responsibility for getting better once we are aware?

The awareness suggested above would produce a *"wipe[ing] mistakes off the blueprint".* In this sense, awareness produces recognition of truth and a resulting reversal of energy, producing health. This may or may not involve *doing* on our part. It would be logical to avail ourselves of the medical help that is available.

Christ said: *"Forgive them Lord, for they do not know what they are doing."* A lack of awareness implies that we do not know what we are doing or did. Once we see the results, we gain awareness and with it responsibility. Could it be possible that psycho-emotional based illness will respond to our raised awareness, yet environmental, chemically induced and genetic illnesses are much more resistant or even unalterable? Chances are, that a person with a very high awareness level to start with has a much higher resistance but will it give him or her immunity? Would such a person even care about immunity since the fear of suffering, separation and physical death (the dark side of life) has gone?

Unresolved traumatic stress turns life's everyday stresses into a threat to our safety, health and self-image.

Intense emotions limit our ability to see the big picture. Our view becomes polarized and we lose our ability to put things into perspective. We personalize others criticism or unhappiness as *our* problem and move to defend, protect, withdraw, or strike (blame). We take on their issues and add our own issues to it. Now we are fighting a fight on several fronts without realizing it. Some of us become sick or injure themselves. Others lash out, at times, at innocent bystanders. When our body begins to show the stress through physical symptoms, we move to cure ourselves by outside means: through drugs, substance abuse, through diets and exercise. It works…for a while.

Illness as a defense protects us from a threat in a variety of ways:

- It distracts us from something that is scary;
- It allows us to delay what we don't feel ready to deal with;
- It allows us to take a time out; take a break and retreat;
- It slows us down and allows us to look after our needs;
- It becomes an excuse to avoid an unpleasant situation;
- It attracts attention and sympathy from others;
- It allows us to ask for help;
- It becomes a way of punishing ourselves;
- It becomes our silent voice to motivate others to look after us.

Psycho-emotional needs cannot be met with any permanency by the physical.

If we only stepped back for a moment and thought about it, it would become clear that physical, emotional, mental and spiritual needs have different dynamics, different laws so to speak. It makes only sense that therefore they must be fulfilled in different ways.

Being alive we are painfully aware of having needs. From our most basic physical needs to sexual fulfillment and emotional needs for safety, feeling in control, having a sense of belonging and connection. Again, it is not the *having* of needs that is the problem. The true problem lies with attempting to meet all needs in the same fashion. Physical needs are and ought to be met through the physical. When we attempt to meet all of our needs through the physical, we attempt to control what cannot be controlled. We then attempt to gain emotional peace and joy by re-arranging, controlling and manipulating our body, our physical world and the people in it.

Relationships Are Our "Emotional Home"

The people we love and who love us become our emotional home.

She was a businesswoman in her forties still looking for a husband...Her mother had had a chronic illness and was in and out of hospital all through her years growing up. When mother returned from one of her hospital visits she would be distant and strange. Life felt scary and unpredictable. It wasn't safe to be close to her.

In our relationships, through the people we love and who love us, we find connection, belonging and meaning. Connection with mother was our first form of love. Now the people we love are our *emotional home*. Feeling connected gives us a sense of security. Bonding and connection play an all-important role in forming healthy relationships and families.

When, as a young child, we weren't able to bond securely, we will tend to struggle in relationships. Weak bonding between mother and child leaves the child open to attempt to compensate by seeking for connection elsewhere. At times, the child's relationship with father (or other family members) may be unusually close. This leaves the child prone to *throw out the baby with the bathwater.* The *baby* in this scenario is all the good and valuable the mother has to offer. It leaves the child stuck in idolizing one parent while rejecting the other parent. This is a conflict that is taken inside as well as experienced outside in our later relationships (or the lack thereof).

Children's needs are for parental and family unity.

Family consistency and continuity are important for the emotional health of children. Children are the innocent bystanders of parental conflicts exaggerated by divorce. They pay an often invisible emotional price. Here adults and children's needs converge without an easy answer in sight. Most likely, we made our relationship choice when we were young and blind. As we mature and discover our partners limitations, we instinctively fall back onto seeing the source for our happiness in *their change*. Once again, the source for what we want and need appears to be on the outside.

One of the primary purposes of marriage is not our emotional bliss but to be a safe haven for our children to grow and blossom. Emotional bliss is temporary and doesn't truly need institutions like marriage. Self-realization, found on the relationship path, needs commitment. As we find ourselves *not in another but through relating to another,* marriage rightly undertaken, can serve our evolution and our children's healthy development.

We feel like the severed arm of a sea star desperate to attach…to anyone.

The businesswoman shook her head…the men she dates show themselves as losers she exclaims. Unlike her, they lack a career and accomplishments and need her to take care of them! They aren't trustworthy or responsible. "I feel so lost and lonely! All I want is someone who has their life together; someone to love who loves me!"

We expect that the people closest to us should fill our emotional needs (present and past). This unspoken expectation causes many battles, losses and only temporary victories. Governed by past experiences, we expect our present day relationship choices to be the source for what wasn't given *then*. We unconsciously empower our spouses to be the physicians that are supposed to heal us. We hand them the task of being our *emotional home*.

Once our emotional equilibrium becomes dependent on someone else loving us, the source once again is with others. Now a loss can be devastating and shake us to the core. What has given our life meaning has been taken. Once we have given our sense of self away to someone else, we are vulnerable to second-guess ourselves. However, our sense of self is not to be confused with the vulnerability love demands.

We become self-critical, defensive and insecure and get caught up in people pleasing. Just like the severed arm of a sea star ready to attach itself to anyone for the sake of being attached, we too become desperate to belong.

People are people. They can withhold what we crave.

We sell ourselves short in relationships just so as to have someone who *looks like* they love us. This makes us very vulnerable and powerless. If we have entered adulthood lacking a clear sense of who we are, we are especially prone to lose ourselves again.

The opposite reaction is common as well...we won't allow ourselves to become truly related, intimate and committed. We over-focus on our career (etc.), something...anything that seems more within our control. *Why risk if it all can be taken away?* Instead of truly being in a place of choice, we react by avoiding commitment and the surrender love asks for.

We become capable of finding *our emotional home* when we *resolve the dictate of our past losses on that present significant other in our life.* Our emotional self needs a home just as our physical self does. However, different from the physical, a permanent emotional home is built on the inside before it is experienced with someone we love. Balance is an outcome of being home on all levels.

We habitually confuse love with dependency and sacrifice.

Love towards others rests on self-love. We cannot truly give what we don't have to give. Self-love is being self-caring, therefore loving others cannot be, at the same time, unloving or depriving with regard to our needs. If we don't have a clear idea of what love is, we are going to confuse love with sacrifice.

Love belongs to our inner state of being. It preexists. We can be aware of it and act on this awareness or we can lose awareness of it and act on our fears, but we cannot abolish it. When we disown or deny or talk ourselves out of what we truly want, think and feel, we lack moral courage and self-love. Yes, our actions may look loving and we may have ourselves and others convinced that we are acting from love; however, true love cannot grow on a mixture of denial, confusion and sacrifice.

To the degree that we are in touch with self-love, are we independent of needing to be loved by another. To that very degree are we actually capable of truly loving another and in turn know that we are loved. Our fears of being left, rejected, abandoned, or hurt, lose their power over us. This moves us beyond a righteous, selfish (and infantile) demand to be loved now the way we think we should have been loved then.

The businesswoman realized that she was still looking for the consistent unconditional love her mother wasn't able to provide. "Just love me for who I am!", part of her cried and demanded. At the same time, she wasn't able to love the men in her life for who they were. She realized that as a reaction to the lack of predictable love from her mother, she had idolized her father. No other man was ever good enough in comparison to him. Unwittingly, by choosing "losers" her dad remained securely on his pedestal.

We truly are capable of being emotionally home once we have mastered the concept of self-love.

If we don't first consider what a loving action towards ourselves looks like, how can then our actions be loving towards the other? Our actions may be self-sacrificing, they may be well-intentioned, but love cannot grow in deprivation of oneself or another. Such love is a confused idea of selflessness. Self-love and loving others are intricately entwined, connected and ultimately inseparable. Others, confused as we once were, may not approve.

Self-love looks at others as equals. As equals they are capable to solve their own problems. It is never our action that will show or prove what our inner intentions or state of mind is. Love is always an inner affair. Love is an extension of self for no reason at all. It does not demand recognition for its nature is self-completing. Self-denial and sacrifice in relationships with adults is not love and will surely lead to resentment, unspoken expectations and over time distance. Selflessness is different from self-love yet rests on a deep inner foundation of self-love. Without this secure inner foundation, selflessness quickly becomes self-sacrifice and self-deprivation. *Self-caring* is very different from being *selfish* or from a confused idea of *selfless.*

When in doubt ask yourself: "Is this self-caring?" "What is my underlying motivation?" "Do I feel deprived?"

Once the pink bubble of falling in love has burst true relationship work begins.

The underlying relationship conflicts that all of us bring to our later relationships can be undone while we are in a relationship. Conflict is uncomfortable. Conflict is also a necessary stepping-stone to *come emotionally home. It is the people closest to us that will challenge us to mature. If they provided us with everything we needed and wanted, we wouldn't have a stimulus to grow.*

Many people avoid conflict and rather settle for the comfort of *seeming* peace now. They hope that things will blow over or somehow go away. Avoiding conflict is one of the chief causes of troubled relationships. It is as if we are still stuck in wanting immediate gratification instead of being willing to work for what we want. When we avoid conflict and neglect to draw our lines in the sand, we remove ourselves from our true nature. We end up sabotaging ourselves and inadvertently the relationships we are in. *If we are not willing to be in conflict, we are not willing to be truly related.* Often we haven't had role models in our parents that taught us that conflict was a natural part of being in a relationship. The end result of tolerating necessary tension is that the relationship is even better after then it was before.

Liken it to a rubber band. Without tension a rubber band cannot propel itself forward. It is the amount of tension that will determine the distance and the possible breaking point.

Conflict is different from aggressive (and sometimes abusive) confrontation.

We deal with what feels uncomfortable and dissatisfying until a better place, a common ground, is found. It most likely will be frustrating and exhausting. Frustration is part of the journey. At times it may seem futile. Yet, if we persist, it is often at that point that unforeseen help arrives. Others have endured much more than frustration when standing by their convictions.

Truly engaging and relating brings a healing and sorting out of what is *"valuable"* and what is "*valueless*[7]" in our relationships. Only then are we truly ready to relate to the other without losing ourselves.

We avoid conflict because:

- we don't know how to be assertive and stand up for ourselves without arguing;
- we are tired of fighting and want to avoid the hassle;
- we do not know what we truly want;
- we doubt that we have rights;
- we feel all responsible and helpless in the face of our partners disappointment, dissatisfaction, or demands;
- we believe conflict is dangerous and means the end of connection and love.

We "toot our horn" about how we are going to change our life.

One day we may suddenly realize that we feel incomplete and unfulfilled inside. We cannot any longer ignore the nagging sense of emptiness and blame our mates. They are standing in our way and dragging us down. They have denied us the emotional home they first promised. The power to transform our boring life lies with them we insist.

In actuality, we may have done little about our own dreams. It was much easier to look for fulfillment on the outside than face the struggles that are inevitable to further our own development. When we shirk responsibility for ourselves, we typically have an affair or break up our relationship and cause many people much pain.

We avoid the self-realization crisis that comes with true relatedness by looking for another as yet *conflict-free* mate. This new mate will solve all our problems and make us feel like a hero or heroine. We end up changing the mate but the pattern is the same and it leads to the same way of life. We can't escape from ourselves, we take our deeper dynamics with us no matter where we go.

---

[7] Foundation for Inner Peace, *A Course in Miracles.*

What needs changing for mutual and maximal growth to happen needs to surface! This puts our relationship under great stress and will strain our ability to love and commit. We are *relationship animals* and the quality of our relationships is therefore important to us. If we can't be ourselves, we live in a *safe but suffocating prison*. If loving or being loved feels suffocating, stifling and makes us feel trapped, we have sold ourselves. Yet, our partner isn't necessarily to blame. Individuality means self-actualization. Everything inside of us yearns for that state of recognizing and being who we truly are. A very young child may answer with a hint of defiance when offered help: "*Me do it myself!*"

Nature wired us to strive for independence and self-realization.

We are preprogrammed to strive for *"Who am I"*. It is one of our deepest longings. We yearn for it as much as we yearn for the love of another and a sense of belonging. Relationships can offer us both or deny both. We are the ones who are doing the choosing not necessarily our mates. Connection with our mate and our sense of individuality (experienced as freedom to be ourselves) can happily coexist. Once our sense of individuality has been clearly re-established in our relationship, we can say that we are standing on our own two feet while sometimes "*touching--We*".

Ask yourself: "What adjustments have I made because I thought I had to?" "What conflicts have I avoided in doing so?" "What is the pay-off? "What is the pay?"

Our relationship out of all places needs to be that safe haven for our vulnerable self.

As Ernest Hemingway observed, "*Few men are willing to brave the disapproval of their fellows, the censure of their colleagues, the wrath of their society. Moral courage is a rarer commodity than bravery in battle or great intelligence.*"

No one can be fully an individual unless he/she is fully related first. These two aspects of life are linked together by some deep mysterious and ancient bond. They are two sides of the same coin, two faces of the same reality.

We find our *emotional home* within ourselves and by relating to someone we love. To be truly related we can't have skeletons of unmet needs and old hurts in our emotional closet. Intimacy grows on vulnerability and disclosure of our soft underbelly. "*If it is not safe to do that in your relationship why are you there?*"

Relationships bring us face to face with our denied and immature self. They are the stepping-stones to *go emotionally home.* There may be times when we feel like crawling back to the shore we left from licking our wounds.

As in the biblical story of Sodom and Gomorrah, once you start walking following a higher vision don't look back! You will turn into a salt pillar--salt standing for crystallization and stagnation.

Like-mindedness and Inspiration Become Our "Mental Home"

Sharing the same thoughts and beliefs as others allows us to join.

When we find people who think alike, we experience connection and acceptance. At times, we find like-mindedness through books and philosophies. Likewise, gossip and judgment will tempt us with a sense of connection. In joining through secrets with special others and through judgment against others, we as well establish a version of like-mindedness.

It can be exhilarating to meet someone who thinks the way we do! We sense an uncanny kinship. Inspiration leads to invention and problem-solving sometimes of the highest order.

Most young children are adamant about the values and beliefs they incorporated from their parents. As teenagers, we learn to distance ourselves and begin to find our own way of thinking about the world. Sometimes we discover a world that is very different from the one we grew up in. The pursuit of knowledge can be fascinating. To be *understood* (and to understand) when not experienced sufficiently during childhood may be a life-long journey. We now *crave* to be understood. And, we seek it by joining those that seem to hold strong beliefs and lofty ideas. It has become an outer quest where it should be an inner experience. This leaves us open to seek for it in the wrong places.

Rigidity and righteousness are a substitute for inner safety.

Sharing the same values, attitudes, goals and priorities provides us with safety. To think the way the people around us do gives us the comfort of predictability. Like-minded others provide a safe haven from our fears. If they think as we do then we must be right, we reason.

He grew up in a family with extremely rigid religious beliefs. He was told that God would punish those who didn't do as the Bible said. When his best friend's father had an affair with another church member and left his wife, he felt bewildered and torn. Could he still be a friend with his best friend without offending God?

We all create some form of mental map for ourselves that brings order and meaning to our lives. Often religion provides this map for us. Most young children will absorb without discrimination the values and beliefs they are given by their parents. Families pass on these mental maps and therefore strongly influence the child's understanding and outlook. We may call this map our values, beliefs, worldview, principles, or hopes for the future.

We are taught to be good by thinking and doing the way our parents do. This form of like-mindedness provides us with an essential feeling of belonging, safety and approval. It may also create a deep sense of divide when our feelings tell us otherwise. As teenagers, we begin to question and hopefully as adults find our own way of thinking about the world.

Righteousness keeps fear and chaos at bay.

There is great comfort in insisting that we know what is right or wrong, good or bad. We gain an illusion of safety and control, even a *sense of family* with others who think like us. *Strength lies in numbers!* "*If all of us agree that this is right then it must be!,*" we conclude. We overlook that truth doesn't abide by that principle. Truth doesn't become more truthful depending on how many people believe in it. Like a young child, we assume that if we only do the right and good then life (or God) will reward us.

In times of trouble our sense of personal values and beliefs can be a great help or a great hindrance. If we rigidly adhere to what we have previously accepted as right and good, we do not have to question and face the uncertainty that follows. Our life seems orderly. We overlook rigidity and righteousness. Our world remains the same, a safe haven that we do not recognize for its prison walls.

Our outrage and righteousness becomes a great limitation that keeps us from growing and maturing. Safety remains in outer rituals and accepted values and norms. *Growth and maturity rest on our courage to throw up the pieces of our life and then rearranging them in a new fashion once they land. This is how inner safety is fashioned.*

A joining of the mind is exhilarating and inspirational.

When we find people who think alike we experience fascination, connection and acceptance. Books, like friends, often provide a source of mental kinship. It seems miraculous when we open a book and read about an understanding that we just grasped hours earlier.

Our mind and intellect can be a refuge from our emotional self or it can be empowered by it. Being in touch with our feelings enlivens our body and stimulates our mind. When two minds join something mystical happens. We are able to experience ourselves beyond the ordinary and known. We are able to imagine new ideas and at times become filled with inspiration. Our mind becomes creative and senses endless possibilities.

He had joined a debating class. The intellectual discussions about science and philosophy were fascinating. Other members of the group sounded so inspired, convincing and confident that he wanted to be just like them.

Like-minded others open up the freedom to say what one feels and thinks. This establishes trust and closeness. We feel reassured and valued for whom we are. We are capable of finding a *mental home* in our shared thoughts, values, hopes, beliefs, ideas and goals. The family we grew up in hopefully gave us our first experience of like-mindedness:

- to be understood and listened to,
- to experience ourselves as smart and valued,
- to be capable of reasoning and solving the problems we face,
- to follow our creative urges,
- to trust our intuitive knowing,
- to learn from our mistakes.

"Know thyself", is a Greek aphorism inscribed in the forecourt of the temple of Apollo at Delphi, Greece.

What makes us human and leads us to evolve is the ability to know oneself authentically. The pursuit of self-knowledge is an age-old quest. It is not for the faint-hearted. To know oneself as the very human being one is, with all of one's fallibility, shortcomings and selfish interests brings freedom. We become free to accept what needs to be accepted and change what can be. It is fascinating to come to understand the laws of the psyche. It is inspirational to consider how many men and women have walked before us on the same quest.

"The saying, "Know thyself", may refer by extension to the ideal of understanding human behavior, morals, and thought, because ultimately to understand oneself is to understand other humans as well."[8]

To truly come to know ourselves requires the development of open-mindedness. Open-mindedness allows us to truly hear other people's opinions. When we are truly receptive to others, our mind doesn't already prepare an answer while they are still speaking. We are capable of respecting views and beliefs that differ from our own. We learn to use introspection and analysis to see into ourselves. Open-mindedness is an outcome of self-knowledge and a prerequisite to truly arriving *mentally home.*

Beliefs too can and often will change as we mature. Our understanding of what is right and wrong evolves. Inspiration is fleeting. If what we believed in as the truth becomes suddenly discovered as false, we may undergo an identity crisis. *"Who am I?" "What am I?" "Can anything be trusted?"* Most of us sadly succumb to the lure of safety and comfort of like-minded righteousness. But a few do dare. "*Are you going to be one of them? Or are you going to follow the path of the many?"*

[8] Wikipedia, Know thyself

Intuition allows us to know in an almost supernatural way.

There is a power that begins to grow inside of us as we clean up what clutters our psyche, our *inner house*. Intuition perceives what is hidden and underlying without knowing why one knows. It is an instantaneous recognition of a situation or solution. It produces insight. It is one of our *psychic abilities.* History shows that many great breakthroughs in understanding were the result of intuitive perception and insight. Some people are gifted with a trans-personal form of knowing beyond our everyday personal reality.

Because intuition is not rational, we do not have the logic explanations that our intellect may demand. Maybe we cannot trace the steps on how we arrived at what we *know* or proof that we have a *right to know.* It may be in conflict with what reason tells us.

It has become fashionable to *"channel"* our inherent ability of trans-personal levels of knowing and perceiving. It takes courage to own our gifts. We are afraid that no one would listen if it were *"just us". It is so much more sensational the other way.* We cannot evolve personally as long as we don't own ourselves.

As a society, we focus on developing the intellectual, left-brain functions of our brain and neglect or even discourage intuitive perceptions. What is valued and furthered are rational, analytical thinking and the capacity to accumulate information. At times, therefore others or ourselves will dismiss our intuitive insights as guesswork. We become afraid to be regarded as *weird or crazy.*

Intuition can easily be confused with assumptions based in our past experiences. Therefore most of us have learned to not trust, refine and develop our hunches. Our *ego* with its need for self-glorification gets in the way.

Increasing our awareness does not by itself necessarily change our experience.

More often then not, we actually turn the very tool that would set us free against ourselves. In particularly people who are prone to be self-critical indulge in this. The best way of dealing with judgment is to dismiss its validity the moment we become aware of judging. In other words, immediately correct your judgmental attitude. There is no point to judging yourself for judging or despairing over your judgmental attitude. Take the power of belief out of your judgmental thoughts or words.

When we get caught up in self-criticism, we counteract the positive outcomes of awareness. Judging others out loud is verbally abusive or becomes gossip and slander. Either version shrinks our awareness. We become less. Judgment divides our world into *you and me.*

What I judge in others I now have to judge in myself and, what I judge in myself I will judge in others. Once we step beyond judgment, we can find a new level of kinship with that other person. Underneath it all, we share their fears, hopes and needs.

Our mind has the power to deceive us about what is truly meaningful.

The way we habitually manage our thinking is a bit like attempting to ride a horse sitting on it backwards.

Let's say for a moment you want a new car...and you have all kinds of reasons for why this new car is important to you. (By the way, there is nothing wrong with wanting a new car and indeed getting it.)

Maybe you don't have the money and therefore part of you feels frustrated. As a result you feel deprived. You can't help but keep thinking..."If I only could afford a new car!" It looks as if having this new car would bring you happiness. Happiness seems outside your reach. The resulting feelings lock you into all kinds of secondary negative feelings and possibly actions. Your focus is on what you think you cannot have.

Just for fun let's change the dynamic for a moment: ask yourself how you would feel if indeed you were able to buy this new car today and park it at home? How would you feel falling asleep tonight? Let's take it one step further...having that feeling how then would you feel about yourself?

Your answer will be individual...but let's assume your answer is that you would feel "important". This feeling...(of importance) is most likely an experience that has a question mark attached inside of you (for some reason). This feeling...(of importance) is not something you hold as an accepted fact about yourself. It is something you seek outside of yourself, in this case by buying a new car. If this was not so, you would not carry strong emotional energy about owning this new car.

Our mind is meant to be a tool.

The thing is, this feeling (of importance, etc.) is truly an inner experience. Seeking it through outer accomplishments or re-affirmation by other people will not put it inside in any permanent way. It is only you who can cement it in your psyche by claiming it. It is within your power to think and treat yourself that way.

Your mind may tell you otherwise. And, by believing that your outer searching has nothing to do with your inner self, you share like-mindedness with millions. Once you discover the deeper meaning of your upper level wanting, you can buy a new car or you don't have to buy a new car. The new car is now just that, a new car. It does not come with any other hidden emotional attachments that you somewhere inside of you hope to fulfill.

Substitute something that seems to elude you for "the new car" and find out what is hiding underneath...your mind has become a tool of self-discovery. You are ready to take responsibility for your dreams and true feelings about things.

We remake ourselves daily when we finally accept who we are. Once we have become willing to open our eyes and have found acceptance of the unacceptable, we become who we want to be. This isn't an easy task. It involves dealing with the limitations that have become so normal, so habitual. It rests on becoming our own best friend. *"Who am I?"* is a question answered again and again on a new level, each time we ascend to a new level of awareness. All evolution just like DNA is spiral in nature.

Whenever you feel upset ask yourself: "Who do I want to be in this circumstance?" Start with a blank slate for yourself and others daily.

Like-mindedness is not always found through our spouse.

When we meet our future spouse, we assume like-mindedness due to the blinding qualities of romantic love. It is truly a challenge if the person we married holds very different beliefs and values then we do. *To think alike* is the basis for many relationships. However, a spouse cannot possibly agree with us on everything.

As the everyday drudgery of routines, responsibilities and their boredom take their toll the initial closeness we experienced becomes dulled. We think of all the things we differ about. We feel not valued and appreciated for who we are and what we do. We want to go places we have failed to go and do things we have failed to do.

If we ever looked at our ideals and dreams objectively, we would see that we could do most of these things within our relationship and the life we have. The true reason is not that our mate stands in the way and that he or she doesn't think the way we do. The true reason is that we haven't been willing to take responsibility for our dreams, our true feelings about things and risk. Tolerating the tension of conflicting wants and wishes that will naturally arise in any relationship is very uncomfortable, to say the least. However, without this tension we cannot find a new common ground and grow in intimacy.

We expect our mates to give up their way of thinking, feeling and acting and adopt ours. Or, we give up our way of thinking and feeling and adopt theirs. Either (unnecessary) adjustment is avoidance. It is time to consider helping ourselves. Not all mates are capable of being our like-minded others in every aspect of life. Because we do not share like-mindedness on all things does not mean that our relationship is lacking. True human love rests on acceptance of who we are and who the other is. We find our *mental home* through inspiration and self-knowledge. We will find like-minded others if we reach out. These like-minded others may not always be the people in our family.

The Mystery of Life Brings Us "Spiritually Home"

"To a frog that's never left his pond the ocean seems like a gamble. Look what he's giving up: security, mastery of his world, recognition! The ocean frog just shakes his head. "I can't really explain what it's like where I live, but someday I'll take you there."
Jelaluddin Rumi, poet and mystic

There is lawfulness to all of life, our inner world as well as our outer world.

When we lose touch with a deeper underlying connection to life itself, alienation, emptiness, greed and strife enter. It is the integrity of our personal life that each individual either lives or doesn't live, that produces and leads to ethical responsibility. It leads to the mastery of good and bad in human nature and therefore ultimately in our own nature. It leads to an experience of inter-connection bringing meaning and fulfillment to our every day mundane tasks and interactions that make the same *not mundane*. Meaning rests on feeling rooted through our bodies to the earth, the *"I am"* experience of being alive. Purpose is an inner sense of direction on how to contribute to the betterment of all.

Our inner being is experienced as immeasurable and incomprehensible, us, and at the same time not us. Our inner being is our *spiritual home.* This part of us is independent of any outer person, thought system, or place while at the same time allowing for and balancing all of them. It is this *spiritual home* that ultimately satisfies our need to be home. It is all-inclusive...there is beauty and purpose in a physical place we call home and meaning in being with people we love and who love us. We find inspiration, safety and belonging through relating to like-minded others. Our spiritual home offers us something that cannot be found in any other way...inner safety, connection and belonging, untouchable by outer change.

When we lack identification with this innermost part of us, we experience ourselves as a fragment cut off from the world around us. We experience alienation and feel separate. *We then have to be very careful with our physical existence, possessions and our emotional connections.* Or, we become careless and irresponsible overriding our fear and sense of meaninglessness. We feel set adrift and alone in a big and dangerous world where our existence seems constantly threatened. We keep ourselves busy and distracted.

Are you carefree, neither "careful" nor "careless", in your interactions with others and with your responsibilities? Which areas of your life tempt you most to lose yourself in either "careful" or "careless"?

We create a God in our own image.

My parents looked at people who went to church as foolish, weak and deluded. When I went on hikes in the nearby mountains I found where I believed God lived. I could hear a voice in the gurgling water, the rustling of the trees and in the sunshine throwing its surreal light onto the hills. I had found something magical that touched me deeply. To this day I find my spiritual connection through being out in nature.

No matter what we were taught growing up or have come to believe, most people do have a sense of something beyond their physical existence. This place of wonder and mystery allows us to step beyond the underlying fear of our human lives and brings meaning and purpose during troubling times. The types of spiritual beliefs we hold are strongly influenced by what our families taught us. If we were encouraged to question within a framework of trust, we had the necessary space to develop our own understanding of the mystery of life. Our family's beliefs then provided the foundation from which we could push off into finding our own deepest convictions.

If our families' teachings were rigid, we learned that only our beliefs and those of accepted religious authorities were the right ones. We had to either submit to what our family would tolerate or risk losing their approval and support. This strongly influenced what we today believe about our essential nature. *It leads us to create a God in our own image.* This sadly often is a punishing and vengeful God; a God who loves the good and hates the bad; a God who is separate from who we are. Conflict within us or with others is an outcome of that inner division.

Without a deeper reverence for the unknowable our thinking, feeling and acting become fear based.

Our faith into the supernatural gives us safety and order. Without it we are easily tempted to experience ourselves in times of trouble as helpless, hopeless and alone. In our nightmare we thrash, attack and defend. It requires shifting our identification beyond being a mere finite human to begin to relax. We then can experience ourselves as supported by the safety net of spirit and matter. Separation becomes individuality, distinct yet connected. Our identification shifts from the physical and material to our inner state of our being. We become *I am, versus I am this...*or *I am that.*

Imagine spirit as vertical lines and matter as horizontal lines forming a net. The little squares created are our individual lives. When we are aware of this net, we know that we are supported and part of both spirit and matter. We are connected to every other square in the net. It is impossible to be disconnected. The net cannot exist intact without any of the squares. The squares make up the net and the net creates the individual squares. To know ourselves as one with all and as irreplaceable is to know that we (the little squares made of spirit and matter) are an intricate part of the net.

Now fear is meaningless. Experiencing ourselves as just a "little square", "disconnected" and "alone" is to deny our true nature. Then all we are is the body and we better be very careful with our physical existence, possessions and our emotional connections.

Truth has been inherent in the human soul since the beginning of time.

It is only the way we express truth that changes through the ages. As our intellect grew we were able to express and comprehend it in an ever more conscious, logical and exact way. There is a truth, grasped by our intuition, which is the mystery of life. This is a mystery we generally call *God*, the quantum physicist calls *Unified field,* the priest calls *Soul* and the esoteric philosopher calls *Consciousness.* If our curiosity and wonder was encouraged, we naturally learned to discover what is true for us. We learned to discover our own personal truth. To know our truth in a situation, we need to be able to share what we think is true. In expressing what we assume to be true, we find if it is so for us or not.

Many families live by an unspoken motto of *don't say what you truly think and feel.* Instead of being taught emotional honesty we are taught to deny and hide. This weakens our ability to know what is right for us. The expression of who we are becomes clouded. The good news is that as adults we have the power to undo and correct what might have gone amiss. To get in touch with our truth, we have to first learn to become more truthful with ourselves in the safety of our own mind. We have to learn to *admit to ourselves* without plunging into remorse, self-condemnation and guilt. And, we need to learn to question the messages we were given.

How to live and act in order to live a meaningful life?

This question is what through the ages has been communicated to us. *How do we gain this deeper wisdom that speaks to the very basic questions of life?* We are told that ours can be an understanding that moves us from intellectual knowledge through psycho-emotional insight to intuited spiritual vision. That it holds the deepest interest and meaning for people allowing them to overcome the most excruciating hardships, even the fear of death. This is an indisputable historic fact. The many religions on this planet speak to it in their own way. It is like a memory of an original harmony and unity that is lawful.

This guiding ideal of harmony and unity leads us to find joy in our daily life for no reason at all. It is an intuited understanding that life is a gift to be shared by extending our love and joy to others. It calls us to share the unique contribution we are capable of with those that come into our life. It rests on using our ability to think, use foresight, past experiences, introspection and deliberate over our actions to live wisely. When we allow ourselves to react to daily experiences in a habitual and almost instinctual way, we reverse our own evolutionary movement. Now alienation, emptiness, greed and strife enter. We experience ourselves as a fragment, terrifyingly vulnerable and finite. Our energy withdraws in a protective stance instead of expands in a creative stance. Our thinking, feeling and acting become based in fear.

Our relationships and life itself are the testing ground for our spirituality.

We touch the divine when we can see it in another's eyes. We touch the divine through the wonders of nature and at times of mental inspiration. It is in our interactions with people that we are forced to put into practice what we say we believe.

In Christianity, we are taught to not have any other source before God. When we expect others to meet our emotional needs, to make us happy and fulfilled, we make them into our source. When we buy things to buy happiness, we confuse the origin of happiness. When we seek self-worth through accomplishments and success, we remove ourselves from what is truly meaningful.

Committed relationships are a mutually beneficial practical arrangement and an opportunity for sharing and companionship. Committed relationships are a necessary safe haven to grow healthy children. They are a meeting place between two self-sufficient and equal individuals producing personal growth and allow us to occasionally touch the divine.

The root of the word *spirit* comes from the Latin *"spiritus"* breath. Our breath is essential to our physical existence. Our connection with spirit is essential to our sense of self, meaning and purpose in life. *"To be in the world but not of it"* is the mastery that leads us beyond what our senses tell us touching another realm of self and life!

We sometimes touch the divine through the physical. Our physical existence and experience can become imbued with the wonder of the spiritual. When our feelings are a vehicle for healing and connection then we touch the divine through the emotional. When our mind is filled with fascination and inspiration, we touch the divine through the mental. When we become still and sense the mystery of life, we touch the essence of spirit. We stand in awe of life and the universe. *Finally, we are home.*

How to Bring About Changes We Want

"You cannot hope to build a better world without improving the individuals. To that end each of us must work for his own improvement and at the same time share a general responsibility to all humanity."

Madame Marie Curie

With every new beginning there are changes.

When we choose change we eagerly say YES to what we regard as something good. We anticipate and strive to bring about something new in hope for a better future. Change can be exciting and full of promise. Even good and desired changes are stressful! Some changes are initiated by us others aren't. It is important to have a plan "A" and "B". It is equally important to realize that our own plan for happiness is just that, a plan, *subject to change without notice.* Challenging as this may be, life asks us to move with trust where it wants to direct us.

Some changes are presented to us by life itself or other people unasked for. They are completely unexpected and at times disturbing, frightening and painful. They arrive on our doorstep at the most inconvenient of times. We typically do not recognize the heavy hand of change as an inner need for progress. We weren't taught to say to ourselves: "*Something good will come of this!*" "*Sure don't know what it possibly could be right now (all I can see is what has been taken from me) but in time I will see*".

Most changes appear "done to us" by someone or life itself.

And because we lack the faith to *"find the silver lining in the rain cloud,"* at times, *"the rain cloud becomes our life.* Change is a guaranteed constant in life, for the better or worse. The stimulus for change may be the choices we made along the way. Sometimes change happens because of choices *made for us* that we would never consciously choose.

Change may be due to an opportunity that is exciting yet unravels the life we have known. A crisis teaching us to question and reconstruct the roles we had assumed. Or, we find ourselves facing the same problems and saying the same things over and over until all becomes too painful or too empty and we finally decide to make a change.

Our greatest teachers are the people in our immediate environment. Yet, entering a relationship with the intention to change the other usually backfires. The need for change has to be an inner recognition for it to translate into positive action. It typically is difficult to accept our mate as the initiator for positive change. At times, we need a crisis coming from any other direction but from our close ones to be able to accept a new direction in life.

We usually want the other to change so that *our feathers won't get ruffled!* We want them to come around to our way of life; it obviously is better then theirs! It would create commonality and connection. Changing old ingrained patterns and insecurities isn't quick or necessarily easy, our own or our mates. It takes courage and discipline to look to the inside for a *fix* instead of insisting that it should be on the outside (only). It takes courage to accept others for who they are instead of trying to remodel them into who we want them to be. It takes courage to accept the consequences. Change is very rarely straightforward moving from "A" to "B". Its nature is spiral. It takes patience, commitment and time.

Human beings are creatures governed by motivation and habit.

As long as we can, we will take the known or easy way out. There has to be a reward or a consequence for us to relinquish what's habitual, convenient and self-serving. We all bring attitudes and behavior patterns to our relationships (personal and professional) that are not workable. Actions and attitudes that don't nourish our relationships and our life keep us stuck.

Change progresses in a spiral fashion. It vacillates between well-intended but quickly aborted attempts to first successes to setbacks to accomplishment; to be revisited on the next spiral.

A man walked down the street. There was a large hole filled with water that made the street impassable without getting wet. He proceeded and got wet. He walked down the street again forgetting about the hole and got wet again. Once again he walked down the street and noticed that there was a large hole filled with water but too late, he got wet again. Next time he turned to walk down the street he remembered that there was something, but too late he got wet again. The time after that he reminded himself to not walk down the street that had the hole but he forgot. After several more occurrences of getting wet, one day he remembered, as he was about to turn to walk down that street and decided to take another street instead. Change is like that.

Others respond to our attitudes and behaviors.

All relationships maintain an innate energetic balance. If we crystallize in one extreme, we unconsciously support our mate to move to the opposite end. If our mate is crystallized in one extreme, we will instinctively want to balance things by moving to the opposite viewpoint or behavior. This is true with our children as well. This is why business types are married to artists, lazy types find industrious and capable mates, irresponsibility is balanced by over-responsibility and people who are prone to self-doubt attract opinionated counterparts. We do usually very clearly see the need for change in our partner. Seeing our own imbalance, what needs to change in our attitude, is much harder.

Changing the way we relate to others will produce a change in the relationship. It is the only change we truly have power over. Once we change it becomes uncomfortable for the other to maintain their old position. We in effect expose their hang-ups, closed-mindedness and imbalances. This may produce change. Now, this form of exposure is definitely not the same as crucifixion since it lacks judgment. Others are usually not inclined to be grateful (at least initially).

The other will have to adjust to stay in balance. This may be done with loud cries of disapproval and threats, seeking to pull us back to the old ways. *Have you ever watched a bunch of crabs that were thrown into the same bowl? In their attempt to escape, they pull the ones who almost succeed in climbing out, back!* Creating change takes courage and the perseverance to maintain our new position while *all hell breaks loose*.

To bring about change we need to resist the temptation of compensating or picking up the slack.

Relationships don't tolerate a vacuum. If our partner is not ready to grow with us it will become apparent. This may be terrifying because we anticipate loss. The old comes to an end, yet the new is still illusive. Deeper fears of *being alone* may surface. All change gives us an opportunity. Life-long relationships contain an unlimited potential for growth for the individuals. That doesn't always make them easy.

Changing oneself has many benefits: we learn to deal more constructively with the people who won't change; it allows us to make peace with our own unmet needs from the past instead of demanding that our significant others in the present meet them; we have a chance to sort out which of the expectations we carry are realistic and which aren't; it will clarify for us what rights we do have and what demands are legitimate. When focusing on changing ourselves, we learn to get in touch with our own inner world. *What is our payoff for overcompensating for others and not holding them capable and accountable to do their fair share?*

Model change by:

- Changing the way we respond and relate;
- Focusing on what *we can do different*;
- Holding firm to what is important to us; being willing to risk what still may seem at least partially in our best interest on behalf of our conviction.

For change to happen we have to first sincerely want it to happen.

We have to be emotionally ready for change to happen. We have to be willing to do what it takes on our part first. At times, we say we want change but are not yet ready to do what it will take. Old habits, our old sense of identity and our fears get in the way. Our very first needs as infants were for constancy, predictability and consistency. When these needs have not been met sufficiently when they should have, then change stands in contradiction with these needs. *We may not like what we have but it is known and predictable.* Some relationship patterns are so long-standing, habitual and ingrained that it takes a *brick hitting our head* before we get that something has to go!

Our mates are human and therefore not capable of fulfilling all of our relationship dreams. In some ways we may be very compatible and in other ways quite incompatible. There may be little we or others can do about personality characteristics that are innate to their being. However, there is a lot we (and they) can do, when asked to act more constructively. *Where there is a will there is a way!*

What are our own motives? Are we set on proving that the other won't be there when we need them...that the other is incapable and weak...that they don't truly care? Is that what we truly want?

What we resist persists.

If we resist shouldering the responsibility for how we feel about something, we become incapable of doing anything about it. Our emotional reactions are in charge. And, we inadvertently put others in charge by demanding or expecting that they should change. Since we cannot *make* them change, they now hold power over our emotional equilibrium.

When we don't look for deeper insight into the soil within which our problems have grown, we may snip off a leaf or two but won't eradicate the weed. Judging others or ourselves for the problems we face will only serve to intensify them. All problems serve a function. They are a defense mechanism put into place to protect us from something that we experienced as threatening. They are a product of what we have failed to learn.

"People's pain often comes from the gap between how things currently are in their lives and how they wish they could be."
Carolyn Foster, *The Family Patterns Workbook*

This pain is an outcome of repeated unsuccessful problem solving, a belief in loss and a confusion of what would make one truly happy. It rests on the belief that we can be harmed by our or others' lack. What we do not readily recognize is the fact, that what we have in our life serves a function, consciously or subconsciously. So, it may make us miserable, it often also offers protection from an imaginary something we fear even more. It is a call by our soul to grow.

"To know what is right and not to do it is the worst cowardice." Confucius

Some people have such an aversion to conflict that they rather sacrifice their (and at times their children's) best interests then stand up and speak up. True, others probably won't like it when we voice opposing opinions. We may even be (rightfully) afraid of them becoming abusive towards us. Deep down people tend to be self-serving. Voicing our opinions takes inner strength and courage. We carry a deeply seated fear about being separate from the group. Nature and experience (our own and humanities) has taught us that it makes us vulnerable. Speaking up takes wisdom and foresight. We may have to face later that we were wrong! We may need courage to find out that those we thought were our friends or had our best interest in mind didn't after all.

Depending on our background, conflict has many different associations for the individual. For some people conflict equals abusiveness. There are people who thrive on confrontation. They have learned to control and manipulate others into letting them have their way by using their aggression so as to intimidate. *"Divide and conquer"* is an old maxim that is not outdated for today. It takes courage to face these bullies and not flinch. Being prepared is essential! Our lesson may be that we are capable of protecting those we love and ourselves.

There is a difference between conflict and confrontation.

If our past has taught us that conflict will put us into harms way then why risk? Anger frightens people. We feel frightened by other people's anger but also by our own anger. Women in particular tend to repress anger for it is socially unacceptable for a woman to be publicly angry. As such we do a big disservice to others and ourselves.

It is as if we buy a coloring set at the store without the color red, pretending we have a complete set. We need our fangs and claws to protect and defend our ground, our loved ones and ourselves. Other people aren't always fair or well intentioned. Life isn't fair. To pretend otherwise is to live in a fantasy world.

Pain and conflict then become the motivators we cannot ignore that will allow us to grow. *"We are seldom upset for the reason we think we are."*[9] *Deep-seated feelings are our baggage we carry and therefore our responsibility. Feelings of not important, not capable, not good enough, not wanted, not protected, etc. have tentacles reaching way back into our past.*

We can try and fool others but we can't fool ourselves.

We may avoid conflict in many ways. Some of us pretend: "*Oh, it doesn't matter!"* Each time we belittle or minimize our feelings about things, we also belittle and minimize ourselves. My question to you is: *"If you wouldn't be happy to live with this for the rest of your life, why is it OK to live with it now?" You may have a legitimate reason. Do consider however, that the way things go, if you don't change it now, it will be even more difficult to change later.* Things are actually best addressed before they have big feelings attached, have become an ingrained pattern and before they led to numerous disappointments and failures.

What is the price you pay? What are the unfulfilled hopes, dreams and wishes you hide, ignore, or have given up on? Others aren't there to save us from ourselves. They have a big enough job of saving themselves! If it irritates you now, what makes you think it won't irritate you tomorrow or the day after? What adjustments will you have to make to be able to live with this ongoing irritation? How are these adjustments, little by little, going to erode what is meaningful to you and remove you inch by inch from your true

---

[9] Foundation for Inner Peace, *A Course in Miracles*

nature? And what do you think this constant irritation will do to your health and the intimacy in your relationship? Bring you closer?

All advances for mankind have involved some form of challenging the established and habitual.

This is true on a personal level as well. Change requires that the status quo is being questioned and challenged. Societal change and personal change are interdependent. This isn't a call to attack, blame, leave, or think that another's change is where it's at! It is a call to claim what is yours foremost inside of you, both, what you regard as good and bad. It calls to stand by your convictions and expose what needs to be exposed without demanding to see blood or have others sacrifice their first-born.

When others challenge us to change, our first reaction may always be to see ourselves as unjustly treated. We tend to first blame and obsess about the why, how and what another did. Step back for a moment before reacting and ask: *What is my part in all of this? If anything, what am "I" supposed to learn? Why does it upset me the way it does? What do I need to do to get a different result?*

"An error does not become truth by reason of multiplied propagation, nor does truth become error because nobody sees it. Truth stands even if there is no public support. It is self sustained."

Mahatma Ghandi

Ultimately, it is our responsibility to set boundaries and make changes when we feel dissatisfied with our relationships and life. We have to be willing to ask for what we want and need and stand our ground with regard to it. Blaming others, in particularly behind their back, is a way of avoiding and taking the easy way out. Blame keeps us swirling around in an upper level emotionality without resolving anything. Constructive problem solving incorporates the other person's complaints or pain as equal to ours and finds a mutually agreeable solution. Setting boundaries is stating what is acceptable to us and what isn't. As such, it has natural consequences. It is often at this point in our evolution, when unforeseen doors could open, that most people miss their true opportunities.

Don't try and teach a pig to sing.

It will frustrate and dishearten you and it will certainly either annoy the pig or be completely wasted in influencing it.

Some people, who hold very rigid, outmoded, and immature ideas about relating to others in relationships won't respond to anything else but clear and consistent ground rules by which to play. We are all creatures of habit and convenience. NO is so much faster and easier than YES. In such a case, it would be wasting our creative, intuitive and well-intentioned efforts by trying to convince the other of a new and better way. We may have to take our situation to a higher authority.

Reasoning with someone who can't or won't hear us is a futile action. They simply may not be interested in what we have to say at all. They have their own agenda. Our request may be like the irritating buzzing sound of a housefly. They eagerly long for the fly swatter.

In such a case, attempting to communicate what is important to us will definitely fall on deaf ears if not be used against us. Any display that appears emotional and vulnerable will be judged as irrational and therefore weak, a behavior to be ignored and criticized. Working towards win-win solutions is as yet a foreign language. Now, extending oneself and showing one's vulnerability is the wrong thing to do! This is a time for *tough love* and passive resistance.

Learning to draw lines in the sand.

People have to first be willing to relinquish selfishness, developed empathy and surrender the idea that they know best for another. Only then are they capable of seeing the situation through someone else's viewpoint. This allows for working towards win-win problem solving. We have to be willing to fall back onto simply saying NO!! Setting down clear, simple and consistent boundaries is the only language that has a chance of being successful. Self-change now means learning to communicate clearly, in short statements what is OK and what is not OK. It calls for refusing to withdraw into fighting back or giving up. Creating change rests on being aware of what we think, like, feel, knowing our rights and knowing when someone else has crossed the line.

Set boundaries while maintaining a dead calm and resolute energy. Remember any display of emotion might be used against you. Just as garbage will pollute our environment careless emotional energy pollutes our shared emotional environment. People who are careless with their emotional energy are indeed polluting common emotional living space.

Take the opportunities that life gives you.

Gratitude is a virtue! Remember to be grateful for what you have. Our mind at times becomes obsessively focused on everything that is wrong with others and the life we live. We are often tempted to over-focus on what we don't have instead of focusing on everything that is right with our life. Make sure to remember to be grateful for the good in your life as a daily routine. Remember to find joy daily if you have a reason to or if you don't. Life is too short to be miserable.

What works for children works for adults! We all like to hear what we do right to please others. No one likes to constantly hear what is wrong with him or her. Sometimes, we have to look for something good to say. The people who love us want us to feel loved by them. If we tell them what we want instead of complain about what we don't have, the likelihood is, that they will make an effort.

Even the most well-intentioned mate feels reluctant when asked to undergo a personality change.

We want them to change so as to care-take our wounds. Despite that flaw in our thinking and the fact that this strategy has failed us many times before, we steadfast hold on. We keep hoping that the others change will save us from a repetition of our past pain and provide happiness now. What we don't want to look at are our feelings and the unavoidable consequences if we would accept the reality that is. Attempting to change others, fooling ourselves that it is possible to change them into what we want them to be, allows us to avoid.

Ask yourself: *"What feelings come up, realizing my husband's (significant other's) limitations?" "What is my investment in him changing?" "Why do I want him to be a certain way?" "If he was to change then what don't I have to feel?" Look for answers beyond simply happy/great. Find adjectives that describe your feeling.*

A strong sense of who we are and what the world is all about grows from a secure foundation of trustworthy care during the first six years of life. Later, significant trauma may upset this experience. Yet, our early associations carry the power to do the most harm. Consistency, continuity, predictability, gentleness, guidance and not feeling judged for who we are, are basic requirements in early childhood. Within such an environment, the child can experience itself as safe and secure to *express, experiment and explore.*

As unfashionable and outdated it may be there is truth in allowing and encouraging men to *give* and women to *receive*. Many women are poor in receiving others help. Many men are unskilled in giving of themselves emotionally.

Remember many *today(s)* have a way of growing into a lifetime. Start with living the relationship you want to have and the person you want to be today. Once we have taken this step, the changes that need to happen will happen. Maybe we don't need to hold on so tightly in affairs of our security and our hearts.

As we take our first tentative steps in trusting that the hand of life will hold us, we learn that changes are helpful and that the new directions they point us to are good.

We habitually assume that we know.

Our Thoughts Determine Our Experience

"It is not the facts in a situation that tend to disturb us. It is the meaning we give to those facts that upsets us."

Usually we do not question what we assume our eyes see or our ears hear.

"I saw it with my own eyes!" "I heard her say it with my own ears!" "It is a fact!" Facts, however, do not necessarily make us angry, judgmental, hurt or upset. They are simply observations of what is. As observations they lack preconceptions and need to be interpreted as to the meaning they have for us. We mix what is with what we assume is or we fear will result.

Experiments have shown that different people observing the same accident will give different descriptions. We know now that our hopes, wishes, fears and beliefs will override what we could swear we saw or heard. Fear, in particular, has a disproportionate influence on the assumptions we form. Some people will habitually respond to kindness with suspicion. Low self-esteem predisposes us to perceive rejection where none was intended. We are capable of finding something wrong even in a truly good person.

Ninety three percent of what we communicate is based on our body language and energy or tone of voice. Our beliefs, unresolved issues and insecurities govern this communication. *What do we see because we expect to see it? What interpretations are we placing on what actually is? How do we react to innocent gestures of others?*

The nurturing we received influences how we perceive, communicate, learn and problem-solve.

"*Early life experience has a disproportionate importance in organizing the mature brain*," writes prominent U.S. neurobiologist Bruce Perry. "*Both a lack of critical nurturing experience and excessive exposure to traumatic violence will alter the developing central nervous system.*"

Early childhood is a formative time of deciding who we are in relation to others and the world. Our early experiences determine and shape our future emotional health and how well we will be able to learn and communicate. They influence the level of confidence with which we approach various life situations. They determine our sense of ourselves as loved, loveable and loving. Our early experiences become the bedrock in which many of our later limitations are chiseled.

"Critical nurturing experiences" are often subtle and their lack is hard to establish. They are dependent on the maturity and awareness level of the adults who care for us. They are subject to the peers that either include or reject us. Even if our childhood was relatively harmonious, we did take from this time beneficial as well as limiting associations and ideas and their resulting interpretation patterns. Exposure to frequent fighting, unpredictability, criticism, lack of understanding, or neglect predisposes us to becoming hyper-vigilant towards the slightest sense of disharmony.

What wasn't given leaves us wanting.

Conclusions and interpretations become the basis for our habitual way of thinking.

Our habitual thinking may be equated to a computer program: *input determines output*. This idea promotes hope, for input can be changed. Input is part present experience and part past experiences and decisions. We have choice in what to think. New decisions can be made. The result is a different output namely a different experience.

The meaning we give to our seeing (perception) arises as a natural by-product of the conclusions we drew during the first few years of life and along the way into adulthood. This giving of meaning becomes habitual. We see and expect what we were taught and our past decisions dictate. To see something as good or bad is, in a sense, predetermined by our mental habits. These conclusions are part interpretation and part fact. They are strongly influenced by our maturity level and innate personality tendencies.

Whenever you notice yourself indulging in negative or judgmental thinking imagine yourself pushing a "delete button" that erases the thoughts you just had. You may add a mental note…"Cancel, cancel", etc. and consciously choose what you want to think. Add a statement to dismiss what you just thought or said. In other words, deny your judgment its validity as in: "…this means nothing!"

"Why" a silent voice asks.

We form assumptions about *why* certain happenings and incidents occurred and what their meaning is. Part of the meaning we gave to things that happened to us was strictly an inner process. Part of it was influenced by our innate personality. Part of it was strongly influenced by our upbringing. Aware and in-touch-with-themselves parents parent well. Unaware and immature parents will parent poorly. Yet, certain experiences were simply beyond our parents control and dictated by the hand of life.

"My mother had to go to hospital when I was six months old." "I don't remember, of course, but my aunt tells me that I wouldn't stop crying for days."

The younger the child the more likely is mother's absence experienced as extremely distressing. A multitude of different conclusions may an individual child associate with the fact of mother's absence.

One child may experience abandonment and the accompanying emotion of helpless rage. Another may feel rejection and the feeling of "I am not good enough". A third, take on the fault for her absence and therefore feel guilt "It's my fault". A fourth, might conclude that there is nothing to worry about and trust that she will be back in due time.

How well mother and father (and our extended family) are able to mitigate the experience will minimize the traumatic impact on the child. Yet, it is ultimately the child that will decide on how to interpret the experience and what conclusions to draw.

The most significant and influential part of any conclusion drawn is the meaning it now holds.

"If mom left because I wasn't good, etc. then this means that I am???" These conclusions personalized turn into decisions about oneself. They become the foundation for our self-image and self esteem. As the building blocks for our emotional health and attitudes they determine our future success in life and relationships.

A very young child will experience his/her environment from a point of observation. His/her mind is as yet open and relatively void of preexisting assumptions. The child has to be taught and will conclude what meaning to give to what it is encountering.

The baby played with an orange. "Ball, ball," he exclaimed excitedly. "No," his mother said. "That's an orange!" We learn to give meaning to things. Part of that is a necessary step of functioning in life. Yet, it also can be our biggest limitation.

"What course of action does my old conclusion and emotional reaction dictate?"

"What if I dealt with this in a completely new and different way?" What would this new way be?" (If all fails, try the opposite to what you habitually feel drawn to do...if nothing else, you will surprise yourself and others.)

Maturity requires us to question the conclusions we draw and the roles we adopt.

Part of becoming truly adult is to sort out the present meaning (truth) from habitual interpretation (untruth) and see every situation as *new.* The truth then needs to be accepted and digested, which is a bit more involved then this statement implies. The untruth needs to be dismissed.

The meaning we give, associations we have and interpretations we place produce the emotions we experience and determine how we react and relate.

Our thinking, seeing and experiencing is subjective. We habitually indulge in fantasies of imagined negative outcomes. Interpretation begins to surround and often distort the present. In the process of developing our personality and individuality, we all make decisions about what we want to identify with and what we don't.

Remember thinking as a child that you would either never be like your parent or wanted to be a firefighter like Dad?

We learned to distinguish between what is valuable and what is valueless often according to the acceptable norm. Some of the guidance we received was beneficial. It taught us how to lead successful lives. Part of becoming a mature adult is questioning the conclusions we drew, the values we were given and the roles we adopted. These determine what we experience today.

Prejudices are taught!

Our families and the community we are raised in passes on to us preconceptions towards other people and life in general. *In this fashion "the sins of the father can become visited onto the son".* The habitual interpretations and expectations we place on ourselves and others become a self-imposed prison. Open-mindedness is a minute-by-minute choice. It requires that we step beyond preconceived ideas and judgment. It rests on the recognition that it is our own sense of guilt and insecurity that closes our mind.

Children aren't born as blank slates to receive the parents and societies imprinting as their *only way* of relating to the world. Even so these influences may be very powerful, they are born with innate predispositions influencing their perceptions of the experiences that will shape their life. It is nurture, nature and personal interpretation that blaze a path for us.

Ask yourself:

- What choices have I made that are opposite to my mother or father?
- What is (was) my role in the family?
- How is my spouse like my mother or father?
- How am I reacting to people in the present the same as to those in the past?

Our thoughts determine how we interpret.

He had been reading about the power of thought. The more he attempted to not have negative thoughts the more he couldn't help thinking them. "Thoughts are creative," the book stated. He looked at his goldfish and thought: "I am surprised you have lived this long!" The next morning the goldfish was floating belly up in his little tank. "I have killed my goldfish!," was his first reaction.

Obviously, he hadn't done anything to kill his goldfish. Yet for a moment, he felt as if he had. "Why did this happen? Because I had that thought the night before."

Thoughts are all powerful with regard to our *inner world.* They determine how we *interpret what is. "Why did this happen?"* They therefore determine our experience of what is. *"Is this good or bad?"* And, they determine our reaction to what is. Our reaction to *what is* has the power to *influence* others' reaction to us. Confusing the power our thoughts have with regard to the outer world *instead of* our inner world is a common mistake and generates fear. If we had the power to influence creation (the outer world and the things and people in it) with our thinking we would be omnipotent. *He would be able to bring his goldfish back to life by simply thinking so.*

Personal power wants to indulge in magical thinking.

Very few people (if any) can stake claim to having conscious, deliberate access to a higher level of thought that is instantly creative at any given time. On the other hand, our thinking does have a major impact on how we experience. This is confusing to many people first starting out on the path of self-awareness. It is tempting to assume that the super-human potentialities we explore are ours to yield. We readily fall back into the magical world of the preschooler. We are tempted (and sometimes taught) to surround spiritual reality with magical thinking.

Personal power wants to stake a claim to super-natural power. Omnipotence, (*I can affect creation: My thoughts killed my goldfish*). Omniscience, (*I know what will happen before it happens: My thoughts predicted that the goldfish was about to die*). Omnipresence, (*I am present wherever and whenever I am needed: My thoughts told me to be there to save my goldfish*). These are powers that don't belong to our individual personal selves.

To overestimate the power of our thoughts with regard to others and creation (the outer world) and to some degree even with regard to our body becomes a form of magical thinking. It leads *to throwing out the baby with the bath water.* The truth that is inherent but distorted by our confusion becomes lost to others and us. We lose credibility.

Again, our thoughts interpret what is, determine our experience of what is and produce our reaction to what is. As such they are all-powerful with regard to our inner world and can affect our environment inadvertently through our reaction to it. Other people have choice in how to respond to us.

If our mind is open, it will perceive and allow us to seize the opportunities that exist. We align ourselves and as a result often end up in the right place at the right time. Our habitual thinking process affects our body but not exclusively, heredity and environment do play their role as well.

How can the blind lead the blind?

Many of our problems appear to be about what is happening now, yet they are rooted deeply inside of us. We feel frustrated and helpless by their repetition. They seem to appear in ever-new versions with ever-new faces. Our best efforts fail. We feel stuck. Since they repeat themselves in patterns, they can be deciphered and predicted. Part of the solution to what produces discomfort, pain, disappointment, or hassle in our lives is coming to understand our personal inner connections with the problem we are struggling with. Our life doesn't have to be an obstacle course.

"What experiences have repeated (and are repeating) themselves in ever new versions in my life?

"Where in my body do I carry the vortex of that experience?"

"When have I felt this vortex (experience) for the first time?" (How old was I? Go with the first thought coming into your mind).

"What conclusions did I draw about myself, others and life at that time?"

As long as we don't figure out the underlying dynamics, these problems will happen again, with new faces or in new circumstances. Since patterns follow time lines, they repeat themselves cyclically. People are creatures of habit and do what is familiar. People also see what they expect to see. Our mind has the capacity to see selectively for the better or the worse.

Our Mind becomes Master or Servant

What distinguishes us as humans is our ability to think and reason.

The ability to think about our actions and motivations, others' actions and motivations and reasons for happenings is an important aspect of what makes us human. Our ability to analyze allows us to learn from past experience and as such lays the groundwork to living a more successful, conscious and loving life. It helps us to anticipate what is to come, be prepared and take constructive action.

Misused, analysis becomes mind-chatter. Our thinking spins around in circles obsessing about the injustices received at someone else's hand or life. *Then analysis becomes paralysis.* The inability to take constructive action on our behalf, lost in *trying to figure it out.*

To function in every day life, we need all the functions of our mind. Our intellect allows us to acquire factual knowledge gaining ever-greater understanding. Analysis allows us to learn from the past and predict and anticipate the future. Intuition allows for insight and to comprehend beyond what our senses feed us and our intellect can grasp. Foresight assists us to live in the world wisely.

The mind ultimately is a tool to help our experiencing, experimenting and expressing in this world. The trouble is, *most people have never learned how to not think without the help of alcohol, drugs, or TV.* The tool has become the master.

Our opinions are intricately connected to our feelings about things.

Thoughts and feelings are intricately connected. For most of us unresolved and unexamined feelings become the energy that motivates thought. They are *the something* that clings to our judgments and invests them with power. These emotions hold information about the pre-assigned meaning (our past conclusions) we have given. They will provide us with insights into our deeper fears, needs, motivations and goals. Many people are very uncomfortable with their feelings and therefore hope to retreat into their mind as a refuge. To be rational and analytic is seen as superior to being emotional.

When one feels unsafe to yield the power feelings have, feelings are dismissed and avoided. The intellect with its reason and clarity lacks the *messiness* of our emotional world.

We are used to claiming that our thinking is superior.

Staying on an upper mental intellectual level of analyzing, explaining, complaining, justifying, or disassociating by overriding feeling, won't resolve the deeper issues. Our whole being experiences them. Our opinions and our problems are not simply ideas or behaviors to be dealt with solely through our mind. We feel our struggles in our body, our muscles, our posture, energetically and in our interactions with others. Attempting to control our behavior with will power by only changing our thinking is only a short-term solution.

Mind over matter truly is a modern version of a long-standing attitude. Overriding our emotional life by over-focusing on our intellect is avoidance. We attempt to control what needs to be disciplined and directed. True mastery will elude us. When change becomes part of our personal evolution, controlling our thinking takes on its natural helpful role. Now it is us who are changing not just our thinking.

When the turbulence and intensity of our emotions remains in need of mastery, we are tempted to seek refuge in our mental life. Now analyzing and thinking isn't any longer a tool but an escape that becomes a way of life. Equally, seeking the stillness of our inner being can be used as an avoidance of our human side. Mastery implies the ability to use all aspects of self as their function dictates.

Prayer used to be the tool of choice to accomplish quietude of the mind.

Today meditation has become the new popular choice to accomplish this task. No matter what the tool, the goal is to experience the quietude, relaxation and rejuvenation that come from the no-thought-no-emotion-silence of our inner being.

For most of us thought will either precede or trigger a feeling or a feeling will initially arise without thought and then need a thought to grasp its content. As such, thought will remove us from this inner state. In prayer or meditation we are able to access a part of us that is beyond thinking and feeling in a human sense. This part of us is empty (of thought) yet full. It is devoid of emotions yet quietly peaceful, joyful and content.

This quietude of thought and emotion remains unknown or becomes inaccessible as long as our mind is *master.* We need to turn the *master* back into a *servant.* Physical activity, prayer, meditation, creative activity, etc., we have to find the discipline that works for us. Learning to take a break from thinking and feeling may be accomplished through focus or through relaxation.

It is in our daily relationships that the degree of mastery becomes evident. We can gain access to the stillness of our inner being while still not having achieved complete mastery of all of our human aspects. We may have achieved mastery in some aspects and still struggle with others. The same holds true for other areas of our life. We may have very good communications at work but lack the same ability in our personal life.

Whenever we do not feel joy and our energy does not extend itself for the sheer joy of being, we are not where we are meant to be. No matter what the stress or circumstance, joy is an inner state chosen...or not.

Make it a habit to feel this joy at least once a day no matter what else is going on in your life. Simply, for a few moments, set everything aside...imagine yourself diving beneath everything to the joy of being alive. Look at your surroundings through the eyes of that joy.

We can avoid ourselves only for so long.

We state (with an air of superiority) that all that counts is living in the present. As a result, we become unable to learn from the past and therefore seem *doomed* to repeat it. The mind, instead of being a tool that works for us, has become a tool that works against us. In a misguided attempt to free ourselves, we claim that the past is unimportant. We may take refuge in an absence of feeling, in substance abuse, or in our spiritual endeavors attempting to override the messiness of our human life.

The past will dictate what the present is, as long as, the past stays unexamined and not assimilated.

The average man may numb himself with alcohol; the scientist may hide in his intellect; the spiritual seeker may hide in the spiritual realm as an answer to life's ups and downs. Substance abuse, intellect and spirituality often become misused by the man who doesn't know how to or doesn't want to deal with his psychological self. It becomes an attempt to side step having to deal with the mess of our emotions and the pain inherent in living in a finite physical body and a human world.

If taking a break becomes disassociation it only adds to our problems. To use our emotions, mind and body rightly produces serenity. Pain then is recognized as an obstacle not as something to be feared. Pain is unmasked and faced. Our physical, emotional, mental, psychological and spiritual aspects are in balance. *We live in the world but are not of it.*

Without emotional mastery "thinking" quickly becomes denial.

One of the functions of our mind is to discern between what is good and bad, valuable and valueless and right and wrong. This sorting out and decision making of the mind is necessary to live wisely. When the mind is master it turns this function against the self and other people. Judgment now becomes a way to disown one's shortcomings by seeing them in other people. This produces divisions and separation. It generates fear.

Habits are not always easy to break. We may find that disciplining our mind and abstaining from judgment and blame is not as easy as one might assume. Since emotions give thoughts their power, it takes achieving emotional mastery (to be OK with whatever feelings we have) to truly be able to master our thinking. Judgment is based in feeling *right.* It therefore carries emotional energy. *Righteousness* is a feeling and thinking state.

It is a misuse of our knowledge, values and morals by making them universal instead of keeping them personal.

There is a way through the circles that our mind wants to spin.

Judgments are simply *thought bubbles* if we do not invest the power of our emotions into them. If we find it difficult to let go of being right, we have emotional investment (are emotionally *hooked*) and need to look deeper for our inner discomfort with the issue.

If we address our habitual judgments as *thought bubbles,* we are able to withdraw the emotional energy we habitually give them. We don't have to take these thought bubbles seriously! They are only dangerous to our peace of mind if we believe in their validity and act on them. Then inner division creates outer division and disharmony.

- Thought bubbles, just as soap bubbles, are easily *popped. "Changed my mind...I don't believe this!" "Blessings, blessings, this means nothing" "What kind of a silly thought is that... go away!" "This is not what I truly want (etc.)!"*
- Willingness to change one's mind is the prerequisite: *"I know I am right but just for the fun of it I am willing to be wrong."* (This doesn't mean that I am necessarily wrong; however, I am willing to see another side.) *"My responsibility (my side) in this is..."* We can begin with *"being willing to become willing"* to let go of being right.

Mentally stepping back allows us to think about our thinking.

Once we shift to a neutral observer position, we naturally step beyond our need to be right, our need to blame others, or to see ourselves as unjustly treated. *We cannot truly manage energy as long as we judge it and with that push it away.*

Now, as we have learned to step back, we can think about our thinking, past connections and a course of action to choose. The space created allows us to use the mental capability of analysis in its right form. This is probably the most helpful step in aiding our own development. We untangle the distortions that our past superimposes on the present. Our righteous ego mind has lost its ability to hijack us. Changes come when we learn to interject a *pause* and actively choose to find a different way of looking at the circumstance. Choosing to pause does not mean to withdraw and avoid or ignore an issue.

We may take our ball and go home for the moment but then we come back to the playground. It is an active relating to oneself and others:

"I need to think on this…I'll get back to you!"
"There is another way of looking at this!?"
"What past associations do I have?"
What is the original hurt that now makes me vulnerable?"
"Looking through the eyes of love and trust what do I see?

One insidious version of out-of-control thinking, is succumbing to the "critic" that lives inside all of us.

For some people (due to their early childhood upbringing) this *critic* has taken on a dominant position in their psyche. If getting in touch with how we think and feel is confused with getting in touch with the self-critical messages living inside, who would want to?

Nothing is gained from self-reproach or self-blame just as nothing is gained by placing blame and judgment on others. The critic that lives inside of us feeds off our self-blame. It is like a monster that grows larger and larger the more we feed it. We have to take a stand towards this inner voice, as in: *"Speak up when you have something new and constructive to say!" "Otherwise be quiet!"*

We will fail our own expectations and values, all of us will. How we deal with when we do, is what shows the difference between those who have healthy self-esteem and those who don't. Healthy self-esteem says: *"I messed up…I'll try to do better next time!" "In the meantime, what can I do about it?"* Poor self-esteem says: *"I messed up…what is wrong with me!!!" "I am such a loser!" "This is hopeless!"*

To starve the monster of poor self-esteem we have to make it a practice to start each day with a blank slate. We have to actively look for something nice to say about ourselves to ourselves, no matter how insignificant.

"Each night before you fall asleep think about all the things you did right today!" "Bless or dismiss (as a work in progress) everything that comes to mind as having gone wrong!"

Self-judgment is the ultimate attack.

Our wound deepens. Truly, others are only bystanders to this dynamic. Hiding, compensating, explaining, justifying, defending, etc. will only serve to make the fault more and more real. In defending ourselves against others' (or our own) criticism and judgment we give it validity. We operate from a belief that we have to protect our inner selves from an outer threat. We ignore that it is *our* self-judgment, uncertainty and lack of self-acceptance that has the power to inflict the wound in the first place. As such, we keep it open and festering.

Even positive affirmations can be used in this fashion, as a defense against what we truly believe to be true. If we use them as a tool to protect ourselves from what is now seen as an inner threat, our self-accusations, they become yet another tool used against ourselves.

We only defend ourselves if we feel attacked, believe there is a basis and truth to the attack and that our own defense can safe us.[10]

This establishes that the attack has the power to diminish who we truly are. And here lies the illusion of it all. In making something real in defending against it; it becomes real. We make it real. We invest it with power it does not have by itself. Then we move to undo it. *What is wrong with this logic?*

What is unreal needs no defense or explanation; it simply needs to be dismissed! It is at best seen but ignored, given as little energy as possible. This is denial used as a tool working for us.

We say to ourselves: "I know you (judgment) are there and part of me believes in you as a reality but no longer...I won't believe in you any longer!" "Be gone!!!"

"I will choose what to think and feel!" "I will accept that I am an imperfect human being." "I can and will learn, little by little!" "My self-

---

[10] Foundation for Inner Peace, *A Course in Miracles*

worth is not dependent on what I did or didn't do, it is a birthright". "I will claim it as such!"

The tool of positive thinking and affirmations has become widely popularized.

We can choose what to think. We can choose to have positive thoughts. When we choose our thoughts, we learn to stay focused. We are disciplining our mind. The ability to focus our thoughts can be a valuable tool in times of stress when our thinking would want to slip into fear. Since our thoughts come attached with feelings or will trigger feelings, choosing our thoughts will determine our emotional experience. *"I am so stupid, look what I have done,"* will trigger a different emotional experience then, *"Oh, well, mistakes happen to the best of us."*

To think and interpret experiences in a positive way can help develop a positive attitude towards life. Our emotional equilibrium rests on our ability to talk ourselves out of our doubts and fears. We have to learn to minimize our shortcomings and failures to gain perspective. Affirmations used in this way can be an essential element in life success and good health. What might appear to be a failure can become a hidden blessing. Now all experiences can teach. Positive thinking and a positive attitude become the fuel for success. They begin to align us with our inner state of being.

At times, the more we affirm one state of mind, the more we experience its total opposite.

Affirmations have another side. They will keep mind-chatter at bay. They will generate a positive feeling state. And, they will also stir up any energy that may live inside our psyche that is not in alignment with our affirmations. Rightly understood, this is an opportunity to sort out and relinquish. Old wrongful conclusions need to be undone. A divided mind cannot create.

An affirmation is a declaration that something is true. We may desire or wish for something to be true consciously, yet not wish for it or believe it subconsciously. Affirmations that are repeated mindlessly and therefore lack emotional energy stay for the most part ineffective. They are just words. Affirmations need to be fueled by our belief and emotions, at least our willingness to believe. Then affirmations are capable of becoming a tool to take charge of the inner critic.

Affirmations are a form of autosuggestion in which a desirable (and in truth preexisting) condition of the mind is intentionally focused on. This is usually done through repetition. Affirmations can be seen as a mobilization of one's inner already preexisting resources. We may have to *"fake it"* (trusting that they do preexist) until we *"make it"* (know they do). The key word here is *"inner"* as in *"I can do this"; "I am deserving"; "I am going to be OK", etc.* The words we choose in our affirmations don't have to be pretty or exalted as *in "I am beautiful and magnificent".* We have to be able to feel them. *"I like the way my hair looks today".* Affirmations become brain washing and an attempt of manipulating reality when super-imposed onto the outer world.

Most of us want an easy, no effort solution to our problems.

We are gullible to promises of an easy, no effort and immediate and permanent cure for our ills. We want a magic pill (or program) that will do all the work for us. Affirmations and positive thinking are, sometimes, seen (and sold) as such a promise. This is rather too simplistic. Our psyche is multifaceted and so are our problems. Attempts of imprinting our subconscious mind with minimum conscious effort on our part is a form of magical thinking.

Mental and emotional mastery are earned. Altering our judgmental and limiting thoughts, beliefs, attitudes and emotional associations we have developed over a lifetime takes *"elbow grease".* Shortcuts are temporary.

When used rightly, affirmations and positive thinking generate a positive emotional experience. This experience is by nature expansive and self-completing. *One might say like attracts like.* We are open to approach and interpret experiences in a more positive light. With more confidence we open doors that we wouldn't have before.

Trust solves most of our problems. It opens us to receive the good that comes our way. Accessing our preexisting inner resources through affirmations is akin to understanding the laws of physics.

For example: a positive magnet (our inner state of being) will attract iron particles (that which is akin to it). The more iron particles it attracts (the greater our awareness of and ability to reside in our inner state of being) the stronger the magnetic field becomes.

Affirmations become our reality when they become accepted as the truth about us. That is why negative self-talk is so detrimental. Positive affirmations in combination with visualizations can be a powerful tool to suggest a new way of thinking about us to our subconscious.

Why are You so Different from Me?

We come from different backgrounds that taught us different values and morals and offered different degrees of support, guidance and care. We look at another person and our senses tell us that since their physical appearance is different from ours, they are different from us. This world that we see is built on perceiving differences, in inequality and on competition. Yet, we fear being different as much as we crave being different. On the one hand, being different gives us recognition, a sense of individuality and even safety. On the other hand, being different alienates us from others and makes us unsafe.

The differences we see and the separation that we experience are, for the most part, a product of our mind. They are super-imposed on all levels of experiencing. This state of being is like a feverish dream in which we believe that we have different interests from others and are only able to gratify these interests at another's expense. We take, bully, judge and impose.

Our emotional experience appears to be uniquely ours and no one else can *truly understand*. The world and other people are seen as being there to serve our needs. It is a win-lose worldview. Ultimately it is our striving to want something different from what we have, that creates our dissatisfaction and pain just as it helps us better the life we live.

Where do these initial divisions come from?

Zoroaster or Zarathustra (circa 1000 BC) was an ancient Iranian prophet and the founder of Zoroastrian religion. Like many others, he saw the foundation of human existence as the cosmic struggle between *"Aša, The Truth,* and *Druj, The Lie"*, which is akin to the *"Western Good and Evil"*[11]. Scholars see Zoroaster as the first prophet to proclaim the initial division of divinity into *all good and all bad* by rejecting the forces of nature in favor of a moral order.

He can be seen as one of a line of prophets who have progressively revealed an understanding of divinity. Prior to this

---

[11] Wikipedia, Zoroaster

evolutionary step God was a *nature-God*, seen as both life-giving and life-destroying. Humans imagined themselves able to influence the circle of creation and destruction through offering sacrifice.

This attitude towards the mysterious that holds power over daily life and ultimately divinity is akin to the magical world of the infant and toddler. A toddler, just as early man, views life and the powers that appear to direct it as containing both, *good and bad* without division.

Inner divisions are experienced as outer divisions.

The journey of separation (*loss of paradise*), struggle with *good and bad*, and promise of eventual union (*heaven*) is humanities journey. It is the journey of each individual on this planet. It is a journey of self-awareness, duality and identity. Every child born undergoes this same evolutionary journey and eventually transcends the magical world of *preconscious at-oneness* and the associated omni-powers. We enter what we call the real world, a world of opposites and vulnerability. And, there we are... struggling with the duality that we experience in daily life and intimate relationships losing sight of heaven (a state of union).

Her eyes looked at me with an expression of surprise and bewildered recognition. Suddenly it all made sense: the feelings of "I can't do it by myself"; the immature boy friends that needed her help; the frustration over feeling stuck in an unsatisfactory job that she had wanted to leave for many years, yet was afraid to. Her early experiences showed an uncanny similarity to her mother's. The conclusion she had drawn and her mother had unwittingly reinforced was: "I can't do it alone".

Invisible walls separate us from those we love and what we desire most in life. Others' different wants and actions drive us *crazy*. No one ever told us that this struggle is a normal and a necessary part of reaching maturity. We weren't taught that the war we experience is ultimately fought in our mind. It is in our thoughts that we erect *me and not me, what we can and can't do, etc. It is our mind that first makes room for fearing a negative outcome. It is our mind that divides experience into good and bad.*

Assumptions, judgments and underlying fears are the food that gives our sense of separation and alienation life. All we know is that somewhere deep inside, we remember and yearn for connection, a world of sameness and safety. We cannot go back. We can move forward, *beyond the opposites* that our minds perceive. This other state (heaven) bridges both good and bad (what we want and what we fear). There, connection and safety are established on a new level, *a conscious experience of at-oneness.*

Duality is a necessary step in our development.

It brings psycho-emotional individuality and resolved, eventually, a new understanding of *oneness.* Duality is the condition of one thing having two sides, parts, or faces. Duality is really a mental struggle. When we are caught in a life governed by duality we are caught in the interplay of the pairs of interconnected opposites. Neither half can exist without the other no matter how hard we try to rid ourselves of what we regard as the *negative half* (beauty-ugliness, in control-out of control, lazy-industrious, light-dark, right-wrong, good-evil, mature-immature, etc.) We cannot escape being affected by others just as *night needs day*. Others become the mirrors of our forgotten self.

She realized that the immature boyfriends resembled what she felt underneath her apparent strength. Long ago she had generalized a one-time experience of "I can't do this alone". Instead of being a correct assessment about one particular incident it became an assumed fact about her capabilities.

In her relationship choices today, her boyfriends reflect back to her "I can't do it alone". She could see for them that it wasn't the truth about who they were. The problem was, they couldn't see it. She felt exhausted by her efforts to help them and frustrated by their apparent inability to help themselves.

Those closest to us provide us with enough irritations to last a lifetime. Their being in the world may seem so opposite to what we hold dear and value highly. The resulting discord is exasperating. Looking to resolve our discomfort by demanding for our spouse or child to be a carbon copy of us *isn't the solution.*

With every loss there is a gain. We lost paradise (preconscious at-oneness and the associated omni-powers) and we gained individuality and self-awareness (with its shadow side, separation and helplessness). Now the world has become a world of differences.

It must have been bewildering to experience ourselves as helpless, separate or bad.

The (inevitable) loss of paradise is experienced at one time very young and then *unknowingly, by most,* relived ever after. This loss has as many individual versions as there are people but the experience is the same.

Our perception of ourselves was jeopardized…with it our sense of connection was challenged…doubt entered…we suddenly experienced ourselves as unsafe…a split occurred.

In a frantic attempt to come to grips with what was happening, we reasoned (gave a meaning) as to *why it was happening.* At that moment, we lost our sense of indivisible connection within ourselves and with others. Suddenly there was a *not me,* an awareness of need and loss, the possibility that someone we needed could leave us, an experience that we were all alone in this, a traumatic recognition of how vulnerable and helpless we were, a potential to be unloving, bad, evil (on our or someone else's part). It was a necessary evolutionary step…to become self-aware and enter the world of duality.

In self-defense, we began seeing the cause of our pain (*the why, the bad, and what we needed)* as outside and/or took it on as our fault. Our fear screamed: *"You are not worthy, not accepted, not understood, not capable, not loveable, not important, not wanted, not…"* We instinctively moved to protect ourselves. We had to maintain ourselves as good to be loved (or maintain the one we needed as good and loving).

Just like Adam and Eve, we ate from the tree of good and evil, became aware of our vulnerability (nakedness) and were kicked out of the paradise we previously knew. In a desperate attempt to restore what we feared was lost, we searched for the *reason* of what had happened. We never questioned and still don't question that maybe what we feared was not true; or that there was a *deeper truth undisturbed and untouchable* by what happened.

We need the means to bridge the abyss between our different worlds.

At times over night, other times gradually, we discover how different our mate or child truly is and find it very disturbing, frustrating and at times hurtful. On one level we re-experience the original splitting of what was up to then whole. We lose sight of the commonality underlying our upper level differences. We now have to find the common ground that can hold us both. Words and actions are important now. No matter what differences we struggle with on the surface, once we have truly loved, we will always love (which doesn't automatically mean live with)

"I like my house orderly," she says, "Why does he always have to leave the cupboard doors hanging open and his stinky socks on the kitchen counter?"

Sounds reasonable, doesn't it? Well, maybe it is. It also is a perfect example for the allegorical (relationship)-straw that will break the camel's back and frustrate the *"bajeebers"* out of us all. On further questioning Jane starts to speak about her husband's easy-going manner as first attracting her to him. Now it has become a cause for friction.

Speaking with Ralph, he argues that Jane is just too uptight about the house. When he is home he wants to relax and not have to worry about everything being so neat. I can just hear them argue, each feeling right and justified in their outlook on things.

We all have our points of conflict in our relationships, different yet similar to Jane's and Ralph's. We need to recognize that it is not the upper level issue we are fighting about that is the problem. Our attitude of crystallizing and withdrawing into opposite corners on an issue is what gets us into trouble. We lose sight of the underlying commonality that connects us. We need to resist giving into the temptation of closed-mindedness. Only an open mind can discern what tentacles the present may have to the past.

We are different...we can fight it or value it.

At first glance, for both Jane and Ralph, the root of their discontent lies in their difference in personality style. Jane sees and values herself as orderly and organized. Things are to be in their place, it is easier and more beautiful that way, she says. True! Ralph sees and values himself as relaxed, easy-going and casual. Life is less stressful that way. One has a chance to focus on what is truly important, like being together and having fun, he says. True as well! Each partner needs to value and claim the good in the other.

Underneath the obvious they both want the same: to be valued and respected. In Jane and Ralph's case these are the needs that still have a questions mark attached in their inner world and therefore appear challenged in the outer world.

Reclaiming the good and useful and respecting the other for who they are, allows for addressing the underlying unmet need brought into the relationship. It reestablishes connection. There lies safety in being right, that it is the others fault. This form of right has tentacles reaching back to old wounds. Surrendering the need to have the other acknowledge that they were wrong is just another version of *needing to be right.* Letting go of being right forces us to turn inside for acknowledgment and become *emotionally independent.* Not a prospect we may necessarily fancy. *Emotional independence* may be confused with *not love* and a *lack of connection.* It is so much easier to demand change of the other.

We have to grow up a little and not expect our mate to be all things to us.

There exists the myth of finding a *soul mate*, a mate who predictably will be able to relate mentally, spiritually, emotionally, sexually and on a practical day-to-day level. This wish is a wish to return to the fusion of *preconscious at-oneness*. All mates come with hang-ups...only the degree will vary. Duality guarantees occasional struggle. Finding a common ground between individuals is the hallmark of all mature relationships.

Because all relationships keep a delicate energy equilibrium, even if only one partner changes their attitude it will affect the equilibrium of the relationship. It forces the other to *do something*. Like water in a glass, the energy equilibrium in a relationship keeps adjusting itself constantly. If our mate is reluctant, too afraid, or too closed-minded to change he/she will typically attempt to crystallize into the opposite even more so as to push us back into our old place to balance him/her. We may be tempted to compensate for what the other leaves empty. We may lose ourselves many times before learning to insist on common ground. The equilibrium in a relationship will be established one way or another.

People closest to us will challenge us to question who we thought we were.

Our mental categories, the boxes we built, will need to be re-examined. To meet others as adults (not the parents we didn't have or the idealized mate we hoped to have) and accept what they can give and receive is our challenge today and every day. Once we make that commitment, we stand at a point of balance along the lines of the pairs of opposites. To find this balance means to find maturity, wisdom, joy, synthesis and psycho-emotional health. It is to move beyond to a place where we can see both sides, both perspectives and the value in both experiences. In essence, we then become freed from duality.

The idea that opposite sides always transform into each other is the philosophical foundation of Taoism, founded by Lao Tzu's writings. Yin and Yang are considered to be complimentary aspects of the Tao that create natural order in the world. Yin is a feminine energy. It is thought of as the breath that formed the earth. Yang is masculine energy. It is thought of as the breath that formed the heavens. It is important to note that Taoism maintains that without Yin there is no Yang and without Yang there is no Yin. Everything in nature must have both Yin and Yang. It regards Yin and Yang not as polar opposites but complementary aspects of the same idea.[12]

---

[12] Wikipedia, Yin and Yang

The woman in the above example recognized that assuming: "I can't do it alone" was a misunderstanding. By the same token it would be a misunderstanding to assume that life was about "I have to (want to) do it alone" (its polar opposite). Dependence and independence eventually mature into interdependence. In relationships they are intricately connected. They "transform into each other" and are the "complementary aspects of the same idea". An individual equally capable of both becomes freed from both and truly interdependent. Interdependence is a prerequisite for relationships based in equality. Equality leads to true relatedness and intimacy.

We are too used to interpreting all actions through our own peculiar polarized view of the world.

We quickly assume to know for the other...*the splinter in another's eye always looms larger and magnified than the beam in our own.*

Like a teeter-totter on a children's playground, if we sit on the opposite end our partner has to move to the opposite end as well for the game to work. The swing or stalemate created is synonymous to what happens in relationships. If we are ready, prepared and committed to *get off our end* the other has to get off their end. In other words, do *something* to maintain the equilibrium or depart all together.

It can feel as scary as sliding from the top of the teeter-totter to the middle. We are afraid of losing control and getting hurt. In relationship terms this means losing the relationship. The differences that attract and repulse us are the growth opportunities to be properly assimilated. We are connected with one another. Our lives are tied together and there is a link in which we can see one current running through all.

Jesus said to them, "When you make the two into one, and when you make the inner like the outer and the outer like the inner, and the upper like the lower, and when you make male and female into a single one, so that the male will not be male nor the female be female,..., then you will enter [the kingdom]."

The Gospel of St. Thomas

Our mind wants to take sides.

When we allow our mind to only perceive one side of an issue psycho-emotional energy and with it our identification becomes limited to one side of the pairs of opposites. Now our conscious mind will side with one perspective against the other. Seeing one as *all good and desirable* and the other as *all bad and undesirable,* we lose sight of the aspects that are beneficial. These aspects are now outside our conscious control to be used when needed.

The baby goes out with the bathwater. We have lost our ability to be gentle. We overlook the good and beneficial. We respond to even a one time minor occurrence as if it were a major character flaw or a black spot on someone's essence. Our conscious mind has taken up arms against a part of ourselves, against our own humanity and cast it out. Now our view of others and ourselves is unconsciously influenced by it.

The task of developing our sense of self is difficult; it comes without a "How-To"-manual.

We are thrown into this journey before we know how to walk or talk. We are left to our own devices without any clear instructions or our own personal guru, utterly dependent on our fallible parents. We all deny and judge certain aspects of our personality as unacceptable. The only defense we have as children is to deny the negative so as to be loved for the positive: *"Wasn't Me!"* We pretend that we can slice good and bad apart; keeping the good to ourselves and giving the bad away to others. This limiting of our perspective to half of a totality or continuum is the hallmark of our human condition.

Regaining the bigger perspective and choosing this perspective consciously, allows for stepping beyond the opposites we see. This *other side* may be a positive state of mind or a negative state of mind. The other may be right or wrong, guilty or innocent. *Ultimately this does not matter.* As humans all of us will *mess up* sometimes. All that ever is judged or forgiven is a human fallibility. Learning to integrate our opposing thoughts and feelings is a step in the right direction.

Working with a mental picture (visualization) has proven itself to be a powerful tool to suggest change to our subconscious. What is necessary is the ability to ask for help and the willingness to see things anew![13]

- Take a few deep breaths, relax and close your eyes to allow you to focus inside.
- Imagine that the attributes you struggle with either in yourself or another (stupid–smart; responsible–irresponsible; to be abandoned–to abandon someone, etc.) are like mini personalities that function inside of you. They do come in pairs; where there is the one there is the other.
- Now imagine one of these mini personalities (the one who is abandoned, etc.) as sitting in your left hand and observe its characteristics. What does it look like? What are its attitude towards life, work and other people?
- Now identify the opposite to this mini-personality (the one who abandons others)--sitting in your right hand. Again, identify what this part of you looks like, etc. Ask it the same questions as above.

Take a moment to identify the positive function they serve for you, for they each do. This may not be obvious at first, since you may have a strong preference for one or cannot identify with having experienced both.

Make a list of plus and minus attributes for each side.

Take a moment to list all attributes for both parts. You may realize that their services to you are complimentary…if one allows you to be assertive; the other allows you to be liked and therefore be connected to others. You will notice that the negatives of the one side balance the positives on the other side.

- Introduce these two mini personalities to each other. In all likelihood they have never met before but taken turns as *underdog* and *top dog* at different times in your life.

---

[13] Adapted from a workshop by Chuck Spezzano Ph.D., Hawaii, 1984

- Ask them if they would be willing to work together in the future. (No, they do not have to know how that would be possible.) Assuming that you get a YES answer, it is time to call on someone that you regard as wiser then you. This is not necessarily a person but may be a wise figure of history or your religion, your Higher Self, a spiritual power.
- Imagine this person or power to have the ability to *melt* these mini personalities so that only their pure energy (like a puddle) remains. Then ask this person or power to join these two puddles together and watch what happens next. (It is important that you not attempt to do this yourself, but have it done for you!)
- You may receive a new mini personality containing the blended attributes of both. You may receive a symbol that holds meaning for you. You may be left with a feeling, typically your body will take a breath; something has shifted.

We may temporarily retreat into "alone" before we finally find "heaven".

At times, we feel we cannot succeed at relationships. The state of duality we experience just seems too overpowering with its conflicts. We exclaim, *"The more people I meet the more I like my dog!"* We may temporarily retreat into *alone and give up* relationships. It gives us a chance to heal our disappointments and failures, *a chance to lick our wounds,* reconsider our attitudes and behavior.

We aren't omniscient! Others have the power to deceive us without any fault of ours. Others actions wound us. We assume that somehow our shortcomings led to what they did. This is magical thinking. We do not possess the magical power of making someone else *act stupid or careless or hurtful.* We become vulnerable when doubt enters. There are deeper connections for why we (or they) made the choices that were made. Just as there are deeper connections for why we are affected the way we are.

Unless we plan to live on a mountaintop, however, we cannot get away from relating to others. How well we do will to a large degree determine our sense of satisfaction with life. Eventually alone becomes too lonely and we will once again find ourselves in a relationship. As people we are relationship animals. If we have used our time wisely, we are better prepared this time. If we only bid our time, we recycle our old mental perspectives, repeat our old patterns and hurt again.

Whenever we hold more then one thought about a situation the good things we want will elude us.

Consciously we want all the good things in life. How often do we say to ourselves: *"If only this or that would be different, then I would be happy?"* We are unaware that there is another thought inside of us that often wants the opposite to what we want consciously. This deeper thought is a form of protection from what we fear.

Whenever we hold more then one thought about a topic our energy is divided. We consciously believe or want to believe one thing but deep down believe the opposite. Divided energy cannot create. What we don't have but desperately want keeps eluding us. Our intentions are genuine. We feel frustrated and we blame others or ourselves. We break up our relationships or leave our jobs only to find the same in a new version. Unaware or helpless with regard to this inner resistance we struggle on in futile attempts. We cannot see that we are our own biggest roadblocks.

Answer the following open-ended question as spontaneously as possible (insert your own words). "If only...(for example: My partner would be emotionally available)", then:...(I would feel safe in the relationship).

Now change the then answer you came up with...(I would feel safe in the relationship) and put "I don't want to..." in front of it. The then answer now would state: "I don't want to feel safe in the relationship."

Most likely this will seem completely ridiculous at first. Everything inside of you may resist. Just for the fun of it, play along.

Now brainstorm on the following open-ended questions as spontaneously as possible (inserting your own words[14]).

---

[14] Adapted from a workshop by Chuck Spezzano, PH. D., Hawaii, 1984

"Not wanting to feel safe in the relationship allows me to??" List as many answers as you can come up with. Be playful; there is no right or wrong answer. Simply accumulate as many answers as you can, no matter how ridiculous or untrue they may seem. Repeat the same line of questioning with: "Not wanting to feel safe in the relationship, I don't have to??" Same as above. "I don't want to feel safe in the relationship, because??" Same as above.

By now you may have noticed a "repeating theme" in your answers. What past connections can you find?

We need to become willing to question the things we hold "sacred".

It is a journey into the *inner unknown*. This journey will allow for something new. Remember, if you always think what you have always thought and always feel and do what you have always felt and done, you will always get what you have always gotten! Not all is lost! It is our mind that can choose to become aware and reevaluate and reconsider what we have accepted hereto as truth. There are pathways to the subconscious parts of us. The door opens when we begin to question the habitual and known. To *not know* becomes the password to our subconscious. We can choose to listen beyond to the deeper underlying connection and truth that exists.

"Is there a part of me that is afraid and does not want what I so strongly believe I do want?" "Can I accept this part of me and embrace it?" What we can accept can change. What we can accept reenters our conscious mind and now our mind has power over it.

At times, we can only see two ways of dealing with a conflict.

When we face a conflict we interpret what we think is happening and decide on a way on how to deal with it. The decisions we make along the way become forgotten or habitual and begin to govern similar situations. This manifests as habitually employing old solutions in new conflict situations.

Once a decision is made all other options are relinquished. Therefore we experience the present as only having the *same old option* to handle what we are facing or *flip to a complete opposite way*. Usually these *solutions* are extremes of each other. We can't any longer see the many possibilities in the middle that do exist.

In emergency moments we tend to fall back onto what is known and habitual. We fall into *all-bad* thinking: *"I either leave or I stay and put up with this!" We get caught in not wanting to lose the good in a bad situation.* This form of *lose-lose* thinking and problem-solving is an outcome of a time when our capabilities were limited and few options were available to us. The present and its potential choices in our life now are unlimited until we make a decision.

Many of our struggles in relationships are a reflection of where we compromised ourselves before. Our mates or important others inadvertently challenge us to take a look by insisting on being as right and justified in their ways as we feel in our ways. Life is funny that way! *It brings people into our life that will remind us of what we would rather forget, or ignore, or not deal with.* The other option, and really the only option eventually is to *work it out.* To face the differences in each other and be willing to question why they bother us as much as they do. *How have we compromised ourselves in the past in this area?*

Our struggles may lead to viewing the body and material things as inferior to spirit.

Now the body and physical life become distasteful. In its extreme *death* becomes an escape to the world of the ideal, *spirit*. Reality becomes divided into two distinct kinds, mind and body, or the related pair, spirit and matter. One side of each pair is seen as superior to the other. The universe is experienced as an arrangement of binary oppositions, such as spirit and body, good and evil, light and dark, male and female, creator and created, etc.

It is our evolutionary path as individuals and as humanity to escape the interplay of the opposites, its inevitable struggles and artificial divisions. *For each one of us this step is taken inside our own mind and lived daily in our relationships.*

The infant had to, at one point, leave the safety of the womb and with that step journeyed down the road of becoming its own separate physical being. To become fully adult, we have to leave the *safety of sameness* to form our own separate mental/emotional identity. This step is taken when we surrender our demand that others think, feel, want and do as we would. We enter into the world of opposites and *have to face*, either willingly or kicking and screaming, its struggles and heart aches.

Eventually, once our struggle has become transparent, we step beyond it. This is seldom experienced as easy. Once our evolving spirit calls us to complete our development, we find ourselves challenged and bewildered.

"...Content with getting what arrives of itself. Passed beyond the pairs, free from envy, not attached to success nor failure, even acting, [s]he[15] is not bound. [s]he is to be recognized as eternally free; Who neither loathes nor craves, for [s]he that is freed from the pairs, is easily freed from conflict..." The Bhagavad Gita

Our struggles can be the "bringers" of new life.

What we cannot accept is an indication of what remains divided. Our own wounds determine our weaknesses. Where we have failed to mature is where we will now struggle and repeatedly fail. It is with the people we are in relationship with that we re-experience this struggle. They become the *bringer* of our inner pain *or of an opportunity to heal.* It is our choice to determine who they will be to us.

This final place (heaven) is a place in which love is known as always existing underneath the surface differences. Connection and love continue and persist independently of others' behaviors. *In a state of union two equals meet as equals with equals.* Standing together but apart, each being a fully developed individual, a third entity is created. This is the relationship itself equally shared and nurtured by both. In a pro-creative sense it is a child. Now commitment is never questioned, there is no other place to be.

[15] Adding an "s" before the word "he" is my addition

We "Freeze" Experiences into Preexisting Frames

The concept that our mind recycles past experiences in the present is foreign.

We never doubt that the experiences we have today are about what is happening now. We experience the procession of time from the angle of the physical. However, different laws guide our psycho-emotional experience. Our experience of the past, present and future is all in our heads so a time-puzzled St. Augustine proclaimed in his subjective theory of time. All moments would appear to be equally real coexisting in a kind of *vast frozen time space*. To most of us this is known as *"déjà vu"* experiences. Our psycho-emotional experiencing in relationships and everyday life are filled with them. Yesterday is today. The battles we *unsuccessfully* fought yesterday are still being fought today.

We keep insisting that today should give us what yesterday denied.

Our subconscious is very much conversation minded. It will recycle and recycle not assimilated experiences in endless new versions until we digest them, absorb the useful and eliminate the useless. Initially painful or liberating as it may be, it is up to us to relinquish the wrong interpretations we have placed. It is up to us to recognize the distortions that fear introduced.

Our memory allows us to learn from the past and anticipate the future.

Experiences are recorded as memories in our brain. When we experience similar events over and over our brain records a pattern for them. One-time traumatic events, due to their high emotional intensity, have a similar effect. Our memory draws on past experiences (consciously remembered or not) as a reference point on how to perceive, interpret and deal with present day occurrences. We go on *autopilot* thinking and feeling the same way and feeling compelled to respond in the same fashion we have responded hundreds of times before.

She had a habit of working harder then anyone else. When others "needed" her she took it upon herself to do what needed to be done. It never occurred to her to question if it was truly her role to carry others. After all, as the oldest child she was used to looking after her younger siblings.

Mental patterns aid our survival.

They allow us to respond without thinking. This extraordinary useful adaptive device has a *shadow side*. It makes us assume that what is happening now is the same as what happened then. *This makes us relate to the present as if it were the past.*

As important as mental patterns are for our survival, they unfortunately often don't support us in being our best or getting us what we truly want. When we react to life in an automatic way dictated by our hurts, unmet needs and disappointments, *then we are not truly free*. Often what we regard as a sign of danger, rejection, attack, or even love, is not a true assessment of the present. It represents a distortion introduced by our own past experiences and their resulting sensitivities and needs. Now we anticipate dangers where we ought not to and perceive kindness where it does not exist. In trying to finally get from the present what the past didn't give us, we set up a new order of problems.

She felt frustrated at work. Without being asked to, she would step in and "help out". Once her boss expected her to handle an ever increasing workload she became resentful. At first she blamed him for being unreasonable. After staying with her feelings she realized that her "helpfulness" came with a price tag. Underneath she hoped to finally be noticed.

Beliefs play an important part in what upsets us.

They are the foundation of our habits, instant reactions and expectations. When the world behaves differently then we expect, we become upset. Painful, vulnerable, or unacceptable feelings and experiences, our fears, our feelings of unsafe become exposed. Many of the patterns we have formed are the protections that eventually prove themselves unsuccessful.

Long ago she had been taught that to not be helpful was being selfish. For some reason she could never be helpful enough.

We have the capacity to relate to the present through the past. We construct a future based on the meaning that we gave the past. Too often we interpret what is going on from the vantage point of a dependent and insecure child. *"I am not wanted"; "I am hurtful"; I am bad"; "I am not equal"; "I am not important"; "I am irresponsible"; "I am selfish"; "If you only knew, you wouldn't want to be around me", "I know that eventually you will leave me", "I am stupid", "You say you love me, but I know you can't be trusted", "It is up to me to fix it", etc., etc.* These old decisions made and then forgotten have become the blueprint from which we now interpret and operate our lives. The powerful emotions these unexamined assumptions trigger promote and nurture our belief in them.

We each occupy a different–even so shared–world.

No two individuals will place the exact same interpretation on the same experience. The personal interpretations that we place on the world we see are therefore uniquely *our* interpretation of circumstances. *The outcome during times of stress is a time warp experience.* We (seemingly) keep re-experiencing the same old hurt, outrage, or sense of helplessness. *Now* loses its true meaning for us.

Our reactions to those we meet in the present then become dictated from a past reference point, obscuring their present reality.

This moves us to treat and relate with husbands as if they are our father or mother, etc. We react to our mates based on our past disappointments, preventing us from recognizing who they really are, now, not yesterday. Exasperated we exclaim: *"You are just like my father/mother!" "Are all men (women) like this?"* What complicates things is the tendency to attract mates that display similar behavior traits as our parents. The phantoms of the past invade and distort our perception. They dictate our reaction. They carry the spots of pain in our mind that direct us to attack in the present in retaliation for a past that is gone.

Understanding the history that set up our present day problems seems tedious.

"I just want it to go away! What do I do to change this!" are the pleas typically made by people who seek counseling. *When we take our TV to be repaired we don't care for a run-down of all its inner mechanics. We want it fixed!* People first stepping out into the path of self-exploration react similarly. They are impatient.

That *understanding* is part of the solution only slowly dawns onto our mind. We can move to a foreign country, leave our husbands, quit our jobs and ground our children. If we don't understand the soil our problems have their roots in, they will happen again, with new faces and in new settings.

The families we come from are our *personal Ground Zero*. It is there that our innate abilities we are born with and personality tendencies we display get shaped, coerced and pummeled, nurtured, or stunted. When we react to life in an automatic way dictated by our past experiences, our habits or conditioning, we do not experience ourselves as free and creative. We feel emotionally trapped, stifled, obliged and bound at one time or another. We are afraid to let go of what is secure and safe, afraid to take a risk or hope and afraid to disappoint. We see and focus on the limitations that exist in our lives instead of the possibilities that exist.

We carry our families inside of us.

We cannot remove ourselves instantaneously from the attitudes and behavior patterns that were formed back then without due self-examination and resolution. The experiences within our family system and early environment created our psychological core experience of how we see ourselves and how we relate to others. These experiences influence if not determine the choices we see, make and avoid or opportunities we seize. They are the basis for our beliefs about life and the universe. It is in our families where we learned what to expect of life.

We crave and demand the love we didn't receive while unknowingly expecting to not receive it again. We do not recognize this self-fulfilling prophecy as a trickery of our own psyche. There is no magic formula for the healthy growth of a human child. Our families did the best they could and knew. *Blame will not solve our problems now.*

We learned or didn't learn that relationships are like butterflies; they fly best on two wings.

If we were given healthy limits we learned that we couldn't always have it our way. It is in our family where we learned to *ignore and override what bothered us or held true meaning for us.* And, it is there where we learned to *take on other people's faults and lacks* as our problem. We learned to assume that they do what they do because we aren't *good enough.* We learned to please others or to impose our will without consideration. It is here where we first felt that we couldn't truly rely on the ones that were supposed to care for us.

As we enter adulthood the pattern repeats itself. We marry men or women like our parents. We fall back into the roles we learned back there. We walk into life unaware of why we do what we do. The crippling effects of our old conclusions are now re-experienced with our partner. Our sense of security remains tentative. This makes us prone to seek security where it cannot be found permanently.

We typically don't question the often unspoken expectations that were passed on to us.

She had joined the group to learn to communicate better. Little did she anticipate discovering that "her learning to communicate better" was simply another form of accepting the responsibility for others, as she always had done.

We feel exhausted, confused, anxious and frustrated at our lack of direction in life. We don't connect that saying NO to others' demands equals making space and time to think, feel and get in touch with our deeper wants. We fear to disappoint anyone and feel guilty when we can't meet his or her needs. At the same time, we resent their controlling and demanding ways. We are afraid of or feel guilty about asking for what we would like, or simply are unaware or deny that we have emotional or relational needs that deserve to be met.

Changing old ingrained patterns and beliefs isn't quick or necessarily easy.

We will revisit the same problems cyclically before finally finding a permanent release. It takes patience, commitment, awareness and time. *Think of it as the "slinky effect". Like the many spirals of a toy "slinky" would suggest, we will revisit and spiral down ever new versions of the same experience until we finally arrive at the core. All of us have our personal inner "slinkies". Change, just like DNA and life is spiral.*

Thoughts about *why* something is happening arise naturally. The meaning we give triggers a specific *emotional experience,* which in turn, leads to making a *decision* about ourselves and others on how to handle what we are facing. The decisions we make will prompt us to *act* in a certain way, with fight (attack), flee (withdraw) or ignore (deny) being our most instinctual response.

As we accept the *thought-meaning-emotion-action* experience as true, it dictates our future perception of often only vaguely similar happenings. Once accepted as the truth, we come full cycle. Our experiencing becomes *frozen* into a *preexisting frame*. It generates the same old meaning given. The same old emotions experienced prompt us to take the same old actions even in new situations. Re-enacted it manifest as a habitual response known as a *"belief".*

Thought ► Meaning ► Emotional Experience ► Decision ► Action ► Belief

Undoing these beliefs takes effort and time. It is unreasonable to expect that something that we have practiced over and over for years should simply vanish over night.

Beliefs and behavior patterns are a form of "forgotten decision making".

What we accept as truth and then solidify by acting on it becomes habitual. What is habitual does not any longer require thinking and becomes unconscious. Once something is largely unconscious it becomes hard to recognize and we typically only know it by its effects.

The woman in the above example had to learn to pause before making a decision on taking on extra work or being helpful. This gave her a space to assess what her true motivation was.

Was her helpfulness truly a covert call to be noticed; an attempt to prove that she wasn't selfish? If so, she had to first revisit and resolve her old feelings.

(Step 1); to "notice" her own needs: her past hurt and associations;

(Step 2); claim that she has a right to be noticed and to make a space for herself;

(Step 3); claim that it was OK to ask to have her contributions be noticed.

This opens a space to make sure that it either didn't matter that she was noticed or that her work would receive the recognition it deserved (from herself and/or others).

This will free her from the destructive cycle of:

Done to Me ►Do It to Myself ► Do It to Others

Once we learn to figure out why we are as upset as we are, we gain power.

It is hard work to begin to view our early childhood experiences and the patterns we took from them clearly. We are so used to them! What is known is interpreted as normal. If we want different experiences in our life, we need to start by changing our internal dialog. *Sounds like a gigantic task? How do you eat an elephant? There is only one way: bite by bite!*

For young children it is essential to feel connected. Connection means survival, physical but also emotional. When we are little we are willing to do anything to maintain this connection with those we love and need. We combine *truth* with *untruth* so as to find a plausible (to us) explanation about the *why* of what is happening to others or us.

Traumatic experiences in particular will have a powerful impact on our developing psyche, but so will ongoing subtle attitudes that are neglectful of our needs. We internalize the attitude that is first displayed towards us. It must be right and good, we reason, anything to maintain a feeling of being loveable and worthy. The roles we learn in our original families and early interactions with others have a way of staying with us all our lives.

Extreme positions lead to blame and alienation.

The young child's *all black or all white* thinking leads to seeing experiences as either all good or all bad. The lack of discernment to separate the *kernel from the straw* leads to the formation of *extreme positions.*

Extreme positions manifest as experiencing our *bubble,* namely our worldview, and someone else's *bubble*, their worldview, at odds with each other. When others *rub our bubble* our first reaction may be to feel right and blame them. We may feel hurt and unjustly treated. We may feel guilty and compelled to appease.

It is only when we pause to inquire into the why this has such an impact on us, that we can begin to reexamine the habitual assumptions and meaning that becomes triggered for us.

Bridges are built with question marks!

The interpretations we placed on circumstances were our way of coping with what was happening.

They were our immature way of attempting to problem solve an, at the time, overwhelming situation. We didn't have a mature enough emotional circuit system to stand in the fire of our feelings. We did what we had to do. Without realizing it, the decisions we made compromised our sense of connection and our knowing that we are loved, loveable and loving.

One might say that these false assumptions are like a building block (of our psyche) that has slipped (a bit like a disc in our spine). As a result our psyche is unbalanced and out of alignment. The resulting psychological pain is what we experience and of course instinctively defend against. However, our defenses do not correct the slipped building block!

If we fail to change our mind about what went wrong back then, we end up with a distorted view of the world and ourselves. Others change won't truly serve our inner conflict so it might temporarily resolve the outer conflict we experience.

Whenever we face a conflict the question needs to be: "If I felt that I was worthy, loveable, irreplaceable, self-sufficient, that no harm will come to me, etc., then how would I deal with this?

Our mind classifies what our senses bring to it according to previously established categories.

These preconceived ideas become the *proof* for what we already believe to be true and have decided to be true...*you don't respect me...you are not reliable...you can cause me harm, etc.*

And others very well may not be. It is not what they are that has power over us, however. What gives them the power they appear to have is us needing them to be a certain way (respectful, reliable, caring). This, in essence, demands that they should not be the fallible humans they are. It gives them the power to *pull our strings.*

The woman realized that her hidden need to be seen as helpful had made her vulnerable to be taken advantage of. All it took was an appearance of someone needing help or an implication that she really ought to help, for her to move into action. She found herself cleaning up other people's messes and denying herself what she wanted.

All experience holds within itself a kernel of truth and wisdom, something that is good, helpful and beneficial. As young children we tend to wrap that truth and wisdom with the misunderstandings of a young child. We either incorporate it completely or reject and fear it completely. It is time to take the good and leave the bad and to assimilate the useful and eliminate the useless.

Moving forward involves looking back and leaving behind what doesn't serve us any longer.

Today, as adults, we do have the emotional maturity to digest and deal with what was so overwhelming and impossible then. Today we can face that at least some of the conclusions we drew were one-sided. We are now ready to give the responsibility to whom it belonged all along. And if it is ours, to make peace with ourselves; and if it is not ours, to grieve the loss we hoped to avoid.

We can come to understand our past in a new way. This frees us to give up demanding from our present day relationships (from our present day *close others)* what those other *close others* in the past didn't give us.

- *Is our emotional reaction appropriate to what is happening in the present? Are we reacting not just to the present but also to the past? A present day conflict will instantly trigger a similar past experience that still lives unresolved inside of us. That is how the present becomes overwhelming.*
- *Are the same (or similar) things happening to us over and over again? If yes, then there is an ant trail we need to follow. There is a trigger we need to explore that sets us off or makes us prone to these experiences. Patterns have time lines attached. What was traumatic and we couldn't resolve at age two, repeats itself in new versions in our life now every two years with ever-new faces. Our original hurt happened at x-mas (in the spring, etc.) and now each x-mas we re-experience a similar upset.*

We can take a journey back through time and decide again what we now want to be true for us.

When something upsetting is happening in your present day life, take a few minutes and allow your mind to wander in a focused way.

The following technique[16] will allow you to explore an event or situation that was significant to the formation of the beliefs you hold today. Often such an event still has unresolved emotions attached. Therefore allow yourself to cry the tears that you maybe never cried originally.

---

[16]Adapted from a workshop by of Chuck Spezzano, Ph.D., Hawaii, 1984

First, locate where in your body you hold the sum total of the upset you are experiencing.

Next, find a way to become relaxed…feel the weight of your body supported by the chair etc. you are sitting in or imagine the feeling of warmth from the sun on your shoulders. Turn your attention inward to your breathing. It usually helps to close your eyes.

Now, pretend that your life is like a movie, running backwards in time. See significant events passing in reverse order in front of your mind's eye until you have reached the earliest time when you felt like you are feeling today.

Become aware of where you were in some detail…your home; the living room etc. How old were you? What were you wearing, etc.? Any sounds or smells? Who was there with you? What was happening? How did you feel about what was happening? Allow for the emotions that arise! What decision did you make at that moment in time? If you would know…what did you decide?

Being the adult you are today, how has this decision affected you? What aspect may not have been true in this past decision (remember you were a young child then)? What would you decide today?

If you have difficulties ask for help! Ideally you direct your request to someone that you regard as wiser then you. This is not necessarily a person but may be a figure of history or your religion, a Higher Self, etc. Ask him or her to go with you back there and help you see the situation as it truly was. Ask to be shown the underlying good intentions or unmet needs of other people involved. Can you identify with these intentions or needs? What job did you take on that wasn't truly yours? Make a new decision about yourself and others!

Return to your life today.

Healing in the present or hurting again…

It is in our present day relationships where we find, see and attract what will bring us healing. This is especially true when it comes to choosing the mates we are with. Relationships are the prime vehicle. We will either now heal and rewrite the past or lose ourselves all over again.

We all make the bed we lay in without realizing it.

Deep inside we have a plan for our happiness made by our habits, hopes, losses and pain. We don't realize the great amount of our creative and emotional energy that is being consumed by attempting to avoid the losses and pain of the past.

We don't recognize the prison we have built attempting to protect ourselves in the present from the repetition of a pain that has already happened. It cannot be avoided. It has left its scars. However, it can be resolved. The scars can become the demarcations of a self born in pain but filled with wisdom, compassion and openness.

"It Is Human Nature to Hate the Man You Have Injured."

Marcus Claudius Tacitus

They were sitting around a concrete outdoor picnic table having their sandwiches and casually carrying on a conversation about various topics. What happened next happened fast. He accidentally spilled his Diet Coke. She laughed and said jokingly that it wasn't necessary to do that just because she had brought up the topic of…!

"Don't laugh at me!," he snapped. She felt hurt.

When we feel guilty, we are tempted to find fault with the other.

She hadn't attempted to mock him with her comment. She hadn't judged him for being so clumsy so as to spill his coke, he had! It was his judgment of himself, most likely an automatic assessment practiced many times over, which moved him to lash out and misinterpret her gesture as an attack.

The best defense is an offense. It all happened so quickly, with little awareness and without any conscious deliberation. An insignificant incident, if repeated and retaliated for with further attack, capable of creating huge waves. This same scenario, played out in many different versions, happens hourly and daily in all relationships. We are all subject to its dynamics and stand guilty as charged. *The self-accusations and guilt we carry move us to attack and blame.*

Guilt disguises itself as blame, anger and rejection creating emotional distance. Guilt is often a fleeting emotion that likes to live *underground* in the dark realms of our subconscious. We *forget* that it is there! We experience it as finding ourselves irritated with those close to us. We find it difficult to immediately identify our irritation and blame as our own guilt. The acceptance of guilt into our mind, directed at us, or seeing someone else as guilty, is always the beginning of emotional distance and unhappiness. It leads to a loss of connection.

The moment we see ourselves as guilty, we become angry.

At it's best, guilt is a psychological phenomenon meant to encourage us towards right moral, ethical and social action. It is a psycho-emotional warning signal leading us to maintain healthy and mutually beneficial relationships.

At it's worst, guilt leads us into a distorted perception of the people around us. Unhealthy guilt is an incredibly powerful psychological force. It sets us up to receive the very injustices that we think we have imposed on others. It moves us to hold grievances towards others for things they, in essence, never did.

Our guilt leaves us with a sense of feeling less. Anger seeks to equalize the situation. We literally *puff ourselves up like a puffer fish* so as to undo the loss of equality and power we sense. This is not necessarily conscious. By finding something wrong with the other, we level the playing field. Our wrongdoing now looks small in comparison to theirs'. We get to feel right instead of less and wrong.

"Forgive me "your" illusions and release me from punishment for what I have not done." A Course in Miracles

Unconsciously, however, the knowledge remains that our attack does not undo our guilt. We are as capable of doing, or not doing (if we haven't already), what the other did, or didn't do. When we turn against the other person, we turn against our own humanity. Now our guilt is two-fold. We are guilty for our original wrongdoing and we are guilty for our attack. Our mind moves to defend our *goodness* through denial, justification and projection. *Guilt doesn't see others or us as having made a mistake but as having committed a moral crime.*

Guilt triggers a reaction of attack by simple association.

It is a bit like fearing, hating and punishing all dogs for the rest of our lives because the mean Dachshund next door bit us as a child.

Unhealthy guilt triggers an automatic all-consuming response towards people's actions in the present because of a vague similarity to the original hurt. We end up punishing our wives or husbands for the sins of our parents. The need to take vengeance on our own and others' wrongdoing manifests in our life as physical pain, illness, abusiveness, accidental injury, aggression, eating disorders, control issues, fault-finding, failure, self-sabotage, never-ending demands, or feeling driven. The power of guilt in our psyche is incredible. It is in our close relationships that we meet its most intense effects.

Blaming someone else or ourselves allows us to avoid our true feelings.

Guilt works hand in hand with denial and leads us into the maze of our defenses. It seldom appears in its real form but shows itself in our remorse and irritation and blame towards others. To make matters worse, if we lack good problem solving skills, the only tool available to us is often an extreme reaction to what is happening.

To quote Abraham Maslow, *"If the only tool you have is a hammer, you tend to see every problem as a nail."*

When we blame we feel *right and justified*. It keeps us focused on the other person's shortcomings or whirling around in a cyclone of self-pity. Don't be too hasty to judge yourself for your self-pity however. Self-pity in essence is unacknowledged suffering.

Blaming is easy. Blame is a form of attack on either others or us. It rests on an assumption that guilt justifies the attack. After all, we (or they) have done something wrong! Another's (or our own) fault is magnified. Blame allows us to pretend that we (or others) have either *none or all* of the responsibility in the situation. We either get to be victim or victimizer, with no in-between. And most of all, we get to avoid our deeper feelings about what happened.

She had lied to him, he maintained. She had met with her old boyfriend without telling him. According to her, to tie up loose ends on the apartment they used to share. Then why lie about it, he questioned. Anyways, it was all over now. He could never trust her again, he proclaimed. He would never have lied to her. She ruined what they had.

According to her, she omitted telling him, because he gets so jealous. Once she felt guilty and attacked she retaliated by blaming him for being insecure and jealous. "Why does he have to make such a big deal over nothing?" "He acts as if I had slept with my old boyfriend!" "It's not like he tells me everything all the time".

Blame will always take the situation out of its real context and exaggerate the facts.

It allows us to avoid taking responsibility for our part (no matter how subtle or hidden) in what happened. As such, it deprives us of being able to acknowledge and correct that we have missed our mark, which is to know ourselves as loving, loveable and loved. Blame allows us to hide from what is underlying our dissatisfaction and pain. It is a secondary reaction to feeling hurt without taking responsibility for one's own part.

It is as if we paddle on top of an ocean pretending we are in a bathtub.

Personal responsibility means we are responsible for being in charge of our thoughts, feelings, motivations and actions, have the courage to admit to them and mop up after ourselves when needed.

Society and the mass media reflect back to us constantly that we are victims. It is easy to fall into the trap of relinquishing responsibility for us. We don't realize that in relinquishing responsibility we as well relinquish personal power and any adult problem solving skills we have. We remain on the surface with the obvious. The deeper connections stay unresolved.

Whenever we lose something, we gain something else, not always wanted or asked for.

It is up to us to capitalize on what we have gained instead of sitting in front of the broken pieces of our life lost. Insisting on being right about the injustice of our pain does not resolve it. It is up to us to fashion something new out of the pieces we are left with, instead of desperately trying to put them back together the way they used to be. It is up to us to find the silver lining in the rain cloud that is hanging over our head. There is good hidden even here. When one door closes another will open. Acceptance will show us the way. Grief, anger and regret will blind us.

When the hand of life reshuffles our cards, we are offered an opportunity to reconsider the status quo.

Painful as it may be, loss will bring new awareness if we are willing to open our mind to what we are invited to learn. There is opportunity for something new, maybe something that we secretly desired but we didn't dare to venture for. Maybe something that was part of a dream we buried or shelved long ago. Loss pushes us into taking a second look at how we live our life and handle our relationships.

What is truly important?

Our first reaction when we feel hurt may be that "I should have known", blaming ourselves.

We may feel as if we, or others, have broken some unspoken contract. If we take the time to follow the *trail* of our thoughts and feelings, it will lead us back to the *omni-powers* we thought we had and were guilty of failing. The super-human powers we took on when we were little. The path to self-knowledge is across the bridge of facing our secret fears. Self-acceptance rests on being able to put our arms around ourselves when we have failed.

Using the above example, his girlfriend had unwittingly put him back in touch with deep feelings of not loved, not special, not there. His strong reaction to her action is a telltale sign that more is going on then what meets the eye.

She felt guilty and hurt by his consequent rejection of her in retaliation. She realized that it was scary for her to face his anger and disapproval. What she had hoped to avoid with her omission, she had reaped many-fold.

How was guilt born?

As toddlers we learned to distinguish between good and bad. With the awareness of these opposites came the awareness that we were capable of doing one or the other. This made us vulnerable to fail and possibly not be loved by those we depended on. To be bad meant to reap parental disapproval, rejection and possibly punishment. We assumed either suddenly or over time that our status of being loved, loveable and loving was potentially or in actuality jeopardized. This initiated a state of emergency. We had to rid ourselves of our badness.

The knowledge and resulting guilt that we had acted in contradiction to what was expected of us was dangerous to our sense of being a good person. Denial and projection were the tools of choice. *"Wasn't me,"* is a phrase used a lot at that age.

If it wasn't me, then who was it? Must have been the other guy!

All of this takes on another level of intensity when realizing that for the young child being good or bad and acting good or bad are undifferentiated. In child-like thinking being bad is a personal essence flaw, something that can't be changed. The underlying assumption that bad actions or failure will jeopardize one's right to be loved, etc. remains unchallenged. This assumption is the real culprit.

Unhealthy guilt cannot be undone by treating it as if it is real.

Atoning for unhealthy guilt only increases its supposed reality. It therefore increases the power of guilt in our minds. We never stop long enough to question its truth. We hide, manipulate, deny, compensate, blame others and do whatever else we can think of, but we rarely question. We neglect to put guilt into its correct context.

"Have I done wrong and made a mistake?" "If so, I need to correct what can be corrected." There is no need for self (or other) condemnation. Once we see mistakes as sins, we become subject to the resulting cycle of guilt and punishment. Ideally, we deal with guilt in a matter of fact way, sorting out the aspect where guilt is justified and the aspect that is a misunderstanding or wrongful conclusion.

Why don't we do that? Because it requires the following:

- a basic belief in our own and others' essential goodness and innocence;
- trusting that others are capable, resilient and in essence invulnerable to our attacks;

- questioning the values, morals and assumptions that we have previously accepted as true;
- the courage to face our deeper wounds;
- and we must take responsibility.

To complicate things even further, every young child lives in a magical identity with its environment and the powers that apparently move that environment. A three-year-old will full-heartedly believe that there is nothing that daddy can't fix.

A 6-year-old proclaimed to her best friend's mother that, since her mother is a school counselor, she knows everything!

Every child (and parent) must eventually awaken to the painful realization that mom and dad do not know everything. At times, they will not be there when we need them the most.

As you look upon yourself and judge what you do or did honestly, you may be tempted to judge.

You may wonder how all of this could be seen as a mistake instead of guilt deserving punishment. Accepting wrongdoing as a mistake that asks for correction (and forgiveness) is based on a basic assumption of goodness (one's own and others'). It is the realization of an underlying commonality, the acceptance of oneself and another as a fallible human being. It is the realization that forgiveness doesn't mean that the hurt we experienced is annulled or belittled. And, it has nothing to do with confusing taking responsibility with retreating into self-condemnation. Only once we make that distinction are we able to escape the trap that unhealthy guilt sets for us.

Who Wrecked the Happy Family We Once Knew?

To most of us the answer comes quickly!

Parents and siblings are the favorite choices. Sincerely asking ourselves this question can lead us back to the unhealthy guilt and wrong sense of responsibility we accepted. This wrong sense of responsibility is now unconsciously *running our life.*

For a moment, assume that once upon a time you had a happy childhood. You don't need to be able to visualize this or even fully believe it. You only need to be able to get a feeling of what such a childhood, had it existed, would have felt like. Once you have this feeling, you hold the doorknob in your hand that will open the door to coming to understand yourself and the roots of your deepest thoughts, emotions and behaviors.

- While resting in this feeling, ask yourself who wrecked this happy childhood. *"If it had been anyone, it was..."*
- Allow the first and immediate response to this question guide you deeper. *"How did this person wreck it? What did they do? They…!"*

Limit your response to just a few words, making them as precise as possible to perfectly describe your feeling. The answer, and at the same time accusation, is what you hold in the deepest recesses of your mind against yourself. This is what you attempt to desperately avoid ever doing or being. Or, this is what you have done in myriad of ways.

Children tend to take on an exaggerated sense of responsibility.

This is a survival mechanism. If it is my fault, then there must be something that *"I can do"* to change the outcome. Many adults are still caught in longing for their parents to be the parents that they never were. They stubbornly hang on to the fantasy that, *"If I only would do the right thing, then my parent(s) would become who I have always wanted him/her to be."*

Instinctively children avoid feeling the tremendous psychological impact of feeling powerless. To be utterly helpless to bring about what one craves but cannot change is terrifying. It is this feeling of helplessness that is at the core of all trauma and ultimately at the core of what makes us human. We *drag* with us what remains unresolved. We *store* it in our body and re-experience it in our present-day relationships.

Without a developed emotional and psychological system, children are left to their own devices. They will instinctively avoid or delay to adulthood having to stand face to face with what could not be changed or resolved. Only an adult can truly face, withstand and sort out the emotional impact of trauma. The problem is, we have thoroughly forgotten and gotten used to denying that *any* type of trauma happened to us. We are caught up in needing to keep those we love good. The idea that someone who is bad is not worthy of love is deeply ingrained into our psyche. That it is possible to love someone who has *failed us or done bad* is bewildering.

The truth becomes surrounded by fearful interpretation and conclusions.

Errors in understanding and unresolved emotions don't allow a child's psyche to assimilate what is valuable and eliminate what is valueless in an experience. The conclusions drawn about oneself and others become accepted as truth. As a result, the conclusions drawn and emotions denied are dragged into adulthood unresolved. What was first done to him/her, the now adult does to or assumes about his/herself. This leads to shame and blame.

Interpretations that we have accepted as truth make us righteous and afraid. The conclusions we drew become the blueprint for the life we lead. What we feel has been done to us, or we think we have done, governs our present-day attitude and behavior. We continue doing…(it) to ourselves in many hidden ways. Given enough stress and pressure, we may do or have done…(it) to others. Or, we are afraid and very careful to not do so.

As a result we tend to either avoid or overcompensate. We may become overprotective, or are in denial and oblivious about acting in the same manner. Overcompensating rests on wrongly accepted responsibility. Being oblivious leads to doing to others, what was done to us and passing the *"sins of the fathers on to the children"*.

► What was done to me (or I think I have done)
leads to abandonment & betrayal; which leads to
► Do (it) to myself
leads to shame; which leads to
► Do (it) to others
which leads to guilt.

Emotional life functions by the law of opposites.

Considerable amounts of energy are now being spent in avoiding the knowledge or repetition of the original experience. When emotional energy is not in balance we become vulnerable. Given enough stress, we will eventually, find ourselves in a situation where we are *doing to others* what was *done to us*. This will happen despite our best effort to avoid such a case. The result is an overpowering feeling of guilt. Guilt demands punishment.

"What better punishments then have someone "do to me" what I think, "I have done?" Unacknowledged and unresolved the cycle continues spiraling into ever-crazier distortions. It wrecks havoc in our relationships, career, health and life in general.

She was three years old when she received a hamster as a pet. She loved that hamster and carried it everywhere with her. One day the hamster was dead. She had dropped her hamster while playing, that was the reason her hamster died, her parents told her. She felt devastated. She never had a pet again.

Even as an adult she could hardly talk about it without breaking out into tears. She had killed the very thing she loved. This experience was her most vivid recollection when she first felt that *"I am dangerous"*. It took a long time for her to accept that her parents had failed her by not providing age-appropriate guidance and giving loving understanding, support and explanations. She was left with her overwhelming feelings. *"Loving understanding and explanations weren't her parents' style," she concluded dryly.* She pushed her feelings away and learned to cope the best she could. She carried the conclusions she drew buried deep inside into adulthood.

As an adult, whenever she began to feel close to someone, she was overcome with feelings of fear. "I am afraid of intimacy", she proclaimed almost defiantly. Deep down she felt like a failure. While she was in her twenties, it didn't bother her. Once she reached her mid thirties, she began to question.

Once we have accepted an assumption as the truth, it will function as such in our life.

The woman in the above example realized that her fear of intimacy was in fact multifaceted. One aspect of it was an attempt at protecting the people she loved from herself.

Young children see themselves as the center of their universe, *omnipotent, omniscient and omnipresent.* They therefore assume that they are to blame for any hurtful experience involving any member of the family.

Accepting this imagined guilt into their minds allows them to maintain their magical state. It also subjects them to an overpowering sense of responsibility. It protects them from being exposed to the core of all traumatic experience, an irresolvable sense of helplessness in the face of what is happening.

"As long as it is my fault, I must be able to do something about it to alter the outcome."

This defense is aimed at maintaining a feeling of power but backfires, for now they have become unsafe in a two-fold way. Believing that they have the power to cause what happened makes them unsafe with their own personal power. Believing they are the cause makes them guilty and severs their sense of connection and closeness with their parents. Doubt enters *"Am I loving, loveable and loved?"* Parents often don't realize that this question is answered inside their young minds.

Make sure you tell your child:

- That he/ she is not responsible for your or your partner's bad mood or upset.
- That his/her failures are normal and insignificant and that success is just around the corner (give a personal example of a similar failure).
- That he/she is loved, loveable and loving (good) and any behavior to the contrary only a temporary mistake.
- That temporary lapses of judgment cannot change who he/she is in essence and how you feel and think of him/her.

All traumas aren't just a one-time dramatic or abusive event.

The most common trauma experienced is subtle neglect and rejection; criticism of who one is versus what one has done, a*nd cheering the crash in someone* instead of minimizing failure. Children can be traumatized by age-inappropriate experiences and information. Most people stand guilty of the above at one time or another.

Once the denial lifts, we have to learn to stand and face our worst pain and what we fear is the truth about us. Often there was no safe adult that was able to assist us as children with at least partially coming to terms with our confusion and pain. There was no one to put his or her accepting arms around us and provide us with guidance. Our only recourse was to use the tool of denial. In self-defense we had to *put-away* our pain, fear and guilt so completely that they now seem inaccessible to us. Our daily life struggles become the mirror of our denied self.

An initial traumatic experience usually holds loss, confusion, abandonment and betrayal at its core. This leads to disconnection from others' love and most importantly from our own (as yet not fully formed) love for us. As a result, we are left with a feeling of not being able to love ourselves. Self-love becomes a strange concept and becomes confused with selfishness. Children internalize the attitudes of the significant people around them.

They learn to value, love and respect others and themselves if they are treated with value, love and respect.

The most confusing experiences are the subtle experiences of emotionally not there.

Since parents are humans and more or less aware, chances are that they weren't always emotionally there when we needed them. They weren't aware enough to recognize when we needed their guidance and understanding. They denied us the freedom to experiment and explore. They criticized us when they should have empathized. Instead of minimizing when we made mistakes, they punished. They overpowered us and didn't allow us to find our own way of doing things. Falling back onto the parenting style of their own parents they used guilt and shame in an attempt to keep us safe. At the same time, we knew they loved us.

We can blame them, and revolve in circles, or we can lick our wounds and then aspire to do better by our children and ourselves.

We don't have power over altering time or other people and circumstance. However, we can pick up the pieces and begin to fashion a new life. We can have an attitude that life wants to reward us and is not out to punish us.

Since God's didn't raise us, it is very likely that all of us walk away from childhood lacking in some way. This makes us prone to fail. Certain abilities, securities and potentials weren't assisted in being developed. We now face the hard work of doing it ourselves. It is up to us now to grow the self-esteem and self-confidence that was never nurtured. What a novel concept! We are responsible for ourselves as adults.

Guilt becomes a teaching device when failure and wrongdoing is seen as a mistake.

Guilt used in its right function is an internalized code of values and morals. It is a warning signal to adjust our behavior towards living a moral and ethical life now and in the future. It encourages us to act with integrity and consider other people's interests as well as our own. It encourages us to make up for when we have done wrong. It guides us to act in ways that will nurture and build relationships and ultimately, helps us realize ourselves.

Guilt that has its base in the past rests on childlike assumptions of a power that belongs to the gods. It is not humanly possible to always be there when needed by those we love. To always fix all the hurts and things that go wrong in our and others' lives and to always know what to do or what others need. This form of guilt that rests at the core of our irresolvable conflicts needs to be unmasked and be seen for what it is.

Healthy guilt doesn't ask for everlasting remembrance of a wrongdoing. Each day holds a question that needs to be answered once again in our own minds:

"Who do I choose to be today with the very obstacles that I am facing at this time?"

The past cannot be changed.

Some may find this is hard to accept, especially if their old feelings about the past aren't finished yet. It involves true grieving to finish the past. *We need to grieve the losses, the "could have beens" and experience the anger and hurt, the disappointments and sadness.*

We need to let go of never having that someone reaffirm us, or confirm that we are worthwhile. We need to surrender our demand to hear that they or we were wrong, that they loved us, forgive us and tell us that they are sorry! The past is gone and we can't in all reality turn back the clock and do anything about it. Neither do we truly need to. Every day is a new beginning if we accept it as such. It takes trust, trusting that good is going to come our way.

In the present, we then become truly able to live in the present. We let go of restoring our wounded self-esteem by insisting that another should restore it for us by acting in a certain way. The past then isn't any longer a license or excuse for lack in the present. There is no room for self-pity or feeling victimized. We are in charge of our own destiny.

Forgiveness doesn't annul the hurt that we felt.

Forgiveness acknowledges the common humanity we share: the underlying fear, the temptation to be selfish and the lure of misusing one's personal power. All of these are recognized as one's own, in reality or potential.

We let go of being righteous and superior.

It recognizes in the one who hurt us the same need for love, safety and protection that we wish for. They too want to be seen (at least in their own eyes) as right and good.

Forgiveness rests on the recognition that someone else carried the *salt* for our preexisting wound or we did for his or hers. They (we) may carry responsibility, yet only partially so. It is the recognition that what they did or didn't do has much more to do with who they think they are. Forgiveness is only hard and seems impossible or phony, when we believe that our wrath and right to punish is justified. When we are not willing to surrender our lofty ideals and open our eyes to being fallible human beings.

When will our wrath ever be fully satisfied? Will sacrificing their first-born do?

This doesn't mean that we now have to continue to allow hurtful people into our *inner circle*. People who lack the awareness and willingness to change are *asleep thrashing around in their nightmares.* It is best to get out of the way for they do not know what they are doing! Forgiveness asks us to let go of judging another and with that releases us from judgment. It allows us to let go and move on. It opens our mind to embrace our own and others' humanity. It leads to inclusion, commonality, and ultimately unity. We are free and the hand of life *will* hold us.

Life is a paradox.

Whatever we choose to believe or how we choose to interpret our or others actions will inevitably affect our experience. Once accepted, beliefs and values have a powerful influence on experience and behavior. With awareness of what we believe must grow our tolerance for making mistakes.

Can we admit to our mistakes without succumbing to feelings of blame and self-loathing?

It is a well-established fact that early childhood experiences have a disproportionately large effect for better or worth on our later life experiences. Yet, our attempts to free ourselves have to be more then exchanging one set of conditioned beliefs for another. Neither is this freedom gained by either telling ourselves we are fine or walking around with a shovel over our shoulder attempting to undo all limiting beliefs.

We need to see the associations and connections that today has to yesterday and recognize that change is always accomplished in the present. The process of recognizing our own inner essence is subtle. It is not something that we can impose but must choose.

We avoid truly facing what we feel.

Feelings Are Neither Good nor Bad

"Don't voice how you truly feel" is an unspoken rule in many families and in our society at large. We disown feelings we have judged as negative for the unpleasantness they hold. At the same time, we use them as the justification for our hurtful acting out.

Feelings are seen as unsafe and powerful. Voicing our feelings is hurtful to others or will embarrass us, we were taught. We attempt to rid ourselves of what we feel. We learn to act out, repress, minimize, control, deny, rationalize, discount, project and distance ourselves from our feelings.

Before we can deal with our emotions effectively, we have to:

1. know and accept that it is OK to feel what we feel;
2. we need to grasp that others may not think, feel and want the same as we do, yet still love us;
3. we need to accept that the responsibility for our feelings lies with us.

It is not the *feeling and wanting* in itself that causes us problems. It is the *acting* on those feelings and wants that often complicates our life. Feelings are foremost just that, an inner emotional experience. Acting on this inner experience is an extra, separate step.

Other people are not obligated to give us what we need or want just because we told them or just because they are close to us. As long as we confuse feeling with acting on how we feel, we scare ourselves and cause much unnecessary hurt to others.

As long as we don't believe that what we feel and want is OK, we are going to find it difficult to deal honestly with others and ourselves.

It is the wise and skillful management of emotions that distinguishes the average man from the advanced man. Handling one's affairs with maturity rests on the acceptance and awareness of one's emotions.

Messy emotional experiencing is frowned upon.

We impose admired traits and worthy goals on our children, others and ourselves. We are taught to feel ashamed or guilty for our upset feelings. This locks us into denying how we feel. To approach these feelings the way we would deal with a bruise, is a foreign concept. We know that a bruise will run its course and that we are going to be good as new after.

She was three years old and invited to her first birthday party at a friend's house. Her mother had been diligent in shopping with her for a birthday gift for her friend and a small gift for her. Her mother anticipated that it might be hard for a three-year-old to see another child receiving gifts without receiving anything for herself.

She was dressed in her party dress and it was time to go. Suddenly she began crying, declaring that she just couldn't give her gift to her friend. She wanted it for herself! She wasn't going to go to the party! The mother tried everything...explaining that her birthday would come soon and she too would be receiving gifts...reminding her that she had received a gift already...talking about how all the other kids will be giving a gift to her friend...how birthday parties are about giving gifts to the birthday child...how much fun she was going to have at the party...etc. But nothing worked, she kept on wailing, a heap on the floor.

No or very little distinction is made between feeling what we do and acting on those feelings.

It is commonly accepted to act on our feelings. As a matter of fact, we may have been taught that feeling a certain way gives us a *right* to act accordingly. Feelings by themselves are not a very reliable decision-making tool. It takes the heart and the head to make good decisions in life. Feelings need to first have a space to be *digested* before they can offer us any guidance for constructive actions.

Instead of learning to first digest our emotions, inquire into the deeper meaning they have for us and then choose our actions, we learned to avoid, deny or react. By the time we reach adulthood most of us have forgotten how to be in touch with, explore, have perspective on, accept and use this part of our psyches constructively. Now emotions are experienced as all engulfing and dangerous; they make us lose perspective.

The mother's first reaction was to make her daughter feel guilty, shame her, or punish her for her behavior but she wisely resisted. Finally she simply embraced her, acknowledging how hard it was for her daughter to give this gift to her friend. "Yes, it's so hard!!!" wailed her three-year-old daughter with heart-breaking sobs…then, two minutes later, still nestled in her mothers arms, she took a couple of deep breaths, got up and declared that she was ready to go now!!!

In stepping back from her own reaction to her daughter's display, the mother was able to teach by example on how to deal with upsetting feelings. Her calm demeanor, lack of judgment and show of support allowed her daughter to accept and fully experience her feelings. And, once her daughter did, her feelings changed and she was free to change her mind.

The nature of emotions is that they will never stay the same when faced, acknowledged and truly embraced.

Emotions are fluid in nature. The moment we put into words what we feel, our feelings may change. We may feel suddenly resolved, as if all we needed to do was acknowledge how we felt and talk about it, not necessarily solve it. This dynamic causes many people much confusion and leads them to question the validity of their and others' feelings. Allowing the natural process that our feelings demand frightens us. Here lies the key to emotional mastery in our lives.

We are confused about upper level emotional experiencing and core feelings. Upper level emotions are like a whirlpool and always lead us to blame, either others or ourselves. Core feelings are an experience of the self, separate from what others did or didn't do.

The mother could have dragged an upset and uncooperative toddler to the party. She could have stayed home and punished her. She could have made her daughter feel ashamed and guilty for feeling the way she did. Any of the above versions would have been a reaction to her daughter's reaction.

Instead she chose to lovingly embrace and accept her daughters messy emotional experiencing. There is little doubt that she probably felt helpless and frustrated for a moment, maybe even challenged in her parental authority. However, this incident wasn't about her, it was about her daughter. The mother wisely resisted taking on her daughter's problem. This taught her daughter by example that experiencing her emotions (in a safe environment) frees her to not necessarily act on them. The daughter was able to rebound from the experience with a strengthened sense of self.

Feelings contain an energetic charge that has a loud nonverbal voice.

When we are young this energetic charge is scary and overwhelming. It takes our breath away, *literally.* When we are in pain, we tend to hold our breath in an instinctual response of attempting to ease our pain. It is breathing that allows for the management and release of pain.

When we truly stay with the feelings we have about something, we free ourselves from habitually acting on them. We give ourselves a chance to digest what these feelings have to tell us and then choose our action. Stating how we feel has to be done *without* an intention to *get at someone.* We can *handle* our problems instead of being handled by the energetic charge they produce.

When we judge what we feel, we *forget* to just feel. Instead of digesting our feelings the judgment we put on them begins to occupy our mind and pushes our feelings *underground.* These feelings now live on inside of us surrounded by assumptions and interpretations.

Feelings keep us tuned in to what is going on inside of us as well as to what is going on around us. They provide useful information if we let them.

The two key-steps to dealing with feelings more honestly are:

1. *Learning to acknowledge how you feel to yourself without self-reproach.*
2. *Learning to acknowledge how you feel to others without blame.*

These steps remain difficult as long as we do not know how to access our core feelings. Blame towards others or ourselves keeps our emotional experiencing on the surface.

When we deny our emotions, we become over-sensitized to the slightest unkind gesture.

Instead of being a valuable tool to experience, experiment and express denied emotions take on a life all their own. *We feel victimized by them or we will move to victimize.* Our judgment becomes prejudiced, our view of the world becomes distorted and our mind closes. We attempt to soothe ourselves with food, substance abuse, work, rules and roles. We seek refuge in our intellect. We hide in our spiritual beliefs...something, anything that is less messy and painful.

All human beings are born with the ability to either fully feel or to self-soothe. We can develop our ability to calm down and manage overwhelming emotions. This is different from stifling and avoiding what churns inside of us.

Taking a time out by going for a walk, counting to ten, going to a safe place, listening to music, shooting baskets, writing in a journal, cleaning the house, etc. all are effective ways to step back from emotions that are intense. Taking a time out gives us a space to explore and digest what we feel and then consciously choose our action.

He grew up with a mother who was in charge and a father who went along. He resented his mother's ways of directing his life. With the limited emotional resources of a young child he simply put the feelings he had away. When his teenage daughter doesn't pack her suitcase the way he thinks she should, he takes over and dictates what she should and shouldn't bring on their trip. His old unresolved feelings move him to be what he swore he never would be!

The only time our negative emotions remain is when they become stuck.

Stuck feelings are denied feelings, unacknowledged feelings, judged feelings or minimized feelings. Feelings that still have something to teach us and still need to be explored. We may appear very emotional yet avoid how we truly feel.

Emotions have the potential to become addictive. Self-righteousness, anger and self-pity tempt us the most. We become junkies to the charge they produce. This form of emotionality is a display. It resolves nothing. We remain in denial.

She was only three when she felt abandoned by her mother. She never truly trusted authority again. As a mother herself, she feels outraged when teachers are inconsiderate or oblivious to her daughters needs. Her anger produced an addictive charge of self-righteousness coupled with feelings of victimization.

What we deny, we do not have conscious awareness of and control over. Denied feelings manifest as the very problems in relationships that frustrate us. These denied emotions now take on the power to distort our view of the present, others and ourselves. Our relationships become infested with our unresolved past. We anticipate being treated unkindly.

The biggest problem with denial is that its very essence dictates that we *don't know that we don't know.* We begin to see in others what we cannot accept in ourselves. Acknowledging our wrongdoings generates intense self-reproach.

After all, we swore that we never would! The last thing we want to do, is do to those we love today, what made us hurt so badly yesterday. It takes a high degree of self-love to be able to admit to what we promised we never would do or be.

For the most part, we feel unskilled in dealing with our own and other people's emotional expressions.

Our helplessness and ignorance moves us to discount, minimize and belittle what others or we feel. *"You don't want that or feel that,!" we exclaim.* We become incapable of simply listening and being there. Instead, we immediately move into attempting to fix it, justify or dismiss what is going on.

Only someone who has become comfortable with their own emotional world is OK in the presence of someone displaying strong feelings, such as sadness, grief or anger. Before we reach this point for ourselves, we don't know what to do to make the other feel better!

We do not realize that there is nothing to be done except to be there with comforting arms.

"I hate her!" "She is not my real mother!" Arms crossed and ponytail flying she came storming into the kitchen. Her father looked up from cutting the vegetables. "Of course you don't hate her. We're a family now!"

As adults most of us are very uncomfortable with children's honest expressions. This is a mirror image of how we deal with our own feelings. We immediately rise to tell our children and ourselves that what they (or we) are feeling is not so. But the truth is, that at that particular moment she did hate her stepmother. In denying our children their feelings we teach them to deny their feelings instead of constructively deal with their feelings.

When negative feelings are high, we need to make a space. *"Boy, you sound angry!" "What happened?"* In the space created, feelings can be explored and expressed which in itself often brings about a resolution. There is a difference between feeling angry and using that anger to blame and attack. Anger, even hatred, is an emotional state that can be experienced without taking an extra step of directing the energetic charge the emotion produces at someone or even something. Emotions are like waves. We need to learn to let them wash over us before we act. Then we can take action to change what can be changed. We can learn to focus on what we do like, when things don't change.

Emotions come in many colors and shades.

The emotions we are capable of can be equated to the many colors in a paint set.

If you bought a set of watercolors and discovered at home that it only contained the colors red or black, wouldn't you think there was something wrong?

Strangely, we rarely appear to question our inability and discomfort to experience and express a full range of emotions. We don't recognize this inability to feel as fear of what we think we cannot handle. Our lack of skill is a learned behavior and based in a lack of information.

Everyone has an inner feeling world more or less complex. We all have feelings but that doesn't automatically mean that we all know how to get in touch with, identify and name our feelings. To some of us this may be the very first time to ever attempt to identify exactly what we feel. We may not be used to naming the feelings we have. Being able to identify and name our feelings is learned.

Just like once we learned the spoken and written language of our mother tongue, we either learned or didn't learn to identify and name our feelings. Just as language can be sophisticated or basic, our feeling vocabulary can be simplistic or rich.

We approach emotions, as if they are a dangerous beast.

Now, we have to negotiate the initial stage of thinking that something wrong, scary or bad will emerge if we let ourselves get in touch with our inner life. Once we feel safe with our own emotions, we begin to feel safe with other people's emotional upsets. As we learn to put loving arms around ourselves when we are upset, we know to do the same for others.

Next time a friend or loved one is upset simply acknowledge what they are feeling as in: "You are angry, sad, etc."

Encourage them to tell you how they feel. Keep reminding yourself there is nothing for you to do except to be there and be a sounding board. In fact, it is best to not take sides…nor your friends or the other persons (nor your own immediately).

When someone is upset the last thing they need to hear is that they don't have any reason to feel the way they do! The fact is, they feel the way they feel! It isn't a matter of right and wrong, of justified or not, of who is to blame.

Empathize; maybe relate a similar incident from your own life and/or help the other see things within a bigger context. Remember that blame is avoidance. The feelings hiding underneath blame are our true feelings.

When something in our life presses us under, we become depressed.

When we are totally overwhelmed or feel completely inept at dealing with what we feel and what is, we become hopeless. An overwhelming feeling of helplessness rests at the bottom of all unresolved trauma. Helplessness is experienced in direct opposition with our ability to make ourselves safe. We can't or do not know how to protect ourselves. We cannot change what is. And, what is appears to have the power to harm those we love or us.

Our first attempt at resolution often is to numb ourselves. We either cannot (due to circumstances) or neglect to seek the help (psychological or biological) we need. There may simply be no help available!

For a toothache, of course, we would consult with a dentist, yet to do the same for heartache?

We may attempt to overcome our helplessness and hopelessness through medication. This may be a temporary practical option, a crutch to be used when desperately needed. *At times we need a life raft.* However, pills can never replace learning to truly deal with and coming to grips with our life.

TV ad campaigns persistently tell us that it is a "*Medication over Mood*" question. Take this pill and feel good again…appealing to our gullibility for an easy solution. This goes hand in hand with the doctrine that we should stifle our emotions for the sake of peace. If emotional instability is an outcome of a hormonal imbalance or illness medication holds validity. Emotional imbalances that have a psychological source ask for a different approach. It is up to us to take constructive action on our behalf.

"Changes we make in overcoming self-defeating behaviors...will always outlast and be of greater long-term benefit than those induced by chemical agents. The promise of success via magic pills fits all too conveniently into our overachieving, fast-paced American lives. There simply isn't enough time for reflection, development of insight and the opportunity to learn from our mistakes."

Dr. Anthony V. Rao; Department of Psychiatry, Harvard Medical School, Boston

We experience and carry our emotions in our body.

Denying or overriding how we feel doesn't mean that the energetic charge of our emotions has disappeared. In her book *"Your Body Speaks Your Mind",* Debbie Shapiro writes how emotional energy has the power to reshape our muscles and held long enough to affect our organs and dictate our state of health. When we protect ourselves from emotions that seem too much to handle, or when we habitually deny emotions, we give our physical body a job it is not naturally designed to do!

Our body's tension and dis-ease now become a *"call for help"*. Emotional energy can be withheld and denied, but it will manifest nevertheless. Our body feels tense, we repeat the same hurtful experiences and eventually the withheld energy becomes dis-ease.

We have to actually consciously recall the emotions that need to be dealt with from the body and commit to dealing with them where they belong...through our psycho-emotional self!

Look at the discomfort or dis-ease that you presently experience and ask yourself what the natural function of that part of your body is? What emotional connection can you discern?[17] *What feelings have you pushed aside and avoided to deal with?*

Pain is how our emotions and body communicate.

When we get angry or sad, notice how our heart starts to beat faster, that subtle zing in our chest, or the butterflies in our stomach.

Debbie Shapiro points to the fact that learning to respect our silent inner voice will put us back in touch with the buried feelings of the past and needs arising in the present. The body becomes our ally.

Our body can be the guide to realizing what we feel. We begin to work *with* our emotions instead of *against* them. It is our body that will give us a signal when things don't feel right. When we cannot or do not express what is happening on an emotional or psychological level we physically become affected. A silent voice speaking through the tension and dis-ease we experience alerts us to what we might have sensed, knew somewhere deep inside, but never fully acknowledged.

When we numb ourselves to the hurtful, sad and angry feelings that live inside, we also numb ourselves to feeling truly good, to knowing what we want in life. We ignore or override the warning signals our body sends us. Physical pain can be an outcome of *not dealing* with emotional pain *when* it happened and *where* it needs to be dealt with.

Getting in touch with our emotions feels good even though it may feel bad to feel what we are feeling.

Strong feelings like anger, hurt and excitement are bold. Feelings of blank, bored, stuck, or empty are subtle. This includes *hitting resistance*. Subtle feelings are harder to recognize and harder to work with. Resistance (no matter what form it takes) is always a sign of self-protection. It asks us to respect our own limits, not to just

[17] For further reading see Louise L. Hay, *Heal Your Body*, and Debbie Shapiro, *Your Body Speaks Your Mind*

barrel ahead, but to stop, respect and inquire into its reason for being.

"What is it trying to protect me from?" "Do I still need this protection?" What we resist persists! Therefore the last thing that is advisable to do is to struggle with resistance. It will give way of itself when approached gently with understanding.

Our bad feelings may show us where our attitude has gone astray. *Do we see the glass as half empty or half full?* How we approach life and other people determines a large part of our experience. *A smile begets a smile!* What we focus on we intensify. As such, our bad feelings challenge us to make adjustments, change our minds and learn to relate to others, food, our environment and ourselves in new ways.

We feel better when we finally acknowledge how we feel deep inside. It is out in the open now. It is known now. I can do something about it now, even if the something is simply to acknowledge, grieve and finally accept what is. Our body let's us know when we have reached the bottom of something by taking a breath. A new understanding arises.

If we do not feel this release but get stuck in feeling bad, we have taken a half step and not truly reached the bottom yet. It is normal to have some difficulty with getting in touch with feelings in the beginning. It is like learning any new skill. It takes practice and persistence.

Emotions Have Received a Bad Reputation

Many people blame their destructive actions on the feelings that "others" caused.

We act as if we had no choice in the matter. Not taking responsibility for what we feel produces the misery we experience and cause. It is so very human to first want to focus on what someone else did wrong. Some people more then others feel criticized when another speaks of their hurt feelings. Their immediate reaction is that somehow they have failed for the other is unhappy with them.

In self-defense they reject the perceived blame that apparently was put on them and begin to blame. Yes, others can contribute or attempt to detract from our happiness. However, happiness is most of all an internal matter.

Undisciplined emotional displays will pollute our and others space just as garbage pollutes our environment. Emotions challenge us to learn to step back and gain perspective. We need to learn to direct our emotional energy wisely.

An uncut diamond is an ugly rock. Unrefined and misused, emotional energy is an ugly display. Taking charge is not a call to control, minimize and deny our feelings. It is also not a call to employ willpower. It is a call to become more aware…to consciously choose who we are today and who we are going to be tomorrow. It is a call to embrace what we feel at the core before we act.

Anger is an inherent energy that can either be used to destroy or to create.

We cannot stop ourselves from being angry just as we cannot stop our impulse to live. When we learn to repress and be ashamed of our anger, for we cannot annul it, we often turn it inside. We become sad and depressed instead of angry. Anger becomes self-hatred and self-loathing expressing itself as constant unreasonable guilt, pessimism, sarcasm and depression.

On the other hand, when we use our anger to intimidate, to control and to make others feel guilty, we misuse our natural energy for self-affirmation. *We may win the battle but we have lost the war.* If we only have access to the simplistic emotion of anger or its counterpart hurt, as our sole response to what life presents us with, *we have a problem.*

The little boy was helping his father with breakfast. Suddenly the milk carton slipped from his grasp. His father was not having a good morning. He was late for an important meeting at work and quietly resentful of his wife. He expected her to fix breakfast instead of him.

"Please get a sponge…it was an accident," he managed to say between clenched teeth. It took every ounce of self-control he had to not lash out at his son.

Anger directs us to protect what is ours and move towards what we want.

Only when we accept anger as normal and natural, something that will pass and is not to be used as a justification for acting out, can we set appropriate boundaries. Our frustration and irritation can show us where we have given up too much of ourselves. We become angry when others take more then we are willing to give. We become frustrated when we have reached a limit, when it is time to take a breath and take a break. We become angry as long as the injustices and suffering we endured hasn't been fully acknowledged. We become angry when we feel guilty. And, we become angry when we can't have it our way.

The basic emotions of anger, sadness and distress can be misused to control the people around us. It is as if we have never outgrown throwing temper tantrums in order to get our way. Anger in particular is used in this fashion. We ask for attention negatively by getting angry. When we cannot face the people we are angry towards, we become tempted to get angry with someone who we regard as *weaker or safer.*

You probably have heard the story of the boss yelling at his employee, the employee upon arriving home picking a fight with his wife, the wife criticizing her son and the son kicking the dog…we pass on what we don't deal with.

When anger turns into violence, we ask why?

Why can't men and women manage their anger without becoming violent and destructive like kinder gardeners? Why do adults harm their relationships again and again?

Violence or depression, other or self-destructive tendencies *have their origin in us.* They are an emotional hunger that is experienced as alienation and ultimately as rage. Either extreme (violence or depression) originates from the same core. They are the opposite ends of a spectrum. Either form is a symptom of feeling cut-off from love and life. We feel disconnected and unresolved. No one gains when we throw our unresolved emotions onto others (as guilty as they might be) or turn them against us (hurting ourselves). In its extreme this alienation and rage manifests as suicide (directed inside) or homicide (directed outside).

Anger and sadness are the flip side of a possible reaction to the same experience. When we are afraid of being furious we become sad instead. And at times, when we carry an ocean of sadness inside, we act out by being mad and hurtful. The apparent emotion as such hides the deeper, underlying core feeling. The underlying suffering remains avoided.

Ask yourself what you are mad about when your sadness doesn't want to resolve…and ask yourself what you are sad about if you can't get over being angry. If you can't get over blaming someone else, what are you blaming yourself for? If you can't get over blaming yourself, whom are you not holding accountable that you should?

Feelings don't come with labels or how-to-instructions:

"Hello, I am anger which means you need to stand up for yourself!" Feelings may present themselves at first as fuzzy, unclear,

vague or intense and overwhelming. Our body tenses. We know that something isn't right or well...but what is it? As we keep overriding these first *whispers* or attempt to dam the initial *tidal wave*, they will accumulate and move us to overreact. Attached to the response that would be appropriate come all the unresolved feelings we haven't dealt with along the way.

Anger is red tomato soup on the stove bubbling over,
It is feeling like you are going to explode,
Anger is red, hot burning sensations coming from your core,
It makes you want to scream, strangle a teddy bear, and rip it into pieces,
Anger does weird things to you,
You don't listen,
And you are not kind to people,
Suddenly everyone is your enemy,
No one really likes being angry.

Poem by Tiana, age 12

Some grown-ups still manage their adult emotional relationships like the toddlers they once were.

Outgrowing our preschool ways in our relationships is truly a heroic effort. We have to challenge insecure people (ourselves!) to face their hang-ups and update their behaviors to more adult versions. To add to the challenge, our society's video and TV culture normalizes violence and emotional acting out. Once insecure people inhabit grown-up bodies, the challenge is exalted. They usually don't take too kindly to being told that their ways of being in the world are rather childish and not healthy at all.

There is always a reason for why we do what we do and why we feel what we feel. You may be forgiven for doubting this. If we carry the bruises of someone's temper tantrums, it is only human to not respond with compassion and understanding.

We may not be able to see the reasons for our actions and feelings but they do exist. The logic of these reasons may be twisted, infantile, selfish or completely irrational. They have us convinced of their legitimacy. Even a murderer has reasons for committing a murder. At the time, it seemed the best solution. Unless we unmask and take responsibility for our twisted forms of logic, permanent change will elude us.

Nothing is gained by attacking those who hurt us.

Our parents or others that hurt us may be old now or gone from our life. The power they used to have over us has gone with them unless *we keep the hurt alive.* Standing up for our rights is different from attacking and blaming. Freedom from the past comes from being truly able to choose how to treat and relate to others in the present. For this choice we need emotional perspective. Emotional perspective is an outcome of resolved feelings.

What may be a step towards healing, performed as role-play in a counselor's office, does often not work equally well in real life. This form of attempting to stand up for us only perpetuates the cycle.

Attack makes us guilty. In a subtle way, we end up doing to them what we feel they have done to us. The initial feeling may be one of righteousness but ultimately it lowers us in our own eyes and it tends to alienate others.

The father knew that his son didn't deserve blame or punishment for spilling the milk. After all, he was only five years old and it was obvious that he hadn't done it intentionally. However, it wasn't quite as easy for him to identify why he felt so irritated and stressed that morning. His first reaction was to get angry at his son for being clumsy and then at himself. As his conscious mind intervened he began to step back from his feelings.

There is no point to speaking *our truth* while we are still caught in our own confusion.

Many of the things that happened to us weren't our fault and not even necessarily the fault of others.

Even though these experiences weren't our fault, we do own the responsibility for the conclusions we drew, for how we reacted and still react. We might have been too young to know better. Most likely we weren't capable yet to protect ourselves or felt overwhelmed by our fears of abandonment or rejection. Nevertheless, we do carry the responsibility to set ourselves free today. It is up to us now to stop the vicious cycle that attack will imprison us in.

- Attack leads to Guilt →
- Guilt makes us feel less →
- Feeling less leads to attempts of correcting the power imbalance →
- We make ourselves more powerful by finding wrong in the other (covert or overt) →
- Which leads to more attack →

On his way to work the father was stuck in traffic. Something inside of him began to relax. His thoughts turned to his son during breakfast and his feelings about it all. Suddenly it seemed crystal clear. Tonight he would speak with his wife and work out a shared breakfast routine. He realized that unconsciously he once again had made himself indispensable and needed by taking on more then his share…just like his father used to. His wife and son deserved better than resentment.

Stuck in traffic, the father began to recall the many times that he had been at the receiving end of his own father's resentment. Still very young he had promised himself to never put his own son into the same unjust situation. A new resolve came over him.

Neglect produces invisible suffering.

Sometimes, we are heavily invested in feeling right, even if that makes us into victims *"Don't ask me to forgive him/her!"* we proclaim. *"What he/she did is unforgivable!"* It may be…as long as we misunderstand the suffering that underlies their acting out. Callousness is born in neglect. Selfishness deprives us of closeness. Cruelty is a sign of extreme alienation and rage. Empathy is learned by experiencing it. Closed-mindedness is a sign of insecurity and fear.

Suffering which everyone experiences at some time during their life such as intense feelings of betrayal, rejection and abandonment is excruciating. Suffering is not always obvious. Physical abuse will leave physical scars. Disinterest, criticism, neglect and control leave invisible scars. Unrecognized and unacknowledged suffering manifest as self-pity, low self-esteem and re-enactment of what our psyche endured. A whirlpool of the same old feelings engulfs us or we become cut-off from feeling.

Be gentle if you can't get beyond self-pity…find the unacknowledged suffering underneath it!

Different feelings prompt us towards different forms of release. Anger asks for action: hit a pillow, scream at the wind, go for a walk, jog around the block, mow your lawn, or clean your house. Just make sure you actually feel your anger independent of acting on it with blame and attack.

Sadness asks for an embrace and comfort: go have a good cry, hide under the covers, take a bubble bath, put on some sad music, or cuddle with your teddy bear. Just make sure that the outlet you choose is safe for you and others.

Feelings are the voice of our inner self.

When we cannot or do not express what is happening on an emotional or psychological level, we lose touch with our inner life. When we ignore or force our bodies to override the signals it sends us, we remove ourselves from us.

Our relationships become distant or meaningless. When our spouse asks, *"What's wrong?" We respond, "Nothing!"* We haven't learned that feeling what we feel and expressing it with respect are okay. Our non-verbal energy speaks loud and clear. Our partner feels alienated. It takes coming to grips with the emotional prisons of ignorance, neglect, isolation, abuse and trauma to truly enter adulthood.

Liken it to receiving anesthesia in one finger but the result being that our whole hand feels numb. When we numb ourselves to the hurtful, sad and angry feelings that live inside, we also numb ourselves to feeling truly good. We forget what we want out of life.

To truly and deeply cry is an art. In crying, we release our pain and recognize our connection with others and ourselves. Going through *the wave* of our emotions allows us to get back in touch with the truth inside ourselves. We are then ready to move on.

Inside every unhappy individual there is an angry or sad child.

Once we can be persuaded or persuade ourselves to abandon our childhood conclusions, we begin to grow into resourceful adults. Social skills take the place of hitting skills, manipulations, control and feigned or learned helplessness. We begin to find our voice. Our emotional and social vocabulary broadens.

Dealing with one's feelings is about accepting, respecting and experiencing what is. It has nothing to do with allowing ourselves to act out our bad or justified feelings. Such displays are a burden on others. We become unjust, righteous and at times cruel. We learn (or don't learn) how to keep emotional ties to those we love strong.

She was four years old and on the playground of her preschool. Her peers excluded her from "the group". She felt ostracized…no one wanted to be her friend…and there was no adult to aid her or give direction. Slow by slow, to stand on the outside became her place. She was too young to realize that what they did to her was based in ignorance.

As an adult this experience is her first memory of feeling isolated from others particularly in a group situation. Without the protection and guidance of an aware adult she was left to her own devices. To this day she experiences groups as unsafe.

As adults we need to be the parents to ourselves we never had.

When we are young we need to feel safe to allow our feelings. Constructively dealing with our feelings is a skill like any other that we either learn or don't learn in early childhood. It becomes our responsibility as adults to make up for what wasn't given.

Looking back she now realizes that experiences like that are commonplace during childhood. She could have asked for help from an adult. She could have fought back...she could have drawn a different conclusion about what happened. Revisiting this experience helped her to acknowledge the feelings the little girl had and make a new decision about the meaning of what happened.

It is now our turn to pay attention to what we feel. It is our turn to be there for ourselves, no matter what. If we don't, we swirl around in blame. We either blame others or ourselves for what happened. We avoid truly being in touch with our core feelings. We miss the good and valuable that lies hidden in any experience. Our psyche doesn't get a chance to grow and mature.

We blame others and ourselves when we avoid our deeper "scary" feelings. Blaming keeps us on the surface.

Fearing Emotional Pain

We have learned to deal with our emotional pain the same way we deal with our physical pain.

What works for physical pain is used to avoid *all pain*. It is easy to reach for a drug to ease our discomfort. *Emotional pain, however, needs to be resolved in a different fashion.*

Otherwise, we become afraid of emotional pain. It takes on the power to disconnect us. We get caught up in a multitude of compensations, each causing its own form of limitations and distortions. When we avoid our emotional pain, we cut ourselves off from the knowledge that we have the capability to master our emotional pain. We remove ourselves from what is true and right for us.

Fear feeds on itself. The more we avoid what we fear, the stronger our fear becomes. Young children have to look under the bed, often repeatedly, to overcome their fear of the *"boogie man"*. When we face what we fear most, we learn to master what was overwhelming. Facing ones pain and crying the tears that go with it, leads to wisdom and maturity.

Suffering that perpetuates itself, repeats itself in endless versions, turns in circles, but never really deals with the deeper pain, is a defense mechanism, no matter how real it seems.

Intense emotional pain is experienced as a form of "emotional death".

Hoping to avoid *emotional death,* we actually end up dying many small deaths instead. When we don't deeply, beyond abandon cry when we feel hurt, our hurt becomes stuck. When we don't let ourselves be angry when someone has crossed us, we remove ourselves from what is rightfully ours. When we avoid the emotional death of intense pain part of us dies by resorting to appeasing, pleasing, avoiding and distancing. We psychologically *flee* from what is happening. We learn to put overwhelming feelings aside, namely inside.

Intense emotional pain makes us afraid of feeling joy or love out of fear that they too will be taken away. We limit our joy or avoid love in an attempt to avoid the possible future pain of loss. This gives us a false sense of control and safety. The result is a life that may feel safe but lacks sparkle and meaning. *To gain we have to risk.* In the process, we will find that we are bigger then our losses no matter how excruciating in the moment.

Modern science has assisted us in developing medications so as to stop physical pain.

As a tool this is very valuable and often essential. Much good has come from our scientific inventions and understanding. As a philosophy and generalized approach to *all forms of pain*, it falls short of teaching us that we are masters over our emotional lives. All experiences carry the potential to expand our repertoire on how to resolve our daily human conflicts wisely. There is inherent pain to living in a physical world where loss of one kind or another is imminent. The future remains unpredictable. It is up to us to *make lemonade if life hands us lemons.*

Crying is a natural psychological function of responding to loss, fear, trauma, overwhelm and physical pain. *We can't deeply breathe and withhold our tears at the same time.* We stop our breath so as to stop our tears and pain.

While we are in the throws of our emotions, all memories of happy days appear to be gone. Happy days or good feelings cannot be forced back...they will return of their own if we allow the natural rhythm of our emotions. *The way to it is through it!* Once we face the core of our pain our body takes a breath. An energetic blockage is released.

Next time you are upset remind yourself to keep breathing. Imagine actually breathing into your pain the way you would breathe into a fire. Just like a fire this will initially intensify what you feel. And, just like a fire it will eventually burn out if not fed.

We develop unique styles of dealing with life's disappointments and hurts.

We build our own unique set of defenses to protect ourselves against pain... the pain that still lives inside of us. This pain becomes triggered and re-experienced with each new loss.

Once again he stood at the crossroads with his present girlfriend. She wanted to get married. He wanted to just continue the way they have been. "Why was there a need to change?," he asked. He didn't want to lose her but the thought of marriage scared him. It triggered feelings of being trapped. It was difficult for him to realize that his fears of being trapped actually were a disguise for his deeper fears of being truly vulnerable. That depth of vulnerability was terrifying.

Sadly, our defenses often bring about what we fear. We drive away those we love by needing them too much. Or, we stay too far away unwilling to invest ourselves. The child who wants his mother or father who isn't there again and again learns that loving hurts too much. It learns to ask for and give little. Or, it learns to overcompensate by giving what it so dearly wishes to receive. S/he becomes a caretaker. S/he learns to protect the ones who are supposed to be the protectors.

Love becomes confused with vulnerability.

The child that felt deeply hurt by its parent, the one person that was supposed to love and protect him or her, learns to associate love with hurt. Emotional intimacy becomes confused with vulnerability and equated with something negative and dangerous. *Why then take the risk of truly getting close to another?* We never learn that underneath our sense of vulnerability lies another layer of our psyche, our deeper essence of invulnerability.

We learn to become parents to our parents or siblings or mates. We learn not to let our survival depend on the help or love of anyone. Independent long before our time, we put aside the helpless, terrified child and with it, our ability to feel and digest our emotions.

Children growing up in the same household did not necessarily experience or receive the same form of parenting. Due to age, sex, illness, birth order, personality style, or other stresses, they are often cared for very differently. Our style of perceiving reality and expressing emotions is uniquely ours. It has grown out of what we were born with, what we were given, and what we decided.

Risk we must if we hope to succeed at life.

In our lives now, we once again have opportunity after opportunity to complete what was left incomplete. To re-parent ourselves means to develop that inner safety net that allows us to unconditionally experience ourselves without judgment. Ultimately, we will reach the maturity that can withstand being rejected, abandoned, or betrayed by those we love.

He realized, that not dealing with his fear of vulnerability would mean the loss of his relationship. Loss was what he wanted to avoid. He couldn't get away from it either way. The choice appeared to be either losing his girl friend or lose what he regarded as safe.

Memories kept flooding back...past relationships. He was only 18 when he was deeply hurt by his first girl friend leaving him. He had promised himself to never allow anyone to hurt him like that again.

His mother had left his father when he was 18 months old. He couldn't remember...his father must have been devastated at the time, he reasoned.

He was going to make a new beginning with his present girl friend. Thinking about this fears, they suddenly seemed childish. Now his feelings just had to catch up with his mental understanding.

Our instinct moves us to fight or flee what we experience as threatening.

Our *animal-brain* dictates that we respond with either a *fight or flight* reaction. Our flight response makes us close our eyes to what is damaging, harmful and unhealthy around us. We try to *overlook* so as to *not rock the boat*. As a habitual way of relating to what confronts us, we end up deadening our inner knowing. Practiced often enough, we then *become helpless to change or fight what should be changed.* Moral courage in everyday life remains a foreign territory.

When we flee what should be fought, the abnormal becomes normalized. When we flee what should be faced, we end up repeating the past. We then aren't able to distinguish any longer what is good or is bad for us. We become unsure what our rights are. Instead of following our gut feelings, we rationalize, go along and surrender to the status quo. We leave those close to us and ourselves open to ignorant, inappropriate, disrespectful and often abusive treatment.

We were told that what we wanted, knew and sensed was wrong. Our parents and teachers were supposed to be our mediators and advocates to the world we faced when we were young. They were supposed to put things into perspective for us. Often, they either weren't there or were the ones who confused and hurt us. As a result we are still like young children in adult bodies when it comes to asserting our rights in our lives now.

We have forgotten to trust our inner knowing.

In *Women Who Run with The Wolves,* Clarissa Pinkola Estes describes how our inner voice that could guide us has become inaccessible to us. We are afraid to risk. Fitting in seems more important than what we feel is true for us. For the sake of peace we surrender ourselves. We confuse peace with ceasefire and defeat.

True peace cannot be achieved on sacrifice. Without a clear sense of our personal power we tend to be overpowering when we should tread lightly. We are meek when we should draw clear lines in the sand. We are too socialized to slam our fist on the table and demand. At the slightest sign of opposition and criticism we feel threatened and draw back.

Different societies and different families have different ideas about how much to encourage and support when their children seek for independence and self-assertion. What is acceptable still often remains split along gender lines. Maybe the people who had power over us didn't allow us to assert ourselves. Or, we were put into situations beyond our ability and level of maturity. Expectations were too high or the awareness what would be age and developmentally appropriate was lacking. (Pinkola Estes, 1992)

Our need for independence and exploration was wronged.

Insecure parents will experience the innocent searching for self as a threat. Many parents and authority figures lack the ability to wisely deal with the power imbalance that exists between adult and child. They are unaware that it is their response that decides if a crisis becomes escalated and will hurt the as yet budding self of the child. They lack the awareness and ability to *appropriately minimize*, putting the experience into an age and developmentally appropriate frame. Only then can it turn into a positive character-building experience.

Writes teacher, psychotherapist and author Haim Ginott, *"...I've come to the frightening conclusion that I am the decisive element in the classroom. My personal approach creates the climate. My daily mood makes the weather. As a teacher, I possess tremendous power to make a child's life miserable or joyous. I can be the tool of torture or an instrument of inspiration. I can humiliate or humor, hurt, or heal. In all situations, it is my response that decides whether a crisis will be escalated or de-escalated and a child humanized or de-humanized."*

We become who we think we should be.

Young children when judged, criticized, or belittled, will often draw incorrect conclusions about themselves, others and life. These conclusions build the foundation of what they are able to do, what is right or wrong, what is safe and who they are. These conclusions are not necessarily what the adults around them intended. Interpretations and conclusions accepted as truths take on a directive power in their developing psyche.

As adults, these former children (us!) will find it difficult to act on their own behalf. We have forgotten who we were meant to be. And, when we do experiment, we feel guilty and bad.

The forbidden becomes an adventure. We feel we have to sneak around to rebel against the status quo. Afraid to step out openly and take risks, we keep hanging on to the old. Maybe we don't like what we have but it feels safe and known. We may *ref up* but then fall back and don't dare.

Once again these now adults (us) tend to surround themselves with people who cannot or will not give the support they need to make a change and step out. Whenever we do step out, we have to face the unknown. This terrifies us. We feel all alone. Past associations flood our mind and begin to dictate what to feel, or do, or dare.

Our doubt becomes paralyzing.

Apathy, confusion, doubt, overwhelming fear and a lack of self-worth annul any whispers that urge us to make a change. We feel as if we are wading upstream through hip-deep water. Everything inside screams: *"Move!"* We just can't find the energy and strength. Our hands and legs won't function. Our fear of failure is overwhelming.

We don't realize that we have a right to our own feelings and our own perspective on things. It is not about being right or wrong. It is about what is right for us, no matter what others think, no matter what it looks like. Failing can't hold us back as long as we are willing to pick ourselves up and try again. It is much harder to get over the missed opportunities and *could-have-beens* than having failed.

Don't look back! Remember the Bible story of Sodom and Gomorrah, ...looking back will turn you into a pillar of salt. Salt stands for crystallization, deadness, frozen in time.

Look to where you want to go or be! Put all your faith into what you want to have, not what you are afraid to lose. Use fear as a caution sign, asking you to proceed slowly, getting prepared the best you can, taking small steps. Too often we use fear as a stop sign.

Whenever you become afraid when you are about to step out and break the mold of the known and habitual, tell yourself: "I can do this!" "Others have done it before me...I can do this!"

We are worthy of all the good in life!

We have a right to a supportive environment, an environment that will support our dreams. Anyone who cannot at least at times nurture our emotional, mental and physical life is not good for us. They are wasting our time and energy. *They support us in staying trapped in a life of less.*

As we must treat others with respect, caring, and value, we deserve to be treated by others in the same way.

In the 1960s, scientists conducted animal experiments to learn about the flight instinct. A dog was put into a large cage, which was partially wired so that the dog would receive a shock each time it stepped into the right side of the cage.

The animal learned quickly and the experiment was reversed; now the left side would receive the electricity. Next the entire floor received random shocks. There was no way for the animal to escape or anticipate what was going to happen. The dog was confused at first, then panicked and finally gave up any attempt to escape the electrical shocks. Next, the door to the cage was opened, but the dog did not flee.

When a creature is exposed to violence or treatment it cannot escape or stop over a long period of time, it will tend to adapt to and *normalize* the situation. When it could gain freedom, the creature will stay. It's instinct for self-preservation has been dulled. This is learned helplessness.

In subtle ways many people carry a version of this learned helplessness. Ask yourself:

- What adjustments have I made because I thought I had to? What is holding me back from challenging them? What would I do if I knew that I will be safe no matter what happens?
- Have I forgotten to experiment? Sometimes, it is better to do anything else than what we habitually do.

Our first connections are the fertile soil or barren lands within which all of our later connections grow.

If these first connections are unreliable, broken, or betrayed, we transfer those experiences to what we deep inside expect from our mates, children, friends and business partners.

We stay in bad relationships too long and we put our children into places beyond their age and developmental readiness. Instead of feeling angry and outraged, we lack warranted feelings and become depressed. As we lose our natural inner knowing inner emptiness follows. This leads to the meaninglessness that is underlying so many of our modern societal problems today.

When being raised to be *too good* has distorted our inner ability to protect, flee or fight what should be fought, we lose our capability to save ourselves.

We now lead secret lives, sneaking bits and pieces of our dreams into our everyday reality instead of living the lives we ought to. The very people who ought to be there for us during times of challenges, which ought to love us, instead appear to hinder us. Everyone needs someone to stand by them!

When Victimization Leads to Victimhood

Victims are people who have been subjected to suffering by others or the hand of life.

Being victimized threatens and assaults the very core of our deepest sense of power and safety. We feel utterly helpless, vulnerable and shaken. We keep reliving the memory of the assault we faced in new situations over and over again. The life we have known before is gone. We are left with pieces of what once was beautiful. It is normal to feel outrage, even hatred. It may seem impossible to envision a new life free of the hopelessness and helplessness we experience today.

The acute phase of emotional processing takes about three to six month if we work with it correctly. Once the acute phase has passed, we move into long-term recovery.

The emotional pain is relived and relived in a spiral fashion until it is fully digested and assimilated. Similar incidents will trigger our old as yet not completely resolved feelings. Delayed emotional processing may occur years later. Each time we are in a similar situation now we have to take action on our own behalf and learn that we are not victims any longer. Each time our feelings resurface, we have to resolve them again, patiently.

Having to face the terror and pain again and again may seem unfair. *"Why me? Our inner rage wants to hurt them back!!* The choice simply is: either revolve in circles of terror and hurt (allowing your pain to become chronic) or take steps towards healing. If we choose the later, we eventually do walk away from it with a new self-concept. Digested and assimilated, these experiences teach us. Our vision of life and what it means to be human becomes widened and we gain a new perspective on what happened to us.

Post-traumatic Stress Disorder[18] is a form of delayed emotional processing.

Post-traumatic Stress Disorder (PSTD) is caused by events of actual or anticipated death, serious physical injury, or a threat to one's psychological integrity, to a degree that our usual psychological defenses are incapable of coping with the impact. It can be divided into an acute phase, a chronic reaction or a delayed reaction. The following experiences are known to cause the condition:

- Childhood physical or emotional abuse, including neglect; also, witnessing such abuse inflicted on another person;
- Experiencing an event perceived as or one that actually is life-threatening, such as a serious accident or medical condition (e.g. cancer, loss of limbs), or a natural disaster;
- Surviving or witnessing physical assaults, including cruelty and torture, experiences of sexual abuse or assault, warfare or combat.

There are common ways of incomplete processing of what was too overwhelming.

1. *Intrusion:* being plagued by recurrent nightmares or flashbacks, during which one graphically re-experiences the trauma; the repetition of destructive patterns in relationships; some behavior patterns and personality tendencies.
2. *Hyperarousal:* being prepared for fight or flight; e.g. the typical hyperactive startle reaction characterized by jumpiness in connection with high sounds or fast motions. At times, its polar opposite: unusual stoic and rigid behavior.
3. *Avoidance:* avoiding contact with everything and everyone, even one's own thoughts, which may arouse memories of the trauma. The sufferers isolate themselves, becoming detached in their feelings with a restricted range of emotional responses *"numbing"*.
4. *Dissociation:* feelings of depersonalization and de-realization; the person is *"in another world"* and in extreme forms this can

[18] Wikipedia, Post-traumatic Stress Disorder

involve multiple personalities and acting without any memory*"losing time"*.

Insisting to be seen as a victim, as unjustly treated by others or life, has a shrinking effect on our psyche.

Healing takes time and gentleness. Life and other people can be unjust and cruel. *It wasn't fair that this happened to us...but it did.* Once we are past the acute phase of the trauma we endured, it is up to us to decide what the impact of the experience will mean to us. *Victimization is an experience. Victimhood is a state of mind.*

The injustices we received may have been excruciating. It is terrible to have to deal with the loss of a loved one, or to endure torture and cruelty. The pain inflicted is unfathomable to people who haven't *been there.* However, if we use what we endured against others it will give us a false sense of control, power and safety, *the very things that were taken away.* It may be emotionally gratifying initially but it doesn't allow us to get on with our life.

Using the injustices we experienced, as an *entitlement* is a defense mechanism. It is a manifestation of *incomplete processing.* In doing so, we avoid having to truly experience the *pain, helplessness and utter sense of vulnerability* these experiences brought. We neglect to realize the one power that cannot be taken, *our freedom to choose on how to react to what happened.*

Incomplete processing leads to living in a state of separation from our denied thoughts, experiences and wishes. We develop a tendency to refuse to consider what *we* are doing to ourselves by either partially avoiding or perpetuating our outrage and pain. We don't have to look at how we continue to make ourselves into victims by continuing to insist that we are. *You owe me* is so much easier than to face and resolve the pain we carry inside and *what we don't have because of the loss we endured and our unresolved pain.* It is easier to blame those who hurt us. Our pain may seem too colossal. The experience seems to deprive us of what we used to have.

Hardship and the utter injustice of loss are part of being alive. Justice is a human invention. To grieve our loss and deal with the deprivation the experience brought to the best of our ability without blaming in retaliation may seem superhuman. It may seem impossible in the moment, yet we are capable of it. We won't know this to be true and know the freedom it brings until we have resolved our confusion and pain.

Victimhood is a state of mind long after the actual victimization has ended.

This state of mind is capricious to our inner state of peace, joy and well-being. It lives off an attitude of neglecting and often refusing to take responsibility for what we have or haven't done. This state of mind shouts, *"You owe me!" "It is because of you that I don't have what I want!"* Victimhood as a state of mind, demands, takes and does not give. It as such is out of alignment with the most basic law of life...extension, the ever-becoming life principle.

To insist on seeing others as victimizers for the rest of our or their lives actually turns us into persecutors and victimizers ourselves. We keep giving them a power over us that they in reality don't have (anymore). We become as unmerciful as they once were. We now do to them *symbolically* what was done to us. This keeps us trapped turning in circles of pain. It keeps us trapped in being right and all we can see about them are their bad actions. Our vengeance cannot make things right again. Our wrath cannot undo the harm caused. We, in essence, lower ourselves. We don't have to pick up the pieces and fashion a new life, *scars and all*. Our psyche doesn't get to digest, grow and mature.

One action or one period of someone's life is always only a partial picture of who they are.

Are humans capable of unspeakable atrocities? Of course! Is life unfair? Absolutely! And we may find ourselves in the path of others' insanity and cruelty with no fault of our own. However, one action or one period of someone's life is always only a partial picture of who they are. Even a murderer is capable of showing kindness and affection.

Others are indeed capable of hurting us physically and they may be ill intentioned towards us emotionally. When we feel victimized by others as adults in our daily lives, we often shirk the responsibility to choose how to react to their behavior. We neglect to set boundaries in a timely fashion or to get out of the way of their insanity. We neglect to take a moment to understand their underlying limitations, hurts and fallibility as humans. This renders us less capable to draw the consequences we should. We personalize their behavior towards us. We humanize or de-humanize their actions and underlying intentions and motivations. We don't realize that in doing so, we crucify not only them but ourselves as well.

Taking responsibility for what is happening to us does not come naturally.

A two-year-old bumped into the corner of a table. She turned and scolded the table for hurting her! To her mind, the table had intention. She wasn't aware of a difference between animate and inanimate.

It is easy for adults to see that it wasn't the table's fault. It is easy to recognize that she is still operating from a magical form of thinking where she assumes that even inanimate objects have intention. However, adults too, assume intentions where there are none and then feel victimized by them. We too persist in a magical form of thinking assigning the laws that apply to the physical to our emotional lives. Victimhood, as a way of perceiving life, is partly magical thinking and partly a learned response.

It is distinctly different from having become a victim, someone who is subjected to suffering by another or life.

Quickly resorting to feeling like a victim when things don't turn out the way we think they should ignore that life and other people have their own rhythm. We can go with the flow, *help direct and shape it*, and find the silver lining of the passing thunderstorms. Or, we can experience the unexpected and unwanted turns in the road as an unjust assault.

This leads to the belief that we can be emotionally deprived, hurt and diminished by others. We miss the opportunity to grow and learn and to let go (of our plans) and trust that there is good hidden in any experience. We miss the opportunity to explore why these same old hurtful situations keep happening to us.

Trust could solve many of our problems.

If someone steals your car, you are upset. Someone has taken something that you perceive as yours against your will. Now, if you had an attitude of..."I will be provided with what I need," you would have a different emotional experience of the situation.

This is not to say that the above is the correct way of responding. It is simply one of many options available to us. It is our attitude towards what happened that will determine our emotional experience of it. It is our belief that no matter what harm someone causes us, that they cannot truly harm us (in the physical, possibly, but not deep down) that keeps us safe and sane.

The funny thing is, if we can make the step into trust at such a time, good things begin to happen. There are times in life to use our will, to take charge and then there are times to let go and trust that all will be well. Learning when to do one or the other marks our human struggles. Other people are capable of abusing us, confining us against our will, even killing us. *They are not capable of making us think, feel and interpret.*

We can let go insisting what already has happened shouldn't have.

Yes, it would be a tall order to maintain peace of mind in extreme situations. Our sense of loss and hurt may be just too overwhelming. To lose a loved one or a child, to endure torture, assault and cruelty, to face a life-threatening situation, always will be excruciating. If we carry the scars and bruises of these experiences coming to terms with our hurt may seem like a superhuman act. However, if we be-devil the victimizer, we attest to our own violence that is directed at them. Now we have lowered ourselves to the same level. As a temporary reaction this is understandable maybe even healthy. As a permanent attitude it deprives us.

The victimhood we succumb to shows itself as a persistent underlying attitude towards others and circumstance. We may have been taught to be compliant and helpless. We may have been taught to surrender ourselves to authority figures *who knew better.* In truth, our will first gets overpowered and broken by those close to us. More and more we begin to operate from fear, mistrust, a feeling that there is not enough for everyone or that we are not safe. Our interests need protection. We learn that only one can win and therefore all others have to lose. We learn to habitually relate from an assumption of lack.

All of us have the option to use our ability to think and problem solve and do what can be done. *God (the universe) helps those who help themselves.* We can let go insisting what already has happened shouldn't have. Otherwise, we end up exhausting ourselves, exasperating others, and *wailing* at the hand of fate. We end up feeling more and more helpless and resentful in the process.

It is excruciating to bear the loss of what we love. There is no doubt about that. Our belief in the reality of loss is a very deeply ingrained psychological phenomenon. Once we have done everything we can do, acceptance comes naturally.

We are not victims to the world as we are not victims to our own inner life, our emotions.

"I just can't help myself," he exclaimed. "She just makes me so mad!" "Afterwards, I feel bad that I lashed out at her."

"I guess, I feel helpless and incapable when she accuses me," came the sudden realization. "I feel, as if she is saying that I don't have any worth."

Emotions become overwhelming because we haven't learned to deal with them appropriately. We become vulnerable to feeling hurt by others or hurting others because we are confused where our responsibility for our feelings lays. Most likely we never were taught that we needed to direct and manage this part of self. As we learn the tools we gain in confidence.

Living in a physical world governed by physical laws, the chance of feeling overpowered and helpless in the face of physical events beyond our control is high. Other people's limitations and often actions will limit what we can do. We don't have power over others. We cannot *make* others be reasonable. However, most of our pain and lack is self-created by our own hang-ups, interpretations, attitudes and fears. We too quickly give the responsibility for it to others, illness, or life.

We can become willing to exchange our fear for trust.

When we realize that our *hell* is largely self-created by our undisciplined, unknown, unsophisticated and habitual thoughts, feelings and behaviors, we gain the power to change. Others don't truly have influence or power over our perception of things. We are not victims to our own thoughts, feelings and behaviors. Now safety lies foremost on the inside. We don't have to protect ourselves any longer from pain, for we have learned to work with our emotions. Life takes on a new meaning and this earth becomes a much happier place!

Inner peace is an outcome of the intention to be peaceful. Would we rather be right than happy? Often our judgments are based in ignorance. Understanding, as the word implies means...*"standing under";* seeing things from a different perspective; recognizing the underlying connections and laws; seeing things through others' eyes. This understanding will naturally lead us to be able to let go of our righteous position. It allows us to accept what is. We are then able to *let it be.* It is a letting go of attempting to change what is; it rests on trusting that there will be an answer one day. Understanding is one of the cornerstones of forgiveness. It will lead to empathy and open-mindedness. Understanding dawns on our mind, as we are willing to be wrong and *not know.*

Ultimately inner peace is found when we learn to surrender. To surrender means to *give over.* We give over our pre-conceptions, the idea that we know what would guarantee our and others' happiness. Eventually perfection is glimpsed underlying all things. We step forward with trust keeping step to heaven's song.

There is no justification for what is unjustifiable just as the present cannot give what the past took or denied.

We cannot regain what was taken from us by others or by life. We can, however, pick up our pieces and *fashion a new life,* a life equally if not more valuable and beautiful.

In Christianity it is Jesus who was betrayed by those closest to him, abandoned by those he trusted, beaten, torn, insulted, wrongly accused and finally killed. His teaching is based in not seeing himself as a victim but in pointing towards the new life, the resurrection.

Our inner state of being remains eternally free and unharmed if we do not allow our mind to tell us otherwise. Freeing ourselves from past pain and injustices is an inner quest. We all endure suffering, some of us more than others. We are capable of freeing ourselves from the emotional prisons of that suffering. How we think of and treat others in our mind and actions is what we teach ourselves. It forms the base of the reality *we stand on.*

How to Resolve the Tangle of Our Old Feelings

As long as we don't deal with our old hurt we remain vulnerable to being hurt again.

Intense emotions close our mind to over-focus on someone else's part in a conflict. All we can think about is what they have done or should be doing. All we can see is how they have wronged us. Intense emotions hinder our ability to think objectively. This leads to a polarized viewpoint. We only perceive extreme options on how to deal with what we are facing. An emergency signal flashes in our brain prompting us to either fight or flee (avoid, placate, etc.) the situation.

As long as we don't deal with our emotional experiences, we stay prisoners to the pain or terror they caused. Unassimilated, they are not able to provide us with the life skills, maturity and wisdom they could bring. Instead, they throw us off course and therefore limit our ability to see what is really happening. We become unable to see what needs to be done in the present. Unresolved, they take on the power to dictate our behavior. *This makes the future predictable… where it should be unknowable!*

We feel awkward, intimidated, self-conscious, easily hurt and rejected. The past is replayed in the present without us necessarily realizing that it is. Undigested emotional experiences return us to being a child again facing the same overwhelming, impossible situations we once faced.

Reestablishing a sense of safety, connection, the ability to take action on our own behalf and mourning the losses the trauma caused are essential to all emotional healing.

Assimilating our experiences often involves crying.

"Crybaby, crybaby," ...a chorus of preschoolers chimed. Tears streaming down his face, his mouth tightening into a determined line…he didn't want to cry but he couldn't help it! Crying made him feel angry and somehow wrong and weak!

Tears are our psyches' natural way of assimilating and dealing with overwhelm, frustration, hurt and fear. If we judge our tears the act of crying can be distorted (used for manipulation and escape) like any other natural psychic function. If we fear crying, if tears make us uncomfortable or helpless, we have removed ourselves from one of the most natural ways of emotional healing.

Boys and men, in particular, are taught to regard crying as *not manly*. They are taught that crying is weak. As a result, they learn to hold back and judge their tears. No one ever told them about the cost of doing this. There was no warning sign along the way to beware of becoming lifeless and stoic in their expressions. Or, that their inability to be emotionally present is a telltale sign of an unexplored and unresolved emotional life.

Compare unresolved emotions to undigested food for a moment. If you eat a steak your stomach's function is to digest it. Without being digested it loses its nutritional value since your body won't be able to extract the nutrients it could provide (not to mention the resulting stomachache!). Our body needs to digest and assimilate food to stay healthy. The same holds true for our psyche and not assimilated emotional experiences.

Tears actually contain and release toxins from the body.

The discovery of toxins belongs to modern science, yet the ancients seem to have known about the healing power of tears long ago. In mythology tears of children are often described as a magic potion that will bring about healing. People who are crying are said to be surrounded by an invisible magic circle that won't let harm enter.

In infancy crying is our very first way of communicating that our needs are not being met. We move from tears of protest to sobs of despair and screams of terror.

If we hold in pain and tears we become filled with unexpressed energy. We may be filled with resentment, afraid of our own anger, or sense an ocean of tears inside. We now have great difficulty to take positive action on our own behalf. We have lost our ability to fight and change what we know is wrong.

Acknowledging what we feel is different from collapsing into overwhelming feelings. Sometimes that is what may happen, of course! There is a difference between dealing with our feelings and simply allowing them to overwhelm us habitually.

Being overemotional is like a whirlpool. We swirl around and around, remembering all the details and injustices done to us. We remember all the times we have hurt like this before. It is exhausting and goes nowhere.

Our feelings are precious.

To wear our emotions on our sleeve in front of people who lack the sensitivity and maturity to receive them is unwise.

Jesus taught us to not throw pearls before swine. Our feelings are the pearls of our innermost self. Not everyone has the eye to recognize their value.

It is part of growing in maturity to know when to let ourselves be vulnerable and when to wisely delay. To experience emotions in a situation where we need to keep our *wits* about us is unsafe. Those are times to set emotions aside. Experiencing emotions makes us vulnerable. We may temporarily lose our *ground.* Sometimes the people around us cannot be that ground for us due to their own limitations.

We need to learn to acknowledge and express our feelings at appropriate times, in appropriate ways and in appropriate places. There is always time and room to acknowledge and accept how we feel in the privacy of our own thoughts. We need to experience what churns inside of us at some time, though not necessarily to express it to others or allow it to be the motivation behind our actions!

- My feelings are my feelings, right or wrong;
- I choose with whom I share how I feel;
- I can choose when to set my feelings aside;
- I can acknowledge how I feel without blame.

We break patterns when we act in new ways with old issues.

We tend to take the easy way out and simply stay with the obvious emotional surface experience, for example, feeling criticized and not valued. It takes effort to truly look at what this whole area of our life feels like. We have to connect past with present. A new direction for the future rests on dealing with what confronts us today with an understanding of what happened yesterday.

He kept arguing with her boss, "I am standing up for myself," he thought. In bed at night he realized why he felt as upset with his boss as he did. He was reliving the same feelings he used to have with his father. "I am arguing with him the same way I used to argue with my father," he thought, "and it feels just as futile."

We relate to authorities in the present as if we still are the guilty, powerless child or rebellious teenager we once used to be. Our strong emotions are seldom warranted as an appropriate response to what happened today. They are reminders of the past, which is what gives them their overwhelming intensity. The people in the present may have triggered these feelings but are not solely responsible for the *deluge that follows*.

We often do not realize that we distort the present with our old emotional business. Unresolved thoughts and emotions, our *forgotten* pain, manifests years later as discontent or repetitive cycles of loss, betrayal and abandonment.

Initially, learning to get in touch with feelings means to be patient.

Feelings are just feelings. They are not all of *who we are.* Dealt with rightly, they point to more constructive ways of relating to others. We need to step away from our old ways of attempting to rid ourselves of our bad feelings:

- lecturing to ourselves, *"I shouldn't feel this way for this, or that reason";*
- blaming others or ourselves;
- going over and over what happened; trying to figure it out;
- pretending that nothing is wrong and that there is no problem;
- distracting ourselves with work, alcohol, food, exercise, illness, an attempt to change others, or shopping sprees;
- telling ourselves we feel fine, etc.

We can't allow our true emotions to emerge unless we feel safe. We have to now learn to be in charge of creating a safe place for ourselves. Expecting others to make it safe for us won't work any longer. *Safe* initially will most likely be a physical private place. Eventually *safe* will become an inner experience.

"Why does this upset me so much?"

The answer involves looking deeper than the obvious...*to pause...to get away from what we have thought before!*

Usually this means getting away from a story of *right and wrong*. Our past conclusions make us feel right. *"I know I am right about this but just for the sake of an exercise, I will allow for the possibility of being wrong."*

To get to a new place, we have to let go of our usual ways of trying to deal with the situation. We need to step away from analyzing, justifying, judging, rationalizing, and blaming and pay attention to our body sensations.

Learning to take a time-out from our habitual way takes discipline. *If we always think what we have always thought and always do what we have always done, we cannot reasonably expect to get a different result!*

Pause for a moment. Step back from the turmoil of your emotions. Take a breath. Affirm your willingness to see things as they are. Be willing to be wrong. Pay attention to how your body feels.

The following techniques have been adapted from the work of Eugene Gendlin, described in his book, *Focusing*:

- Locate the center of what you feel in your body. (Most people locate the vortex of a feeling in their chest, throat or stomach.)
- To locate the center ask: "If there was a place where this feeling lives, it would be?"
- Once you have identified this place observe what sensations this feeling generates...tension, hardness, emptiness, butterflies, etc.

Emotional displays or squelching our emotions resolves nothing.

We are afraid that once we allow negative emotions, they will take over. We are afraid to become a *basket case*, hopelessly out of control. This fear stems from giving into our emotions without focus.

We end up feeling like a raft on a turbulent river without someone to paddle. Emotions in essence are energy. This energy can be equated to an *ocean wave.* It will rise, crest and then break.

When you are at the beach and a large wave approaches what should you do? If you turn and attempt to run it will most likely knock you down or pick you up and roll you like tumbleweed. However, if you face the wave and dive into it, it loses its power over you.

Intense emotions have a similar dynamic. The moment we embrace our intense feelings with focus, they first intensify even more but then subside. We are left with a new insight or feeling of strength. Emotional healing is a natural outcome of finding a new perspective on what happened or is happening to us. We then assimilate and eventually eliminate what was upsetting or traumatic.

For this to happen, we have to learn to *"hold ourselves emotionally". We literally have to learn to put our arms around ourselves.*

Our emotions will take us like a strong current to wherever they decide. We have to trust that we will survive the journey. A focused mind becomes the rudder giving direction to our experiencing. If, on the other hand, we allow our mind to wander, we avoid truly feeling.

"This is how I have felt so often before..."

"If this feeling held in my body (above sensation) could speak or shout out something, it would say/shout...?!" (If you can't get a word or short phrase, begin intensifying the physical sensation you have–notice the associations that come to mind).

If you do get a word or phrase, start repeating this word, statement, etc., using it to intensify what you feel.

The word or words that come attached to the feelings we hold in our body will be *short and simple* if they truly fit our body experience. Our inner voice doesn't speak in long essays of blame. They will most likely intensify what we feel already. There may be a flash of clarity. They are similar to a *"mantra"* that is used in meditation. Repeating to ourselves this mantra (word or phrase or sound) will deepen the emotion we are experiencing until it finally releases.

Tell yourself: "Stay with it; let it happen; let yourself feel; don't be afraid; I can handle it now!"

Keep repeating your word or phrase over and over, allowing your emotion to intensify, until it subsides on its own. Gently bring your wandering mind back if necessary and stay with it until it decides to leave.

When you first felt this way, you may have been young with limited emotional problem-solving capabilities. You may have felt completely overwhelmed and either couldn't do anything or didn't know what to do. *Now you do!* Your emotional system is now strong enough to take charge of these emotions today. Your adult mind is capable of seeing things in a broader perspective.

There is nothing more important to do right this moment but to hold yourself emotionally. In the privacy of your own mind accept what you feel! Once you have fully explored and felt the feelings that arise, you will feel calmer. You will gain a new outlook on things.

Resolution is an inner shift that is felt in the body.

Something releases, we inadvertently take a breath, things seem clearer. It is as if we hit an inner *trampoline* that bounces us back to the surface more whole. As long as we don't experience this shift, our inner emotional journey isn't over yet. There is more to be explored...it is never wise to act on how we feel while we are still confused and upset.

Psycho-emotional processing is a *spiral-like experience.* We may revisit the same old experiences and feelings many times before finding a final release. Resolving present and past hurts and trauma therefore *isn't* a linear process that starts at "A" and ends at "B".

Key elements in dealing with all traumatic experiences are overcoming a feeling of helplessness often experienced as rage, reestablishing a sense of safety and connection and mourning the loss the trauma caused. The ability to change and heal is inherent in every human being.

Our feelings reflect our soft underbelly. As we mature, we find a more compassionate way of viewing what happened and is happening. Once we stop avoiding our own uncomfortable feelings, we learn to trust that we can handle their intensity. We step beyond being victims to our inner world. *The greatest obstacle to change and a different future is our unfinished past.*

We used to receive the reflection of our own attitude from others.

We didn't understand. In our everyday life, we felt puzzled, hurt, or angry with others. We end up in relationships where our mate displays the opposite to what we hold dear.

Or, we may experience ourselves as flipping from one extreme to its opposite. We can and must integrate the energies underlying these experiences. A variation of the above exercise can show us how to deal with old problems in new ways.

- Say to yourself: *"If there was a place in my body that holds how I feel right now* (or how I see my mate--for example: unsure/inferior–insert your own words)...*the place for it in my body would be…?!*
- *And, if I had a place for the opposite feeling…that feeling would be...*(for example: cocky/superior) *and the place in my body for that would be…?!*
- Once you have identified both feelings, their respective location in your body and their quality, practice shifting back and forth between them using your *"trigger"* (the word or words that will call up the feeling) until you have a clear sense of both.
- After you have a clear sense of both feelings decide to introduce these two feelings to each other. Either slowly move them closer and closer until they *meet* or move the one to the other.

- As they meet and flow into each other observe the changes in your body. The breath that your body will naturally take. (Gendlin, 1978)

As we master our emotions we lose our fear of pain.

When we are disconnected from our inner emotional world emotions seem scary, overwhelming and unmanageable. We are afraid that if we start we won't be able to stop, afraid of being out of control and becoming hurtful, afraid because we don't know what is there. *If fear truly had the power to stop the human race we never would have emerged from the caves of our forefathers!*

Once we learn to embrace and *work* with what we feel we lose our helplessness. The sun will shine again. Life holds promise! We cannot truly know ourselves until we have overcome our fear of pain. Once we have experienced the release of painful emotions and experienced the change this release brings, we instantly gain a new sense of power. We are now able to take practical steps and new possibilities open up. Our outlook on life has subtly changed. It is like taking a breath of fresh air.

A festering wound has been opened and cleaned. It hurts, but now it can heal. Like a rain cloud dissipating, the sun shines again. And we realize, that no matter how intimidating the thundercloud of the moment, the sun is only hidden momentarily.

It is time to live from a deeper place.

It is time to move beyond reliving the same old hurts. It is time to let some fresh air into an old wound. *"Deal with it and put the past behind you"* and "*get on with life"* applied prematurely quickly become part of the problem.

It is up to us now to set up an environment that offers understanding, empathy and support. Such an environment has to be set up in *our own attitude* towards us first.

Change begins by being in touch with how we feel. As we have a right to be treated with respect, caring and value, we need to learn to treat our feelings in the same fashion. Once we begin to truly deal with what we feel, we grow more and more capable to simply set our feelings aside until a better time.

We can take a break. We can *take a time out.* We are capable of experiencing joy no matter what troubles us today. And it is a good habit to get into feeling this joy daily, no matter what we are dealing with in our daily lives.

It's a bit like the ocean. At the bottom there is stillness no matter what storms are raging at the surface. Practice setting your troubles aside for at least a few minutes every day and feel the sheer joy of being: "I am that I am."

Betrayal and Abandonment–the Deepest Wounds

All close relationships start out as exclusive.

It is in our close relationships that we experience the full ecstasy of intimacy, belonging, love and the agony of disappointments, letdowns, rejections and betrayals. *Intimate relationships are the hope for happiness free of conflict and differences.* They are filled with unspoken expectations and assumptions. Eventually, when our close ones break character and don't live up to their *potential or our expectations*, we feel upset, angry, disillusioned, abandoned and betrayed. We find it hard to accept...to accept them for the fallible human beings they are...for not being stronger, wiser and kinder, to accept them for letting us down...to accept them for not making us as special as we make them! We confuse human fallibility with a lack of love.

Betrayal and abandonment deal a heavy blow to our sense of self and our trust into life and others. Of all the wounds that our psyche may suffer, it is betrayal and abandonment that most often are poorly understood and remain undigested.

What we do not realize is that letdowns, abandonment and betrayals in their myriad of forms are as intricate a part of relationships as is love. They can coexist. As a matter of fact, they usually do coexist, which is why things get so confusing. Letdowns and betrayals are always a part of close relationships. After all, if we didn't care it wouldn't hurt so *bad*. They always involve the loss of a dream that was dear to us. And, they do make us deeply afraid to trust again. We are simultaneously capable of, which doesn't automatically mean that we know how to access:

Personal conditional love - Personality self
Personal unconditional love - Transpersonal self
Non-personal unconditional love - Spiritual self

The first abandonment and betrayals happen early on in life.

The first form of trust and love we experience is fusion. As infants we exist in a state of unconscious oneness with our mother, father and our environment. *We seem to think the same, feel the same and do/be the same.* This equals paradise. There is no conflict or sense of separation. The abrupt betrayal of fusion is the breaking of an unspoken contract *"If you truly love me you know...(what I want, need, think, etc.)."* We re-experience this when we first connect with others in a close friendship and, in particular, when we fall in love.

My mother left when I was five, she stated dryly. "I don't really remember much...one day she was gone. I didn't see her again until I was ten. My father raised us. I don't really know how I feel about her. I guess I am angry. She at least could have said "Good-bye".

The young woman sitting in the counselor's office had come to seek help because of the recent break-up of her marriage. Her husband left for a business trip and never returned. She received a postcard informing her that he wanted a divorce.

Later as adults, we re-live with our mates the abandonment and betrayals of our childhood.

Parents who failed to love us the way we needed to be loved. They failed to protect us or abandoned us. They weren't there emotionally or physically when we needed them most. They neglected to meet our needs in many small and big ways. They weren't able to translate their love into loving actions so that the child would know their love. Parents governed by their own fears and absorbed with their own agendas that put their own needs ahead of their children's needs.

Abandonment and betrayal are the loss of a simple and innocent faith in others. The early childhood fusion of *you-are-me-I-am-you* is blissful but eventually will and has to give way to the development of our individuality, which means separateness. This is a step that is either taken gradually, gently and naturally or abruptly and drastically. *How it is taken will influence our later experiences of ourselves particularly in relationships.*

Abandonment and betrayals force us to sever the bond of *specialness* we experience in relationships with other people. Now we have to learn to live with them the way they are, fallible and human, or without them.

Abandonment and betrayals are one of the most confusing and hurtful human experiences.

We have to face the betrayals by a friend or a group of peers who betray a confidence, exclude us, or choose another...or the betrayal by those we have been kind to who now turn against us. Nothing, however, hurts like the betrayal by a lover or mate who finds another, who abandons us at the worst of times. *"I should have seen it coming," we cry. "How could I have been so stupid?,"* we blame ourselves.

All we can see is our loss and our confusion and our pain. *We question if love was ever real? What is real? Can we trust our own judgment? Can we ever trust others again?*

We may move to protect ourselves by keeping others at a safe distance, avoiding truly giving of ourselves. We may become suspicious and anticipate danger where there is none. We end up courting and expecting the crash in others and ourselves. *Why risk and try if one can be hurt this deeply?*

When parents and later our mates act like the fallible human beings they are, we feel let down again. We can't understand why they don't know or how they could do this? Our world, the way we believed things to be and the things we assumed about others, collapses. The bringers of justice, stability and most of all safe love have abandoned and betrayed us. We feel helpless and powerless.

In our abandonment and betrayals we have to face the end of a world that we once thought was ours.

"In this wounding the psyche is opened up and new questions begin to be asked about who we are in our depths. These powerful questions need not lead to alienation and withdrawal,...Whether they serve to madden or illumine is up to us."

Jean Houston, *The Search for The Beloved*

When abandonment and betrayal crosses our path before we have developed the inner emotional strength to deal with it, we undergo an identity crisis instead of stepping into a new level of awareness and acceptance of our and others humanity. We wail: *"How could this happen to me? Who am I? Who are you really?"* We feel deceived. Everything is a lie. With this experience separation and duality enter violently. We find it impossible to keep perspective.

The young woman in the counselor's office felt devastated by her husband's actions. She blamed herself for choosing him as a husband, for not seeing what was about to happen, for not being stronger in handling what happened.

"Did he ever really love me?" "How can I ever trust my own judgment again?," she questioned. It took months before she was capable of stepping back and realizing that she was not to blame. She was not to blame for her mother's leaving and not to blame for not having been clairvoyant about her husband's actions. It was his responsibility to communicate that he wasn't happy and take steps within the relationship to change it.

"Hold me above anyone else and I will make you special in return".[19]

When we allow the specialness of childhood to enter into our adult relationships, we turn them into prisons for others and ourselves. We make enemies out of strangers, but worst of all, we set ourselves up to be disappointed, letdown and betrayed.

Specialness must eventually be undone to make room for our soul to grow. The pursuit of specialness in our adult lives will always lead to exclusivity. It will cost us true intimacy and the knowledge that we are altogether irreplaceable.

The young woman still loved her husband. She learned that she could love him yet not want to re-enter a relationship with him. "He will always have a special place in my heart." "I now can see that I need a partner who is clearer about what he wants in life." I know now, that I can get over the hurt."

---

[19] This section on *Specialness* is summarized from the teachings of A Course in Miracles, Foundation for Inner Peace.

Specialness is the need to be the only one.

Specialness has no room to share and it always sets apart, creating a feeling of separation and superiority. Uniqueness rests on experiencing ourselves as equals. There is nothing to proof. Specialness thrives on competition and exclusion. Uniqueness is like a circle; there is room for everyone. Specialness depends on goals that we alone can reach. Anyone else reaching the goal jeopardizes our worth and loveability. Uniqueness has its one inner scale by which things are measured. It allows for the possibility of a joined goal or for reaching common ground.

Specialness makes comparisons and therefore looks for the lack in another. It uses this lack so as to elevate itself and frantically searches for the tiniest speck of fault in others. It cannot rest, for without seeing this lack in another it would be faced with the lack existing in oneself. Specialness sees life as a pyramid where the place at the top cannot be shared. If we are not at the top, then we are at the bottom. Only one can be special to the exclusion of all others.

Uniqueness is the recognition of being one of a kind.

Uniqueness is the mature version of specialness. Everyone is unique. *Once we grasp the concept of uniqueness we grasp that we don't have to be afraid.* There simply is no competition.

Uniqueness teaches that we are irreplaceable for who we are, but not better or less than another. When we grasp that we are unique, all comparison, competition and insecurities fall away. Uniqueness is like a circle...the beginning is the end and the end is the beginning. Our worth and loveability are birthrights we accept and that cannot be jeopardized. We truly grasp that we have a right to be treated with respect, caring and love no matter what our shortcomings are.

Eventually we take the step into seeing others and ourselves as unique. We become capable of recognizing that there are *many starfish in the sea*, all equally beautiful in different ways. Not all versions will suit us long-term.

Let us hope that we can grow and change through the gentle transformation of our attitudes and recognition of our essence without *the help* of the heavy hand of abandonment and betrayal. *Nothing is worse than to experience the agony of not being special without the hope to be unique.*

We abandon and betray ourselves when we belittle our deepest hopes.

When our sense of specialness is dismantled before we had a chance to experience ourselves as unique, we are faced over and over again with an old deep psychic wound. We will feel profoundly shaken, when a present-day promise appears broken. Ultimately, the refusal to deal with the abandonment and betrayals we have experienced leads to self-betrayal. We abandon our innermost wishes, hopes and talents.

The young woman recounted never having been comfortable with the many business trips her husband took. "I never said anything or questioned him. I always felt that doing so would be childish on my part. I wanted more time together...but time was the one thing he never seemed to have."

Self-betrayal is often subtle and may over the years have become an intricate part of our personality. It becomes our way of relating to others. We don't ask for what we want and undermine our ambitions. We minimize our pain. The plans we made are shelved. The dreams and hopes we carry in our hearts stay hidden. We minimize what is truly important to us and as a result become *little, less, stay small and don't dare.* And the irony of all is that in acting like this we end up doing to ourselves exactly what we feel was done to us.

People who are given to self-betrayal court failures in others and themselves.

They are remarkably skilled at giving an endless list of reasons for why things won't work out. They refuse to risk and advise everyone else against it as well. As such they won't allow themselves and others to attempt to become what they could be and have. *They cheat themselves with escapes and excuses.*

We hand ourselves over to a ruthless inner enemy against whom we are defenseless. (Houston, 1987) Self-sabotage is its main accomplice. We don't dare to take the opportunities that life sends our way. We are our own worst critics treating ourselves the way we would never treat a friend.

This inner judge has no mercy. Just when we are about to succeed at something we have worked for hard and long we lose momentum. Our energy leaves us and we are not there for the reward. To allow and deal with the agony and myriad of feelings that abandonment and betrayal brings is one of the great challenges in life.

Undigested experiences manifest as a vicious cycle of repetition.

If we cannot support our dreams we cannot support others in their dreams. Deep inside we know that we are guilty. And the cycle of repetition starts:

"Abandonment and Betrayal by Others" leads to fear, denial of self-love and attempts to control the hurt, which leads to *"Self-Betrayal"*.

"Self-Betrayal" produces shame, self-sabotage and a lack of self-worth, which makes us vulnerable to *"Betray and Abandon Others"*.

"Abandoning and Betraying Others," produces guilt, blame and repetition. It asks for just punishment.

A vicious cycle producing endless versions of pain develops. Having been abandoned and betrayed we may avoid abandoning and betraying others with all the might our conscious mind can muster. But it is not our conscious mind that is necessarily in charge.

Unresolved experiences are given over to our unconscious mind to handle. Given enough stress and often despite our best efforts and good intentions, we end up betraying others exactly the way we felt we were betrayed and abandoned.

Having internalized what originally *"was done to me,"* we now *"do to ourselves"* and eventually in hidden and not so hidden ways *"do to others".* The resulting guilt continues the cycle. One of the psycho-emotional functions of guilt is to atone through punishment. And, what better punishment then having someone do to me, what I feel I have done to someone else.

The cycle stops when:

1. We recognize its repetition.
2. We step away from the hurt, blame and wish for vengeance of the *"abandoned and betrayed"* and the guilt and denial of the *"abandoner and betrayer".*
3. We find the *"abandoned and betrayed"* and *"abandoner and betrayer"* inside of us and emotionally heal the hurt.
4. We learn to say STOP when someone abandons and betrays us, when we are about to abandon and betray ourselves, and/or when we are tempted to abandon and betray others.

When we are young, we don't have the emotional resources to deal with it.

We lock the experience unresolved inside of us. We move to protect ourselves the best we know how. The pain over time becomes hardened as we begin to experience secondary abandonment and betrayals.

Mistrust, suspicion, revenge and withdrawal have a shrinking effect on our psyches. They close our minds. Fear and control become our allies hoping to protect us from further pain. They prove themselves impotent as well. We will reject and leave before we can be left. We expect defeat from the outcome. Pessimism is our inner attitude towards life. *"It can never work,"* we tell ourselves. Holding grievances and being judgmental seem normal. *"Doesn't everyone?"*

Life more often than not seems bitter, futile and dark. We become unable to see the good and only see the bad in our everyday experiences.

The abandonment and betrayals that we experience today may be secondary but they hurt just as much if not more. To transcend our pain we need to allow for our feelings. As overwhelming and engulfing as they may appear to us at the moment, they will one day be resolved, *"if...if we feel them".* We need to find the bigger perspective, the silver lining, within these experiences so they can become a step in maturity.

Today is an opportunity to finish yesterday.

Those who have hurt us in our life now need to be willing to prove that they have changed their ways. A new foundation has to be poured for the relationship. Trust has to be built from scratch. It has to become a conscious choice to be given when deserved. It can be done. No one said it would be easy. It may indeed seem like a task of mythical proportions.

There will be times when it seems impossible to overcome the hurt. It will take time. One day the pain will be gone. We have to pull our energies back from seeking revenge and obsessing about our hurt or the injustice done to us.

If we are willing to find a new perspective through which to view our wounding, we will find a silver lining. There is something to be gained even here. When one has been betrayed or abandoned in a relationship in which one has shared one's deepest self, moving past the hurt becomes an evolutionary step.

Looking back on resolved abandonment and betrayals, we notice how they gave us a necessary shove, unwelcome kick, or outright knee-buckling blow, to release the comfortable, known and familiar. They forced us to step out into becoming more of who we truly are. Old patterns and attachments had to go. They allowed us to move forward towards a new sense of identity, awareness and new people. They provided us with new learning opportunities that would have passed us by. They forced us to relinquish childlike innocent trust and enter conscious trust based on consideration, equality, awareness of human fallibility and choice.

They forced us to see others for the human beings they are, not for the *heroes* we wanted them to be. *Emotional pain is the loss of what is known and safe so the soul can grow.*

We leap into a greater even though temporarily unprotected and scary reality.

Time is essential for the healing of abandonment and betrayals that knocked at our door when we were too young or too unprepared. They can open our eyes to a new and expanded perspective on life. They can also become emotionally consuming and unmanageable leading to bitterness. They always shake the very ground we stand on and make us question what we hereto accepted as real. It will take time to form a new identity, put things into perspective and fashion a new life.

If these experiences are digested over time and assimilated they will become the great bringer of individuality, new opportunities and maturity. Unrecognized and overshadowed by our pain an opportunity opens for us to take the next step in our development. By forgiving and embracing *their* humanity, we begin to forgive and embrace *our own.*

When our soul needs to grow but we ignore the call often loss, abandonment and betrayal enters to shake things up. We generally do not recognize this fact.

To embrace a new life we have to let go of the life we identify with, the safe and known. This movement is embedded in our psyche. It is visible in the development of the infant, child and teenager and adult:

- The infant's first world is mother...to form an identity apart from mother he/she has to let go of seeing him/herself as an *extension* of mother. This leads to his/her first sense of self and to identify with his/her family.
- The same holds true for the teenager readying him/herself to become an adult. To move forward he/she let's go of his/her family as the most important focus of his/her life and peers become important.
- To form a new family of his/her own he/she let's go of seeing peers as most important and shifts his/her focus to a mate.
- Once children are born into this new union, again the focus shifts. And, once the children leave to find their own life, once again the focus shifts.

Whenever a shift in focus occurs, the hereto known has become internalized. The focus cannot shift successfully unless this internalization has happened. It may shift on the surface yet the underlying dynamics do not disappear. When the focus shifts in a healthy fashion and one's world expands, the hereto known doesn't become any less significant. It has become integrated and assimilated not discarded.

In our loss, abandonment and betrayal, the other becomes the key opening the door to knowing others and ourselves as the very human beings they and we are.

We become capable to discover a more profound self-love and gain new and greater horizons of self-awareness. We are forced to face the challenge to forgive more then we ever thought possible. We are challenged to give of ourselves beyond our protective shell. We rise above our humanity to touch heaven. We become bigger than we ever thought we could be. Loving another, we are able to extend ourselves again on tender wings.

We habitually respond to life from fear.

Our Personal Fears are Manifold

"You gain strength, courage, and confidence by every experience in which you really stop to look fear in the face."
Eleanor Roosevelt

He was a big man, at least six foot tall. Yet, looking at him sitting across from me collapsed in his chair, he looked small and defeated. He had lost his job at the ripe age of 54. It was rather unexpected. His company was downsizing.

"I am terrified," he mumbled. "It doesn't make any sense. I suddenly feel as if I am going to lose everything!"

We are afraid to be alone, to be hurt, misperceived, abandoned and betrayed. We are afraid to lose what is dear to us, what we have worked for so long and hard. We are afraid to become sick or dependent. We are afraid to be seen in *a bad light* by others. *What will they think?*

Being afraid seems involuntary, something beyond our control. We feel intensely aware of our human fallibility, vulnerability and limited power to affect things. We often feel personally responsible. There is no faith at that moment. We have identified solely with being a faulty, vulnerable, limited and powerless human being.

When we habitually interpret what happens to us through the eyes of fear, we have every reason to see the world as a dangerous place.

The fear that limits and distorts is a type of psycho-emotional fear.

This form of fear is first a thought before it is experienced emotionally and physically. Other times, fear may arise as a physically felt *warning* alarming us to danger, an instinctual, physiological type of fear. In either case it is what we do with what we experience that determines the outcome.

It is our ability to think, use foresight, learn from past experiences, use introspection and deliberate over our actions that differentiates us. What we do and feel comes from what we think. Behavior is not autonomous of our thinking. Awareness of our inner world governs our behavior.

It is when we recognize and access a deeper faith that most of our fears disappear. *Then change becomes opportunity.*

We begin to re-frame anxiety as excitement. We recognize our deeper underlying psycho-emotional invulnerability. We trust that there is a reason that things went the way they did. We trust that there is a silver lining to be discovered down the road. We trust that we are immune to others ill intentions. This opens our mind to recognize the deeper underlying dynamics that set up the circumstances that are. Glimpsing perfection, even just for a *milli-second,* brings certainty.

Fears, phobias and anxieties vary in severity among individuals.

They come with the package of being a human being. Children often have specific fears of the dark, insects, spiders, heights, deep water, imaginary animals, etc. Some suspect this is due to an evolutionary trait that conditioned humans to fear certain creatures or situations that could cause them harm. And, we feel anxious when we see or encounter something associated with a previous traumatic experience, conscious or not. Many times we cannot identify the cause of our anxiety.

Writes Susan Greenfield in her book *The Private Life Of The Brain,*

"Anxiety is a state of mind that is initiated and perpetuated with very little external assistance. Anxiety,..., depends on the ability to forsake the present moment and anticipate an uncomfortable future."

Anxiety is unpleasant at best. It is often accompanied by physical sensations such as heart palpitations, tension headache, nausea, shortness of breath, or chest pain.

Anxiety is not always pathological or maladaptive. It is a common emotion along with fear, anger, sadness and happiness. It is a protective mechanism designed to prevent us from engaging in potentially harmful behaviors. On the other hand, if we avoid situations, which make us anxious, so temporarily relieved, our anxious feelings will increase the next time we are in the same position. Avoidance increases anxiety. Escaping an anxiety producing situation does not deal with the cause of the anxiety, our underlying sense of vulnerability. We inadvertently begin to limit our life through our avoidance.

There is a fine line between anxious and excited. We have the power to interpret what the feelings we are experiencing are to us. To do well at certain tasks arousal is necessary. When the level of arousal goes beyond what is ideal, it begins to interfere with optimal performance.

Excitement becomes anxiety when we become afraid of negative evaluations and outcomes.

Fears can have a serious effect on our lives.

Many adults experience anxiety with regard to their career, profession, health, or financial situation. Anxiety becomes manageable or disappears when we experience ourselves as able to *do something.* The *something* may be an action to influence or safeguard against a feared for outcome. Or, it may simply be an internal step in trust that *all will be well.*

To find perspective and minimize (at least in our own mind) the effect a potential negative outcome might have on us, is a learned skill.

Fears that have a serious effect on a person's life are clinically diagnosed as an anxiety disorder. The most common are social anxiety disorder, phobias and panic disorders[20]*:*

- *Social anxiety disorder*
  Sufferers experience intense anxiety in some or all of the social interactions and public events of everyday life. For instance, difficulties attending parties or meetings, making a phone call, walking into a shop to purchase goods; anxiety about being judged by others; anxiety about behaving in a way that might cause embarrassment or ridicule.
- *Phobias*
  Fear of a single specific panic trigger such as spiders, dogs, elevators, water, flying, catching a specific illness, etc.; Agoraphobia--a generalized fear of leaving home or a small familiar safe area.
- *Panic attacks*
  Short periods of intense, sometimes debilitating fear. The onset is typically abrupt and may have no obvious trigger. Sufferers of panic attacks report a sense of feeling like they are dying, going crazy and/or experiencing severe heart palpitations, feeling faint, nauseous, or losing control of themselves.

An emergency type of fear is rare.

When naked fear grips us, stepping back and thinking through a problem may seem impossible. On a most instinctual level it will trigger a fight or flight response. The body prepares the organism to deal with threat. Blood pressure, heart rate, sweating and bloodflow

---

[20] Wikipedia, Social Anxiety Disorder

to the major muscle groups increase and immune and digestive system functions become inhibited...*we lose our appetite.*

As our system gears up, because of its physiological impact on our ability to think, our minds ability to rationalize becomes incapacitated. The experience may produce pure terror, not simple anxiety.

My sister suffered from a spider phobia. One evening I found her frozen staring at a harmless house spider. Her eyes were fixed, her face was white and she was in a clear state of pure fear. An otherwise capable adult had lost her ability to rationalize and help herself.

The fear that subtly creeps into our daily interactions is of a different nature.

The type of fear discussed here is akin to an all-pervading underlying current of vulnerability influencing our experience of others and ourselves. A symbol for this innate experience of vulnerability can be found in the story of Adam and Eve in the Garden of Eden becoming aware of their nakedness. Nakedness stands for feeling and indeed being unprotected. Every toddler undergoes the developmental step of recognizing his/her loss of omnipotence and the resulting awareness of vulnerability.

Short of being classified as neurotic, most people allow their perceptions and behavior to be dictated by this experience of vulnerability without realizing it. This hidden and disguised form of fear urges them to withdraw, avoid, or attack in an attempt to protect themselves, often from imaginary dangers.

It is a fear based in their particular contraction: “I am not appreciated”, (important, worthy, smart, seen as capable, regarded as responsible, etc.).

When fear disguises itself and loses its instinctual function of a *warning signal* alarming us to danger, it produces a psychological distortion. Instead of being a warning signal it becomes a *stop sign*.

The confusion that supports viewing life through the eyes of vulnerability is that most of us assume that all that is real is physical existence. We over-identify with the physical and material because our senses can comprehend it. We assume that we are responsible for what we do but not for what we feel and think, for our inner world. We often neglect to be accountable for our attitude with which we approach life. Invulnerability is an inner psycho-emotional and spiritual experience. It cannot be found in the physical.

To experience ourselves as a facet of the diamond of life and the connection and safety that can flow from it is a leap, especially during times of crisis.

Without fear we stay calm.

The clerk glared back at her boss..."I haven't had time yet! Are you saying that I am not responsible?" "All I said was that I had asked you yesterday to clear out the shelf and today it still isn't done," her supervisor, struggling to remain calm, explained. "All I am concerned with is a clear shelf by the end of today!"

Feeling fundamentally vulnerable, we assume dangers and assaults where there are none. Invulnerability and the self-confidence that flows from it, doesn't perceive a threat. We simply cannot be attacked, physically hurt yes, but not attacked in who we are.

A belief in this inherent vulnerability produces paralysis, helplessness and attack. Our mind turns in circles. Eventually helplessness can lead to hopelessness and feeling completely out of control. Or, helplessness disguises itself as aggression, at times, equally out of control.

The degree of helplessness and vulnerability we experience seems to be determined by an absence of the personal inner resources we have. Our self-esteem, ability to rationalize, minimize or make sense of a situation is our safeguard. Our hidden self-accusations keep us vulnerable and helpless. Helplessness is at the core of all traumas. Fear diminishes when we feel that we can take steps to *safeguard* ourselves and what is dear to us.

The store clerk could have responded with: "So sorry, had a really busy day yesterday. I will make sure to get that done today!"

Fear, in all its many disguises, is a symptom of loss of connection and safety.

No matter what often distorted form it may take the fear that reminds us of our inherent vulnerability, is a cry for connection and safety. Fear, gone out of control or living beyond our conscious awareness has the power to become toxic to our psycho-emotional life. It fools us, interferes with capitalizing on our capabilities and opportunities and sabotages our dreams. It pollutes our relationships and moves us to seek in all the wrong places for meaning and purpose.

This type of fear is an emotion that often operates just beyond our immediate awareness. Its' influence on our decisions, perceptions and behaviors is subtle. It wears many disguises. Doubt is fear; guilt is fear; superiority is fear; frustration is fear; anger is fear; hurt is fear; judgment is fear; loss is fear; etc. If we are willing to step back for a moment and look we find that just about underneath all of our upset rests the fear of vulnerability.

This insidious emotion that we call fear has taken on a powerfully motivating influence over our psyche seldom recognized consciously. This form of fear is a state of mind that is independent of external assistance. We *"forsake the present moment and anticipate an uncomfortable future"* against which we instantly attempt to protect ourselves. This form of fear is typically human.

A field mouse in his burrow doesn't dwell on times when it managed to escape the cat. It doesn't worry if a cat is going to pass by. Once the cat is there and it can smell it, its' physiological alarm bells go off. Fear for the mouse is an experience of the here and now.

We often manufacture our own inner hell.

We construct a personal reality inside our minds that often has very little to do with what is happening in the outside world. The replay of painful past experiences or the anticipation of feared for outcomes in the future are peculiarly human. They lead to physiological body responses the same as immediate life-threatening situations. These bodily reactions, when occurring over lengthy periods of time, lead to reactions rooted in stress: chronic high blood pressure, headaches, irritability, and insomnia, just to name a few. Now, our body exists in a state of continuous flight or fight response.

The disconnection and threat that is experienced on the outside is in actuality a form of having lost touch with our *inner safety.*

Next time you find yourself anxious try the following:

- Interrupt the sequence of anticipated negative outcomes. In other words put a stop to the spiral...don't allow your mind to obsess. *"This thought means nothing...go away!"* Take a deep breath.
- Develop the inner resources of talking yourself out of your fear (enlist a friend's help). *"What am I afraid of happening here...what is truly the likelihood that it will? And if it would, what is the worst thing that would happen...and if it did ...then...? What could I do to help myself?"*
- Choose to face what you are afraid of directly (in mini steps) whenever possible. Initially visualizations may be helpful. Imagine yourself putting your arms around the part of you that is afraid. Acceptance allows for change.
- Use positive affirmations to counteract what you fear. *"I can do this!" "What is mine will come to me." "I am going to be OK.," etc.*
- Imagine yourself as a magnet that is attracting all the good in life.

Fear is like a lullaby; it makes us fall asleep.

The Bible states that once Adam ate the forbidden fruit he fell asleep. However, there are no further references about him waking up. *Falling asleep* can be equated to the experience of the majority of mankind. We are asleep (lack conscious awareness) of our deeper motivations and habitual interpretations. We are asleep to the opportunities life holds and often change brings. We are asleep to our psycho-emotional and spiritual *invulnerability.*

Once we ate of the forbidden fruit we became aware, that we were subject to the law of opposites, to act *bad, to do harm instead of good.* We became aware that others intentions towards us may be to harm us.

Reawakening, as the word says, is an awakening from something. It is an awakening to how we allow fear to become the basis for our thinking, feeling and doing in our everyday life. Fear dictates that we protect ourselves. Or protections cause much of the harm we inflict and the selfish interests we pursue. Fear works from the depth of our psyche and influences if not dictates the majority of our experiencing. Once we are awake, we have a choice.

The man who lost his job learned to view his loss without fear of an anticipated negative future. He began to see the opportunity of finally doing what he had longed to do for many years…start his own business. Once he was able to see change through the eyes of trust and hope he was able to see the new as exciting. This very same change seen through the eyes of the fear of vulnerability polarized his thinking previously around what he didn't want which then became all he could see.

Fear leads us into a multitude of self-protections.

Fear dictates worship of what is valueless. We hope to protect ourselves from what we fear by acquiring money, status and power. We seek to overcome our fear by attempting to control our environment, selfishly take what isn't truly ours, hoard food, misuse our body and establish superiority, etc.

By allowing fear to be our motivator, we give it a power it does not of itself have. We never stop to question the assumption of us as a small, faulty human earthling that is born in time and lives in time ever vulnerable. Fear as a motivation for what we think and do is like a subtle current underlying much of what we have accepted as *normal.*

She had decided to take a dance class. Her teacher was flamboyant and clearly talented. The teacher's overly self-assured demeanor at times took on a sarcastic tone towards students. "Why does she feel she has to put people down in front of everyone?" she asked.

Fear moves us to withdraw or lash out in a protective gesture. This may take many forms. The teacher acted superior and used put-downs due to her inner feelings of inferiority based in her sense of vulnerability. We seek on the outside what we have failed to find on the inside. Yet, seeking and even finding on the outside what truly must be found on the inside will not satisfy us. It remains temporary and therefore *valueless*. We get caught in needing to proof our self-worth.

Our ego will move from one accomplishment to the next in the hope that this one will finally put inside what we crave. The stakes get higher and higher. Fulfillment is temporary; easily lost, yet gained with great effort and difficulty.

Fear, energetically, is withdrawal.

Extension is its antonym. Extension is a fundamental aspect of the universe and our deepest self. As such when we withdraw and withhold or lash out we are not in alignment with our innermost being. As a result we feel unhappy. *We have missed our mark.*

If we do believe in love, we automatically believe in God. By definition, God is love (extension), the ever-becoming life principle. That love and extension are synonymous is easily observed when turning one's attention inside. Loving thoughts, feelings and attitudes lead to a sense of energy extending. In contrast fearful, judgmental or upset thoughts, feelings and attitudes lead to a sense of energy withholding and drawing back, typically in a protective stance. Love and extension go hand in hand. One cannot exist without the other.

Our inner being longs for extension. It will not rest until it fulfills its natural state. In this recognition fear can be seen as a cry to return to what is natural...extension, love.

When we extend from love we "make anew".

As such we allow a situation to be seen in a new way, different from what we might have assumed previously. Unforeseen solutions appear. This allows for past errors to be corrected.

Every rain cloud is seen as having a silver lining and perfection is glimpsed in the interplay of the human psyche and the reality that is. No longer is there any need to hold on to ideals (how we think *things should be) before reality. We become capable to embrace what is.*

Alignment is necessary on a body level as well as on a psycho-emotional level to experience harmony. Just as bad posture or injury can throw our body out of alignment so can undisciplined fear thinking.

Once we have become used to being out of alignment physically or emotionally/mentally, it takes conscious effort to return to correct alignment. Being out of alignment has been normalized. Initially correct alignment of our posture as well as of our emotional/mental attitudes will feel foreign, uncomfortable and take conscious effort. We are capable of extending ourselves when we are in alignment.

Fear moves us to believe that some form of lack exists either in others, the world or us.

The dance teacher took from childhood that she wasn't truly capable. This left her with a deep sense of "less". Her low self-esteem sabotaged her being able to capitalize on her talent. No matter how often other people told her how talented she was, she doubted herself at the display of the slightest opposition. She remained vulnerable to other people's opinions and assessments and she deprived herself of refining her talent.

Most of our fears are a reaction to a past that is gone. When we hide the lack that we are afraid of, we begin to withhold love from others or ourselves. We begin to treat a perceived or imagined lack as real. We become quietly desperate. Our self-worth is constantly in jeopardy. Our mind moves to attempt to fill this perceived lack with our own idea of what we think would guarantee our or others happiness and safety...outer accomplishment and recognition.

In our frantic attempt to change what we think is perceived by others we over-compensate. Low self-esteem leads to acting superior, pointing out and exaggerating other's faults. Or, it leads to acting *mousy.* Over-compensating by over-extending ourselves allows others to take. Neither way works, since the lack that is compensated for is an inner affair.

People are people and as such fallible. On the personality level of course there is lack. It is always possible to perceive lack of one kind or another. Lack does and always will to some degree exist. And just because others may agree with us doesn't make someone's lack a reality.

We judge in others what we cannot stand in ourselves (or the opposite to that). It is not necessarily the seeing of lack in oneself or another that is the problem. When we begin to *withhold love from another, or us* we get caught in judgment. Now, the simple seeing of lack takes on its potential destructive power. Lack has no meaning with regard to our inner worth unless we give it meaning. Accepting imperfection transforms it. *"I am imperfect and loveable!!!"* We become invulnerable.

Another way of dealing with fear is through accessing joy.

Joy is an inner experience that lies unperturbed at the bottom of the self. No matter what storm is blowing through in our daily life, joy is accessible to us instantly. It takes setting aside or shelving our fear and worries for a moment or two. They will be there when we return from our vacation. Taking this vacation often allows us to view the fears and anxieties that plague us differently. One expression and at times access pass to joy is laughter.

There is a famous case of Norman Cousins who had been diagnosed with a spinal disease and been given a 0.2% chance of survival. Cousins took things into his own hands and embarked on a healing program involving watching comedy videos. He discovered that after an episode of belly-rolling laughter the sedimentation rate of his red blood cells fell gradually. He claimed that laughter could alleviate pain: ten minutes of belly-rolling laughter resulted in two hours of pain-free sleep[21].

We know now, that laughter releases natural morphine-like chemicals in the body. The result is a sense of well being.

---

[21] Greenfield, *The Private Life Of The Brain*

Laughter and accessing our inner state of joy brings us into the here and now.

Past and future slip away and we are capable of experiencing ourselves free of what plagues us. Laughter and joy are self-generated.

Apparently children find it easy to break out in laughter. The more we mature; the scenarios that make us laugh become more refined. Maybe this was meant in "*become as little children again and ye shall enter the kingdom of heaven*".

Just as for young children, it is the unexpected, that which interrupts the predictability of our lives that causes excitement. The unexpected becomes our doorway into the here and now.

When we learn to approach life with a *blank slate attitude, an open mind, an eagerness to discover,* even the most mundane becomes new. Now life is an adventure. We have stepped beyond anticipated negative outcomes and freed ourselves of fear and anxiety. And when our deeper contractions assert themselves, we now have the means...*laugh them away.*

Once we begin to see through our and others hang-ups, they, indeed, become very comical.

Facing Our Fears

Being alive in a physical body and physical world generates fear.

It always has; it always will. We have a longstanding history with fear. Primitive man didn't understand and know about natural laws. Unusual events were potentially dangerous. He was ever vulnerable. After all it could mean life or death. Our fight or flight response, so deeply ingrained by thousands of years of use, still to this day remains our instantaneous reply. We respond to life from a hereditary feeling of vulnerability.

Once we lost instinctual survival, we became aware of our vulnerability in the face of nature and life. The resulting helplessness is with us to this day. It must on some level bring back that primitive fear of early man. *Acknowledging what scares us gives us the power to change what we can. It gives us conscious choice.*

There is lawfulness to all of life, our inner world as well as our outer world. Science has discovered the lawfulness of the physical world. As a result, it has helped us master many of our fears connected with our environment and illness.

In our attempt to understand the lawfulness of nature we have fallen into a trap. We deal with the totality of life as if it was only physical and therefore measurable and controllable. We seek to counter our inherent psycho-emotional sense of vulnerability through science as well.

There are aspects of life that cannot be understood or measured by physical science. They can only be known through psycho-emotional insight. Our psycho-emotional fears dictate the fearful world we see and experience. We become separate from creation. In defense, we assume the role of creator by attempting to protect others and ourselves with personal power.

Instead of attempting to annul our fear, we need to ask to understand the conditions that made us afraid.[22]

---

[22] Foundation for Inner Peace, *A Course in Miracles*

Psycho-emotional fear began at that crucial moment in time when we first became aware of being separate.

This original moment of losing our sense of safe connection may have been obviously traumatic yet typically is forgotten. It was a moment in time in which we questioned:

- *Am I loved? Maybe we felt not cared for; abandoned, rejected or betrayed; maybe we felt unimportant or not treated as equal, etc. Something happened that moved us to interpret and thereafter decide that our source was not dependable. With this decision fear arose. Our physical or emotional survival was in jeopardy (in reality or in our assessment of what was).*
- *Our picture of ourselves as worthy of love was threatened.*
- *Am I loving? Maybe we became suddenly aware of our bad intentions; we concluded that we were not loving and therefore "bad"; maybe we were told that we were selfish or concluded that we were selfish, bad or hurtful; maybe our actions became hurtful towards another or a pet due to our lack of maturity; maybe we were put into situations beyond our emotional and physical readiness and we experienced ourselves as irresponsible, hurtful, or incapable.*
- *Our picture of ourselves as good became tarnished.*
- *Am I loveable? Maybe we were told or experienced ourselves as ugly, bad, stupid, different or not measuring up; we may have felt shamed; we may have felt rejected or left out; we may have felt guilty. This led us to conclude that we didn't deserve or that something was wrong with us; that it was our fault.*
- *Our picture of ourselves as deserving love became confused.*
  Any and all of these questions made us vulnerable and produced fear.

Our attitude is either love-based or fear-based.

A fear-based attitude towards others and life makes us *withdraw* our energy in a protective or defensive gesture. It is based in a deeply rooted sense of vulnerability. We feel closed and separate. We are afraid to lose or be deprived in some way. In its extreme form it will paralyze us.

Love (the non-personal kind) is an energy that extends. We feel content and capable of giving. There is no threat. A love-based attitude towards others and life keeps our mind open. We can embrace what is.

If we perceive others or ourselves without love, we automatically fall into a perception that is distorted by fear. Perception through the eyes of fear is a mistake. We have missed our mark and are prone to fall into projection and judgment.

Most of our days are filled with perceptions based in some form of fear. It takes discipline to withdraw our fear perceptions. We have to choose to see through the eyes of love instead, minute by minute. We are capable of changing our mind instantly.

Love-based choices and actions are different from being good even though they may look the same. The difference lies in the self-completing nature of (non-personal) love. The very act of giving becomes our reward.

In a conflict situation ask yourself "What do I "truly" want here?

Escape from fear happens of itself once we become aware.

Her parents divorced when she was very young. Her father and mother remarried and had more children with their new spouses. She idolized her father like any little girl. The birth of her stepsister added to her inner conflict. She already felt torn about her sense of loyalty towards her mom and dad. When her stepsister was born she felt as if her father loved her stepsister more than her. The situation was exasperated since she lived with her mother and only spent time at her father's house once every other month.

"I was jealous!," she stated. "Boy, it feels good to just be able to say that!"

We instinctively want to hide what we consider as weak, our shortcomings, bad intentions, unacceptable feelings and stupid actions. As children, we want to keep our parents good. After all, we depend on their benevolence. Once we fully recognize that we cannot hide, especially from ourselves, we may at first become more afraid and defensive. To admit that we could be wrong, that the fault might be with us, or that those we depend on aren't the infallible gods we want and need them to be, is a tall order. To face the shortcomings our parents have goes against what we are desperate to believe. We want to see them as loving, not as selfish. It is difficult to look at all the conflicting feelings we carry inside. It is not until we realize that there is nothing that we *would want to hide* that we truly set ourselves free to grow into mature adults.

Disowning our feelings and putting blame on others creates alienation. We feel distant because we have distanced ourselves from them and us. As long as we attempt to hide, we feel phony and fake and we limit our awareness. Unknowingly, we have removed ourselves from the solution that exists.

She attempted to gain her father's love for a while but felt that she could not win. She never told him how she felt. Over the years of growing up she slowly began to distance herself. It hurt less that way. It did not occur to her how much she lost in doing so until much later.

In self-defense we find fault with others.

We feel bad about feeling the way we do. It is only human to assume that *others* must have caused our bad feelings. All of us will fail at one time or another.

"Why don't I feel close to my father?," she questioned once she was an adult. She attempted to explain the distance between herself and her father. After all, she loved him. A loving daughter wouldn't distance herself. To blame her baby-stepsister didn't seem reasonable.

He had distanced himself from her, she concluded. "But why?" Like any child (adult or not) she wanted to maintain her parents as "good."

As a child she had concluded that it must be her stepmother's fault. It seemed as that she must be the one who kept her father's love and attention away from her. The one who is behind the distance that developed between her and her father. It wasn't too hard to find "facts" to substantiate this assumption and it was safe to blame her. Now an adult and a parent herself, she began to question that old assumption.

We have developed minds that habitually perceive a lack in others as a form of self-defense against what we are afraid to look at. Loyalty and our need to be loved confuse and distort our perception, in particular with our parents. Until, one day, we grasp that those we love are human and therefore fallible. This does not diminish the love we have for them or the love they have for us.

Whenever we try to deceive we make ourselves fearful because we realize in our heart that it is a lie.[23]

Doubt is a form of fear.

"If I am being totally honest," she admitted, "I wanted my father to love me more than my step-sister". "I wanted to stay special to him the way I felt I had been...just like any little girl would. I guess that is what made me afraid...that's when I became afraid that he might love me less! I wanted him to love me more." "That's when I began to doubt." "When I visited my father's house all I saw was how much he loved and cared for my step-sister. Maybe, if I had grown up in my father's house, I would have seen it differently". Today, I can see my own daughter struggling with similar issues.

She realized that she never dealt with the feelings of loss she experienced at the time. First the loss created by her parents divorce. The loss of the home and family she had known. Then the loss of her father being the father she used to have and she wanted him to be.

Doubt says loss is real. If we believe loss to be real, we act accordingly and with that action confirm it to be real. Now we fall back onto personal power to protect ourselves from the feared consequences of loss. This makes loss even more real, and so on.

[23] Foundation for Inner Peace, *A Course in Miracles*

Ultimately, loss is a confusion of identity.

This confusion questions: *"Who am I"*. To believe that: *"I am loved, loveable and loving"* makes us deserving and invulnerable. We have nothing to prove as long as there are no question marks in our own mind. We remain securely identified with having worth, with being unique and therefore irreplaceable.

Her mother had insisted that it was best for logistical reasons that she would spend relatively little time at her father's house. Her father went along. Her conflict was never addressed.

Her father was not very skilled at talking about feelings. She had alienated herself from her stepmother. Her mother either didn't pick up on her conflict or wasn't able to help her deal with it for her own reasons. She was left to her own devices to answer the question marks in her mind.

Once our identity shifts from our inner state of being to what we feel, have and do, we are lost. We experience ourselves as confused and deprived. Once this confusion has occurred it becomes almost impossible to not feel distraught when one's role in life is *taken away*. We undergo a form of identity crisis. Our personal power to protect our best interests and ourselves has failed us.

Doubt leads to a splitting of an energy that in reality is whole.

This is an uniquely personal experience and personal story for each one of us. This original split produced fear.

Let's say that early on in life you questioned if you were "important" (insert your own words). As this question and with it doubt arose you suddenly became afraid that your suspicion may be true. Your experience to whatever degree traumatic reinforced your doubt and increased your fear leading you to believe that it "was true".

Now your survival instinct kicked in and you withdrew so as to avoid pain. The original energy continuum (for example: important - selfless) that was up to this point whole and all aspects available to you became split.

Part of it now becomes avoided or "bad" (for example: important takes on the meaning of self-absorbed and selfish). This now may lead you to feel that you have to proof that you are important yet you are afraid to appear selfish. You may keep expecting others to proof to you that you are important to them. You may become invested in being seen as selfless. You may become afraid of being unimportant or selfish, and so on.

This leads to other people, money, success, etc., to become empowered to either give or withhold your inner state of "*I am important*". Importance is an inner state of being and as such is unchangeable. A young child will look to the authority figures in its life to have this state of being confirmed.

If confirmed sufficiently the child will identify with "*I am important*". If this confirmation does not happen sufficiently, it remains something to be recognized and proven. This keeps the source on the outside and gives enormous power to other people who do not necessarily care to have this function in our life. It generates fear and makes us anticipate what we fear.

What "is" doesn't need proof.

We habitually take things personal. Due to our inherent sense of vulnerability and the fears that result, we interpret others actions as an attempt to deprive or demean us. Our personal fears dictate our perception and override what we know.

The experience of essence *"I am"* is an expression of "*what is". If I know that I am important (etc.), I am relaxed if others reflect this back to me or not.*

Essence has not attached itself wrongly to how I feel, what I have or do. It remains securely on the inside experienced as a reality. Therefore I have nothing to prove. I am psycho-emotionally invulnerable to attack. Knowing that I am important doesn't necessarily mean that I will put up with other's behavior of treating me as unimportant. I can go either way: overlook their error or correct their error.

Either action does not have a hidden agenda of proofing or achieving my importance since the reality of my importance was never in question *in my own world*. Holding them accountable to treat me as important is simply holding them and me to our joint highest good. The same holds true with any state of being.

Our ideas and ideals of "what should be" become the idols of our present day life.

Our energy of defensive self-protection and our assumptions that *we know what should be* are based on our fears. We persistently assume that *what is* will deprive us of what we want. As we confuse *outer having* with *inner having* we proof ourselves right. We miss the gifts and opportunities of the life we have.

Due to her unresolved conflict she wasn't able to receive the love her father had for her. She deprived herself of the connection and closeness she could have had with her stepsister. She also missed out on the gifts her stepmother had to give.

Once we believe that we are deprived of something we want, our perception becomes distorted. These distortions impair our ability to receive. The trick becomes to awaken to receiving and wanting what we have (gratitude for the good in our life) and not to necessarily demand what we think we want. We transcend our upper level wants and discover our deeper wants. Once we are emotionally resolved new doors will open.

In Christianity, we were taught to not have idols before God. These idols in our present day life are the *ideals and ideas* that we came up with, thinking they would guarantee our and others happiness.

All perception of lack is based in the attitude that things should be different than they are.

Our present state is the sum total of choices we have made, beliefs we follow blindly, masteries we seek to accomplish and living in a physical world. Our perception becomes distorted by the idea that the present state is not in our best interest. We function from an assumption of being ever vulnerable, not just physically, but psycho-emotionally as well. We do not realize that our perception of a situation is like perceiving a diamond by only looking at one facet.

Our mind is simply incapable of perceiving past, present and future simultaneously. It is impossible for our human mind to truly perceive the full potential of learning, all past connections and all future possibilities in an instant.

All loss that we experience does in essence involve the body or a limited sense of identity in one-way or another. Energy does not increase or decrease but simply constantly reorganizes. By that definition, loss is impossible. It is a step taken in our own mind. The physical is finite and physical change often becomes emotional loss. This is part of our human experience. To transcend this experience becomes part of our quest in maturity. To overcome fear and our experiences of loss, we need to overcome doubt. Where there is no doubt there is no fear.

"There is another way of looking at this..." "If I don't take this personal, then what do I see?" "What would I do?"

Personal growth begins with facing our fears.

When we finally decide to stop hiding and pretending to be someone we really are not, is when we begin to mature. Admitting our fears, even just to ourselves, may initially make us feel weak and unprotected. Admitting our fears to others conjures feelings of intolerable vulnerability. In reality, it can give us strength.

When we become afraid we shrink back into attempting to solve our problems through personal power. When we are fearful we have chosen wrongly. We now must change our mind not attempt to control, manipulate and avoid circumstances that scare us. This change of mind rests on our willingness to question what we hereto accepted as the truth.

We need to question the assumptions these fears rest on. Once we recognize our fears as having no solid or a wrong foundation they will disappear by themselves. Whenever we attempt to undo fear in any other way, we actually first make fear real by treating it as real and then we attempt to undo it. *What is wrong with this tactic?*

The Dilemma of "Alone"

To stand alone, to be outcast from family, village and society can (and used to) threaten our very survival. Being alone, having to do things alone can make us feel overwhelmed and distraught. We often feel and indeed are vulnerable when we are alone. As people we are group animals. Community offers safety. Every day life is much more manageable when tasks are shared. Yet, the ability to stand alone with strength when necessary is also a sign of maturity.

Fear will disconnect us from others and ourselves. When alone produces fear, it challenges our sense of identity. *"Who am I?"* We know ourselves through our connections. Connection provides us with safety. Subtle disconnection manifests as loneliness, worry and a *need* for outer safety. When we lose connection with our inner life, we feel vulnerable, empty and alienated.

Once our crystallized life of submitting to the expectations of family, community, society and the outer successes they offer is disillusioned, we begin our journey home. We may find ourselves alone, yet terribly afraid to be alone. For many of us it is at our darkest hour, when we have hit *rock bottom* that we begin to find what is right for us.

Our old life may lie in broken pieces and we do not understand *why.* Physical existence with all its trimmings, by definition, is not safe no matter how careful, rich, or smart we become. There will be unexpected and unwanted turns in the road.

The experience of "alone" is about gaining and defining our individuality.

It is an essential stepping-stone towards higher levels of awareness. Every child has and will take the first steps on this challenging path. As adults, we have conscious choice. We can choose to face our deepest fears...or not.

Once we lose our connection with our inner life, our life with all its glamour and riches seems meaningless. We can hide and distract ourselves only for so long. One has to let go and risk accepting the power of choice within one's life circumstances and the responsibility and consequences that flow with it. Learning to be alone and self-sufficient becomes a step in personal growth. We cannot truly be related to another until we are truly OK with ourselves.

If we hear that we are capable and loved, if someone picks us up when we fall and wipes our tears when we fail, we learn *that others will be there when needed.* From there we move on to learning to *trust into the hand of life to hold us.*

To feel "all alone" is to feel cut off from love, safety and meaning.

"I was two-and-a-half years old when I first felt a terrifying sense of being all alone in this world while staring at the night sky. My parents had been fighting...once again. My father had come home drunk and picked a fight with my mother. In an attempt of protecting herself, she left the house to hide in the wood shed. Watching her leave was terrifying. To my mind she was going to leave for good. I attempted to follow her, crying hysterically, but she urged me to go back to the house, fearing that my presence would give her whereabouts away to my father. So I did!

No one noticed or seemed to care that I was standing all alone in the yard in the middle of the night...sobbing...lost!"

"It took many years before I was finally ready to admit that my mother had decided to save herself over saving me."

As infants and toddlers, we live in a state of *preconscious psychological oneness* and gradually or abruptly enter the world of duality and individuality. If the recognition of *alone* is coupled with the sudden awareness of vulnerability, it is experienced as traumatic. We begin to fear and distort *alone.* Instead of being a normal and liberating growing-up experience, it becomes feared. *Alone becomes lonely and disconnected.*

We begin to doubt our self-sufficiency. We feel cut-off. Or, we become overly self-sufficient and don't learn when and how to ask for appropriate help.

"In a crisis, I will be alone," I reasoned. Going it alone became a pattern and eventually a choice. Looking back on my life I realize

that it didn't even occur to me to ask for help when I should have. I made choices that isolated me from support that could have been mine. I became strong."

"Why did I leave when my mother asked me to leave the wood shed? I left to protect her!!! I chose to save her over saving myself. In doing so I became the parent. I became unprotected and vulnerable and alone. Years later I realized that I could have asked for help from a neighbor. I could have exposed what needed exposing, even at age two-and-a-half".

If we are left to our own devices before we are ready, we learn that life is a scary place. Physical vulnerability becomes intertwined and confused with psycho-emotional vulnerability. If the very people that are supposed to help us are the ones that need protection, we don't learn that help is possible. The abnormal becomes normalized. Exposure of vulnerability becomes shameful.

What is the meaning of life?" What is the meaning of "my" life?"

"I was twelve years old when I first felt awestruck looking at that same sky, strangely aware of my own insignificance in comparison. Something stirred inside... what is the meaning of life?"

Our children will ask these age-old questions, asked by our ancestors. They remain a question mark today for us. Our families provided us with the values and morals to function in our society. They were the first ones to teach us about the meaning of life. Parental teaching, however fallible, becomes a foundation upon which future knowledge is built.

Even if our life now looks very different from our parents, very few of us were able to completely escape the programming family and society instilled in us. We have been taught to submit to the roles and the expectations placed on us. We have been taught to find meaning through *doing and having.*

Our need to be loved and accepted made us surrender our inner urges and take on what was expected of us. Some of us may have rebelled during our teenage years but then quietly adjusted to the norm.

Today, we may stand at the threshold of freeing ourselves from the fears that plagued us over the years. Yet, we may feel like choking at the very lack of inside and outside support. It is hard for us to support ourselves since we are still uncertain about who we are. It is hard for others to support us since our relationships were founded on knowing us in the *old way*.

The experience of "alone", when experienced as lonely, alienated and cut-off produces distortions.

"I was engulfed in total misery. I had held on to the hope that true intimacy in a relationship would keep me from being alone. The very feeling of "all alone" I had experienced when I was two-and-a-half years old!" "My partner would save me!"

We attempt to get the safe connection we missed out on and still crave, from present relationships. Once again we are deeply upset when our present day others don't live up to their mandate.

In our avoidance to face what we eventually must, our attempts at self-protection are at times bizarre: we become dependent to the point of allowing abusive behavior; we become lost in helping others who need us; we avoid truly loving another, leaving before we can be left and moving from relationship to relationship, we become strong and capable, yet find it hard to trust our own strength, when change and opportunity beckon, we refuse, we are too scared, etc. The variations are endless.

We do not as yet recognize that *alone doesn't have to be lonely.* Eventually it will be the forbearer of the highest level of individuality we can achieve. To be *only one, uniquely one* is our destiny while experiencing ourselves safely held by the hand of life. Then, we stand as complete individuals next to each other, self-sufficient yet close, *sometimes touching "we"*.

Trust in ourselves, as being intricately connected to the very fabric of life, has eluded us.

"Instead of feeling relieved at the obvious realization that I wasn't two-and-a-half anymore and quite self-sufficient now, I felt even more distraught. Was there ever going to be an end to dealing

with this deep-seated fear of being alone? I was in despair!!! All my efforts had failed".

"Over the years I had exhausted my options of ridding myself of this nagging sense of "alone" and discovered only temporary relief. I knew that my feelings had more to do with myself then whatever lack might exist in my mate."

When our deepest moments of alone are experienced lying right next to someone we love...or used to love and ought to love, we are ready to question and find another way.

In the past our mind was thoroughly confused about the difference between love and sacrifice. Self-love is a prerequisite to being truly loving to others. As long as we fear being alone with its intolerable feelings of vulnerability, we remain cut off from self-love. We remain needy for someone to love us.

Our psyche's most urgent yearning is to align itself. Eventually everyone has to take the step into coming into alignment within and without. Our thinking, feeling, saying and doing have to become congruent. When our spirit needs to grow and we refuse because we are afraid to face what we have to face, life drags us, fingernails bloody and elbows bruised where we could have walked willingly, dancing and singing. Our souls demand is self-realization. The question that keeps sneaking into our thoughts is: *"Is this all there is"?*

We may not feel ready and quite unprepared. "Ready or not," at times, life will say: "Jump!" Those are times when changes seem thrust upon us by fate.

Faith becomes added to trust and puts us in touch with our inner life.

In the past, we may have *talked the talk.* Eventually we are being challenged to actually *walk the walk*. It may have seemed easy before to do this. We knew the answers for everyone else.

Today we fear the unknown. Our inborn sense of vulnerability asserts itself. Fear tempts us to solve our problems from personal power. We have to learn to take a step in trust when we don't truly know what is good or bad, right or wrong, helpful or useless. Often what we thought was useless turns out to be very helpful. Changes that we thought only contained loss provide us with unforeseen opportunities down the road. What we struggled against and hoped to avoid, turns out to be the best thing that ever happened to us. Yet, people around us become resentful or threatened by our change. They want us to be the same we have been.

Our inner world of new beliefs and the outer world that functions by our old values seem in conflict. We experience a distinct sense of duality and find it difficult to patiently look for the door that wants to open. We may flip to the opposite extreme like the pendulum of a clock before finally finding the middle path. For a while, as we learn to explore our inner life, we escape the unpleasant and ugly. Until one day, the old feelings are back with new faces.

"I had recognized that these ugly feelings arrived in a cyclical fashion in endless versions. I felt like I would rather die now then to continue living with this fear of "alone". I was ready to face what had to be faced".

The following poem describes this awareness.

"Amidst the whirling forces, I stand confused. I know them not, for during all my past, they swept me up and down the land wherein I moved, blinded and unaware.

From place to place and point to point, they drove me up and down the land and nowhere was there rest.

I know them now, and here I stand and will not move until I know the law, which governs all this movement up and down the land.

I may revolve and turning, face the many different ways. Face some wide horizons and yet today I stand.

I will determine for myself the way to go. Then onward I will move.

I will not travel up and down the land nor turn in space. But onward I will move. Author unknown

Personal growth is ultimately a growth in trust and faith.

Trust is only difficult as long as we see ourselves as separate. With trust all of our problems are solvable in one way or another.

Trusting that we are going to be taken care of, trusting others to be there when needed, etc. ought to be our initial introduction into this world. If this initial form of trust isn't established or broken while we are as yet too immature, we are left with a *basic sense of mistrust into life.*

"Years later I realized that I mistrusted authority. It took me a while to see that the ant trail went back to my mother and father and that moment in time in the wood shed."

"I mistrusted that authority was going to be aware of and care about my needs. I believed, that authority, in oblivious self-absorption, would act in ways that would harm me. These feelings were intricately connected to my feelings of alone. This conclusion arose with the reverse self-accusation that I too was oblivious to my mother's needs, caught in my fears, and inadvertently just by my wanting to be with her could do harm to her".

"That is why I left the wood shed. I became the protector at that moment, terrified at the possibility of being harmful. That is why I felt so "all alone". I decided to become helpful in reaction to my fear. Of course, this conclusion wasn't true. Yet, that little child I once was didn't know that. I left behind part of my childhood innocence and grew up over night."

"I didn't even consider that help could be available from someone other than my parents. My fears had isolated me. It was up to me! I took on the role to protect my mother (myself) and to make my father (others) aware."

Mistrust into life and others and confusion about our role in life can be found at the very core of people's struggles later on. It will impede our progress temporarily. The truth is, that sometimes people are hurtful even if they are aware of the hurt it causes. They simply are too caught up in their own fears and dysfunctions to care. It is possible to touch a level of alienation that the caring we might have felt at other times simply evaporates.

Our initial form of trust (or lack thereof) colors how we approach life and others. It has a subtle influence on the choices we make. Our antennas are tuned to the slightest hint of discord.

Our initial stage of trust may be developmentally programmed but conscious trust is a choice made daily and hourly.

We learn or don't learn:

1. a basic sense of trust into life;
2. to trust into our capabilities, worth and *goodness*;
3. to trust a higher destiny/power/plan...God to keep us safe;
4. the experience of interconnection and purposefulness...going beyond trust.

Faith is the trust that says: our life has a higher meaning.

Ancient man and modern men alike used and use faith to make sense of life. Without faith it becomes a question of *either there is a God or there is no God.* If there is *no God* life is a finite, fearful and often lonely existence. Then we are truly alone and ever vulnerable! Life can end at any moment without meaning and purpose, an endless struggle for survival. Faith then is seen as an escape, an avoidance to accept the finality of death.

If there *is a God* all things become purposeful. Meaning can be found in everything. We become psycho-emotionally invulnerable and recognize our underlying spiritual invulnerability. Alone becomes *"all one";* interconnection to the very fabric of life.

"Many roads lead to Rome," a German proverb states. Many different path can and will lead us to our essence and with it bring meaning and purpose to our life. They are complementary not contradictory. It is not about the path we choose; it is walking whichever path we have chosen.

At different stages of our development different philosophies and healing techniques and even a different spiritual direction will work for us more efficiently than others. One day we arrive at the realization that we are more than this body, mind and emotions. There is an *"I"* that listens through our physical ears and sees through our physical eyes.

Matter and spirit become the interlocking threads of a safety net. We, being both (physical and spiritual), are each one of the little squares that make up the net. Once we have a body-felt understanding of this experience, it is impossible to experience ourselves as isolated, vulnerable and alone.

Initially, faith is a substitute for what we may have glimpsed but don't know yet through personal experience.

"Turning to the outside in any form or turning to the inside to a spiritual self seemed a total waste of effort. In my despair I completely doubted the existence of a Higher Self or Holy Spirit or God or anything else along those lines. The despair was all encompassing. I felt completely alienated and cut off from everything and anyone, any form of help from the outside or inside. I was totally and utterly alone!"

During times of crisis, when we need faith most, is often when it seems the least accessible to us. Once we have had a personal experience, we do not need faith any longer, we are certain.

"In despair I made a last ditch effort and called out: "If there is something like a Christ inside of me, then this would be an awful good time to be with me. Help Me!!!"

"And suddenly I felt completely calm. The despair had vanished. I wasn't elated, just felt completely calm. I never before had experienced a calm this profound."

The *"I"* that resides at the deepest level of who we are is like the stillness of the eye of a storm. It is there, no matter how violent the storm rages. We are capable of going there. A crisis or emergency may propel us there despite of ourselves.

The rigidity of superficiality provides safety as a substitute for trust and faith.

Our search for love, recognition, connection, success, wealth, safety, meaning and acceptance, on the outside led us deeper and deeper into a superficial life.

It takes courage to risk what looks like loss on behalf of our inner truth. It takes even greater courage to face our inner demons, to stand and give up any form of avoiding. Our bad feelings arrive cyclical. We have to learn to accept even this part of ourselves. Trust and faith are by choice. They don't just one morning wake us up like a lightning bolt.

Remember that the whole idea of trust and faith would be unnecessary if we had no need for it. It is the very fact that we feel scared and not trusting that we need to consciously choose trust and faith. Once we turn to truly face our deepest fears, we find that where we anticipated loss we find relief and certainty. Where we used to be able to descend into despair and the *"dark nights of the soul"*, now an inner *trampoline* bounces us back...more whole.

"In the past, I had felt like I could sink forever into the abyss of my depression or misery. Now, when feeling myself descending I experienced a sudden stop, as if I was held by an invisible safety net protecting me."

Faith allows for a form of deep intuitive insight.

"...No historical evidence has managed to convince the entirety of the community of historians on earth that any one religion is true. For people in this category, "faith" in a God simply means "belief that one has knowledge of [any particular] God[s]". It is logically impossible that all these different religions with their mutually contradictory beliefs can simultaneously be objectively true.

Therefore, most historians with religious beliefs hold others to be "false", or essentially wrong. This is a standard tenet of most religions as well, though there are exceptions. An example of this is some forms of Hinduism, which hold the view that the several different faiths are just aspects of the ultimate truth that the several religions have difficulty describing or understanding. They see the different religions as just different paths to the same goal. This does not explain away all logical contradictions between faiths but these traditions say that all seeming contradictions will be understood once a person has an experience of the Hindu concept of "moksha" (liberation)."[24]

Whenever we experience a break-through, we sense a new glimpse of connection. When our lives go well, we assume that we have found *the way.* We habitually view others struggles through the particular *colored glasses* we wear, through our experiences and what has or has not worked for us.

The outcome of moments of deepest emotional understanding is true faith.

This form of faith is effortless...it just is. It is beyond doubt and fear. As our intellect grows, we are able to express and comprehend *truth* in an ever more conscious way. Yet, true faith is a truth that is intuited through our emotional understanding and grasped with our whole being...the mystery of life. A mystery we generally call God.

"I had the most unusual sensation that where my skin ended I ended. I felt completely whole inside. I was me, only one on this planet, no one else exactly like me!"

"It was the most unusual physical sensation and satisfying emotional realization: "where my skin ended I ended." "I felt this incredible sense of invulnerability, that had the A-bomb been dropped on the city that night, I would have been fine."

"All need had vanished. All despair had gone. I had a sudden understanding that to be "alone" is to be "only one", as there is only one God and each one of us is a microscopic interconnected version. My life had meaning; I had a contribution to make; I had purpose."

"My feelings of "alone" and vulnerability simply vanished. Ever since, when these feelings did attempt to reassert themselves, I may be momentarily confused but then can see through the illusions they create."

---

[24] Wikipedia, Criticisms of Faith

We begin to live a life that is consistent with our true nature.

We follow our *"bliss"* as Joseph Campbell called it. The discovery of one's life work and one's life purpose is a natural result of a maturation process. As we master fear, we discover our voice in the choir of life. We achieve alignment with our true nature. We become freed from the law of the opposites.

There is a Sanskrit term for this; it is *"dharma".* Dharma is that which holds one's true nature. Living one's Dharma means to do what is right for us. To follow Dharma means to act in accordance with divine law. It is a call to leave all cookie cutter versions of living life and finding one's own way in every aspect. We consciously choose what we eat, to how and where we live, to who we are in relationship with, to what profession we choose, to our spiritual practice. *It is to be in the world but not of it.*

True faith allows us to let go of assuming a position we do not truly have. It moves us beyond our hereditary vulnerability to recognizing our psycho-emotional and spiritual invulnerability. We surrender assuming to know how life should unfold for others and us. It is an assumption that we know which lessons we need to learn. Without judgment all things become equally acceptable. All men become equals no matter what their past, their accomplishments, learning, life style, or maturity. There is no threat.

True faith allows us to trust that all things will eventually work together for our good and everyone else's good, no matter what their appearance now. The roadblocks we encounter on our path are seen as a reorientation to find a new direction in life. Being able to embrace ourselves when we have failed, looked foolish, or made a big mistake is *true progress.*

Our mind embodies itself.

"Something inside had become re-connected. I experienced a profound sense of insight; a body-sensed understanding of the ever-becoming life principle. Somehow at that moment, I didn't just grasp this with my mind but with my whole being: my body, my emotions, my mind, my spirit, all simultaneously."

"I haven't since felt that strange sense of self-consciousness that used to haunt me; that feeling of awkwardness in my body when in the company of others; a strange form of invisible division between others and myself. It used to be so common in the past. Any sense of separation, as if there was an invisible wall between others and myself has fallen away. The result and understanding of this experience is still with me today, in every minute of my day."

When we finally surrender our futile attempts of avoiding our deepest fears, we begin to see pain, loss and hardship within a bigger picture. Our mind and body begin to function as a unit. Now being alive is enough reason to live. Our body becomes our connection to life itself. With that understanding, any separation between physical and spiritual drops away. They are the same.

Surrender doesn't mean giving up or neglecting to bring about much needed changes. It doesn't ask us to pull our claws and file our fangs. It doesn't ignore or avoid or override the pain we feel. It *re-frames* the pain.

Surrender is accepting the reality that is without preconceptions. We are capable of seeing many facets of one experience. Our experience of life moves from being one-dimensional to being multi-dimensional. As a result, we glimpse the perfection that exists underneath the apparent surface imperfection or lack. Inner guidance, a small, quiet voice in our heart, will beckon us to follow and do what can be done.

Spirituality really is a personal experience, an everyday reaching for ourselves.

"The initial wonder has evaporated. My experience of myself as a whole individual, however, has transformed the way I relate to others. Since that moment I have not experienced the emotional despair of the "dark night of the soul" that used to haunt me cyclically before. I get upset and frustrated or overwhelmed on occasion, I cry, I laugh, yet something inside now catches me when I fall."

Awareness is quickly gained and sometimes quickly lost until we finally touch the core of our carefully hidden pain. Once we do, awareness simply becomes part of who we are. It frees us. Spirituality is moments of freedom...moments of enlightenment, moments that we choose and moments that choose us.

There is no one path that will take us all the way. There is no one path that doesn't hold at least some valuable message and truth. We will initially lose ourselves in the cultural collective mind patterns and programming we received from our original family and community. Yet, later as adults, we will eventually awaken to where our soul wants us to be. No matter how limiting our childhood circumstances, we will find ourselves *if we are willing to wake up.*

Meaning and purpose rest on feeling rooted through our bodies to the earth. The *"I am"* experience of being alive, versus *"I am this..."* or *"I am that."*

Those Who Seek Will Find

The origin of religion, psychology and science are based on transforming and overcoming our essential fears.

Science and psychology, both, have overcoming what we fear as their primary goal. They aim to aid our understanding of the causes and underlying lawfulness of nature and psyche.

The focus of religion is to overcome fear by establishing a connection with the mysterious. Theologians like Paul Tillich and psychologists like Sigmund Freud have characterized existential anxiety (the fear of death) as a reaction to what Tillich called, *"the trauma of nonbeing."* They describe it as the moment when a person comes to realize that there is a point at which he or she might cease to be (die). As a result he/she begins to fear death. Religion, according to both Tillich and Freud, then becomes a carefully crafted coping mechanism in response to this anxiety.

Religion will become a coping mechanism to deal with the fear of death *if death means the end.* Yet, there is another level of experiencing spirituality. This other level is a psycho-intuitive experience and not an intellectual understanding nor is it based in blind belief. Death then is seen and redefined within the context of an immortal soul. Physical death becomes the end of only the corporal part of human personal existence. It loses its terror and finality.

The very basic of all human wishes is to find meaning and purpose in life.

"What is it that makes life meaningful?" Our search for meaning becomes heightened when we are confronted with mortal danger or the death of a loved one. Suddenly to be alive has meaning in itself or life seems fragile and unpredictable. "*What is the point of meeting our responsibilities if it all can end in an instant?"*

When our understanding of spirituality is in the early stages coming face to face with death can be excruciatingly unsettling. We suddenly have to face a terrifying vulnerability and helplessness. We may slip into an identity crisis questioning everything and everyone. The life we have known appears false. There is no point to caring. We have lost our ground; everything has been blown wide open. Self-gratification is our only comfort. Coming face to face with death can shake us profoundly.

Her mother had died. She was distraught with grief and felt alienated and cut-off. She had been a devout Christian all her life. Suddenly everything felt uncertain. "Is there an afterlife?" "Is there a God?" "I just don't know anymore".

To what degree we understand and experience divinity will determine how we live our life. An elementary understanding of divinity will lead us to *using* religion as a safeguard to counteract our fear of physical death and loss. Once our understanding has moved us beyond blind belief it transforms into faith. Spirituality becomes an inner experience that brings certainty.

Primitive man attempted to influence the mysterious force that held power over his life through worship.

Like a young child would, he believed that this force had either ill or good intentions. And, that these intentions could be influenced by his worship and behavior. Like primitive man, we are still attempting to influence what has power over us. We attempt to accumulate *brownie points* that buy us an *entry ticket* into heaven. Good, instead of being an experience of self, becomes a means to guarantee God's favor.

Many survivors of near fatal illnesses, accidents and other near-death-experiences report having found a new gratitude for life itself. Life becomes a gift. To give of oneself takes on an evolutionary purpose. Physical death becomes a natural aspect of the circle of life. It loses its terror and ability to disconnect us. Near-death-experiences (NDE) can catapult us into a more profound understanding of the mysterious.

NDE-experiences follow a distinct progression:

- An out-of-body experience: a sensation of floating above one's body and seeing the surrounding area in great detail.
- A sensation of moving upwards through a tunnel or narrow passageway.
- Meeting deceased relatives or spiritual figures; encountering a being of light or a light.
- A sense of overwhelming love and peace.
- Being given a life review: rapidly seeing the totality of one's life history, its interconnections to other people; yet without judgment.
- Reaching a border or boundary; a feeling of being returned to the body.

We assume that bad things should "not" happen to good people.

Bad things happen to good people because of life in a physical body. What is good or bad is really a decision of the mind. Our body is subject to the physical laws of this planet. Accidents happen. Others are ill intended. Nature will do as nature does.

Death is only scary as long as we believe that all we are is this corporal existence. Loss is only scary as long as we don't see the multi-facets of an experience. As we live a more aware life and use our body and the physical with respect and as their nature dictates pain diminishes. Most of the bad things that happen to us are *man made.*

Much of our socialization is built on appeasing others, in particular others who hold some form of real or imagined power over us. *God* gets put into this same category. *Good behavior* may appease others but will not influence the hand of life. It will not provide protection from other people's callousness and ignorance.

"Why did God take her," she sobbed. "Why not my uncle?" "He is nasty. He makes everyone's life miserable."

"My mother was a kind woman; always helpful. She would give you the shirt off her back if you needed it. She was loved by so many people!"

Fundamental teachings confuse morality with spirituality.

God is like the sun...it shines on roses and weeds alike. In essence we are all equal. Fundamental religion teaches that we will be punished for our bad and rewarded for our good. It confuses life's consequences with spiritual reality.

Good can be a stepping-stone to align us with the innermost mysterious state of oneness. No one would be unkind to another if he/she recognized this other as *God in disguise.* Then our life is like a fireworks display versus a flickering candle with a five-inch light radius. It delights and inspires. It lights up the darkness throwing its light far and wide. Its life span may be short. Long life has much more to do with our *good genes* than our *good deeds.*

When good is a programmed mode of functioning without deeper awareness of being, it becomes shallow. So it may appear very philanthropic on the surface, it is in essence self-serving. Then fear of mystery, fear of death, the fear in the face of the essential unknown, our inherited sense of vulnerability remains.

"There is nothing divine about morality, it is a purely human affair." Albert Einstein, *The World as I see it*

When we lose our super-conscious connection, we either institute dogma or atheism.

For many, dogma becomes the way to keep fear in check. The rigidity of dogma brings an illusion of safety, order and predictability.

We know where we stand. Fundamentalism tries to find proof for the personal existence of God. We live life with blind belief and look to a God on the outside. This God, a father figure sitting up there in heaven somewhere, with a long white beard, is a moralistic judge, who will either reward or punish us. If we are good, he will safe us.

By definition this is in contradiction with the idea of underlying spiritual oneness. It resembles the first split into a state of duality: *"the creator and the created"*.

A light beam is not separate from its source!

When we confuse blind belief with faith, we confuse symbolic teaching with spiritual reality. Analogies are taken at verbatim. Fundamentalist teachings often pit reason against belief trying to eliminate doubt. Instead, they lead intellectual man to an atheistic view of life, at least temporarily. Intellectual man cannot any longer simply follow in blind belief. Lawfulness and logic have to have their place, even at the risk of uncertainty. Dogmatic teachings eventually become too rigid and restrictive and actually breed doubt. This leads to new spiritual visions leading us to formulate a new understanding of divinity.

We seek refuge in science or in our intellect as a form of a new religion.

Short-term, this brings us a new illusion of safety and predictability. Atheism and a pragmatic scientific worldview become as fiercely defended as fundamental religion. Our intellect turns life into a scientific and intellectual problem. Physical laws can be measured and controlled. They can be perceived by our senses and grasped by our intellect. Therefore they are seen as real. They offer a new form of safety with their ability to be measured and predicted.

When we hide in our intellect instead of search for the truth, we become cut off from the spiritual mystery that permeates all of life.

Over-intellectualism or attempts to compensate in the multitude of ways that we do are the causes for many of our unhealthy distortions in life. Advanced spiritual understanding is a super-conscious intuited understanding of something that cannot be simply grasped by the senses or reason. It cannot be *intellectually understood.* It has to be experienced to truly be known.

Faith describes what can be known through inspiration. It grasps that our corporal existence is an expression of God. Faith establishes connection beyond the physical. Psychologists will speak of the *"Self"*. Priests will speak of the *"Soul"*.

It is what holds deepest interest and meaning to people allowing them to overcome the most excruciating hardships, even the fear of death. This is an indisputable historic fact. The many religions on this planet speak to it in their own way.

We attempt to dominate nature.

We dominate and misuse nature's most personal aspect, our bodies. We forget to see ourselves as an intricate part of nature. We use the physical for selfish ends and seek selfish satisfaction at our own and others expense. Our body, the people we are in relationship with and the earth pay the price. We lust for comfort and safety and a world without pain. Our bodies become the slaves to our desperate outer searching.

The body, nature and the universe are an expression of an underlying interrelated mystery. We are made of the *same stuff* as the universe. Our body and our mind with their desires are not two separate planes. They are interconnected.

Once body and mind reconnect we lose the feeling of being in exile in our bodies and on this earth. It is only here then where we will ever see heaven face to face. If we believe our real home is not here but in a place that lies beyond physical death–if we believe that the spiritual is found only in old books, churches, psychic phenomena, or outside this reality–then we will see this life as a temporary prison to be escaped.

We cannot explain the unexplainable.

"The fairest thing we can experience is the mysterious. It is the fundamental emotion that stands at the cradle of true art and true science. He who knows it not and can no longer wonder, no longer feel amazement, is as good as dead, a snuffed-out candle.

It was the experience of mystery--even if mixed with fear--that engendered religion. A knowledge of the existence of something we cannot penetrate, of the manifestations of the profoundest reason and the most radiant beauty, which are only accessible to our reason in their most elementary forms..."

Albert Einstein, *The World as I See It*

Existence is mysterious. Spirituality brings faith to the mystery of life. As a mystery, life is incomprehensible, unnamable and indefinable. Mystery must not be confused with a mysterious being (yet commonly it is). It is our connection with a super-conscious ever pervading essence of all life and all existence that ultimately brings meaning to our lives. It allows us to make sense of and overcome the tragic moments that our personal life has to offer.

"Nothing exists but God." Spinoza

Today modern quantum physicists talk of an underlying basis of all existence called a *Unified Field*, a field of consciousness. In the 1660s Dutch philosopher Spinoza declared that God and nature were the same, that there was only one underlying essence to all.

"Individual things are nothing but modifications of the attributes of God, or modes by which the attributes of God are expressed in a fixed and definite manner." (Spinoza)

The leaders of the various religions on this planet have over several thousands of years taught that the human psyche is rooted in this perfect order and harmony. And, that we are capable of knowing ourselves as such.

We can deny a spiritual reality or follow religious teachings with blind belief instead of deep personal experience. If we do, we fall out of the meaningful direction of life and the deeper connection to life. We become cut-off and now try to find in money, drugs, sex and fundamentalism, in instant gratification, science and the physical world, what cannot be found there.

The resulting loss of meaning and purpose will eventually give rise to a new understanding of spirituality and new religions. This cycle has repeated itself many times and it will continue to repeat as we grow intellectually and emotionally in our personal life and as a society.

The mystery of existence remains unexplainable.

Living life from a deeper state of wakefulness, or awareness, or connection is our responsibility as adults today. This responsibility is towards the self, others and the world at large. This level of awareness lies beyond thought, emotions and the physical body, beyond any programmed modes of functioning, any conditioned ways of thinking and being.

It is an experience close to feeling completely empty waiting to be filled. Since words are very limited in describing this experience it sounds otherworldly, where in reality it is completely normal. It is a healthy function of human awareness. *It is to be in the world but not of it.* It is to experience one's humanity while responding consciously from an underlying experience of invulnerability and connection. The term often used is *enlightenment*. This is misleading since life is an ongoing experience of more or less *enlightened moments*.

The challenge lies in sustaining these moments without losing ourselves in our habitual thoughts, emotions and behaviors. The challenge lies in not becoming distracted and preoccupied by our programmed ways of responding from fear and the resulting defensiveness, judgment and compensations. The longer we succeed, the more enlightened we are as such, the more light we carry. In other words, we remain perfectly human while responding from a different level of self.

We can turn on the light or we can allow it to dim.

The meaning of our personal life can only be grasped in our inner world.

The expectation that there is some divine being out there who can answer our prayers removes the divine to something not part of us or us part of it. The inexplicable presence underlying all is everywhere inside of us and outside of us and we can never be separated from it.

Whatever the laws of physical existence may take from us in our personal lives, the truth of who we are will remain untouched.

Wherever we are, it is.

Wherever we go, it goes with us.

Whatever we experience, it remains with us being the essence of who we are.

It is only our awareness of it that can change. It doesn't truly matter if we call this essence *he* or *she* or *it*. What matters is the depth of our understanding of us as part of the divine.

Concern for the well-being of our body, others and the earth and all life on earth is not just a matter of human kindness, ethics, or survival. It becomes a spiritual task.

What if midlife crisis is a crisis of having exhausted ourselves in seeking on the outside? What if it is a crisis of recognition, that all of our accomplishments that were supposed to be *it,* haven't done *it.* They haven't filled that nagging vulnerable, empty place on the inside. They haven't brought purpose and meaning to our life. We seek outside what only can be found inside, a deep and meaningful sense of happiness and connection.

"...Verily the lust for comfort murders the passion of the soul, and then walks grinning in the funeral." Kahlil Gibran

The Tree of Life and the Spring of Life

Psychological paradise is a state of oneness.

As infants we live in a state of *preconscious psychological oneness.* We undergo the natural stages of individuation and are indoctrinated into the values and mind patterns of the particular family and society we grow up in. We gradually become lost to the *reality of oneness* and with it the *experience of our true self.* Now our world is a world of vulnerability, helplessness, differences and separation, which could be understood as a *"temporary interlude of self and reality".*

In this state our interpreting of what we call real is based in the habitual, unexamined, immature, or unaware and often magical perception of others and life. Yet the decisions we make about ourselves, others and life is based on this interpreting. They influence us strongly and become our *new reality.*

These decisions have the power to guide our present and future perceptions and experiences.

Truth becomes surrounded with interpretation. Fear dominates our thinking and behavior. We experience good and evil. The state of oneness that once was experienced preconscious now needs to be known consciously to gain both, self-awareness and oneness.

We are driven out of paradise.

The symbol of the *tree of life and the spring of life* are common symbols in ancient history. There are many myths describing mankind as having to choose between drinking water or eating fruit that is destructive or beneficial. Making the wrong choice results in a deadening to the *true reality of self,* losing the *"eternal memory"* of who we are. We wander in the world of shadows or as the Bible says, we are driven out of Paradise.

Different religions and philosophers have spoken to us of true reality as a state of being that can and eventually must be experienced consciously. Modern science has added its voice to this age-old claim.

True reality is the concept of an unchanging, infinite and immanent reality. It is the essence of all matter, all life and any other process in this universe.

Interpretation of what is "real" is influenced by our deeply seated fears.

As humans we spend most of our life in a state of *"temporary interlude of self and reality"*. In this state our experience of reality is governed by fear. Our personal emotional interpretation produces misunderstanding.

It can be equated to a vertebra in our spine becoming slightly dislodged and therefore our whole spine being out of alignment. As a result we experience pain (suffering). We become afraid of further pain and therefore very careful. Our posture is unnatural. Over time, however, we adjust and become used to being crooked. Now to straighten our posture is equally uncomfortable, at first.

The same process happens to our thinking patterns. We become used to fear thinking. We habitually learn to protect ourselves from the possibility of further pain and with it forget that another option exists...life without habitual pain. To change our thinking may feel artificial and phony.

Humanity has been "dead" (with rare exceptions to the contrary) to the knowledge of its true reality.

Small gold plates, dating from the fifth century B.C. to the third century A.D., were found in Italy, Sicily, Crete and Macedonia. On these plates a warning is given to travelers not to drink from a destructive spring on the left and instead keep to the right where travelers will find another spring underneath a white cypress tree.

Those travelers who choose to drink from the spring under the white cypress tree continue on to the lake of memory, where, after responding appropriately to questions posed by the lake guardians, the travelers receive eternal memories and enter into Gods' presence. The travelers that choose to drink from the spring of dirty water on the left become lost (die) and wander in the world of shades.

Obviously the death warned of is not physical death but a form of loss of awareness or psychological death (dead bodies do not wander!). The texts on many of the plates state that those who successfully complete the journey *"become Gods themselves."*

Adam and Eve too have to choose from which of the two trees in the Garden of Eden to eat. The scriptures state:

"I, the Lord God, planted the tree of life also in the midst of the garden, and also the tree of knowledge of good and evil...."

And I, the Lord God, commanded the man, saying: Of every tree of the garden thou mayest freely eat, "But of the tree of the knowledge of good and evil, thou shalt not eat of it, nevertheless, thou mayest choose for thyself, for it is given unto thee; but, remember that I forbid it, for in the day thou eatest thereof thou shalt surely die." (Moses 3:9, 16–17.)

As Adam and Eve's offspring we can attest to that they didn't die in a physical sense.

Self-awareness gained was coupled with the awareness of our vulnerability and fallibility.

It is interesting to note that God did not forbid Adam and Eve to eat of the tree of good and evil initially...he said they had the right to choose but he advised against it. They apparently could have stayed the same. Eve chose to go against God's warning because the tree of good and evil was the "*tree to be desired to make one wise*". It is new discoveries, inventions and ideas that change the established and known and initiate progress. And in fact, they experienced something they apparently hadn't known before, *self-awareness:*

"And the eyes of them both were opened, and they knew that they were naked".

They gained a new level of psycho-emotional awareness and with this awareness they were introduced to recognizing their vulnerability (nakedness) and human fallibility (the choice between good and evil). The form of nakedness referred to has nothing to do with fig leaves hiding our private parts. It is about the psycho-emotional end of paradise. The recognition of separation, vulnerability and fallibility put an end to the paradise Adam and Eve had known. Every toddler undergoes this developmental step.

Who first painted a picture of Adam and Eve covered in fig leaves? Interpreting Adam and Eve's nakedness as sexual nakedness, probably had a lot more to do with that person than the symbolical meaning and advice given in the creation story. After all, when the story speaks of "for in the day thou eatest thereof thou shalt surely die", is not taken literally. Humanity exists because Adam and Eve didn't die even so they ate the forbidden fruit. The death spoken of was a symbolical death. It was a warning that the life they had known would end. The nakedness spoken of is symbolic for experiencing psycho-emotional vulnerability. Obviously, physical vulnerability existed before and after this recognition "their eyes ...were opened". The only thing that changed is their awareness of their vulnerability.

This recognition is truly a *Galileo-moment!* The implications are far-reaching. To see Adam and Eve's nakedness as sexual nakedness is at the core of our attitude towards sexuality.

Every human child experiences the nakedness that awareness brings.

When he/she leaves the preconscious oneness of infancy, paradise is lost. It is a psychological recognition of vulnerability and often helplessness. Every human child faces this human predicament as a normal developmental step. Even in the most physical sense, when one is naked, one is vulnerable to the elements. All humans live with a deeply seated sense of vulnerability and a resulting search for safety. Vulnerability and helplessness is at the core of our human dilemma.

Psycho-emotional nakedness was confused to stand for sexual nakedness and seen as an insult towards God, leading to many unhealthy distortions. This misinterpretation reaches deep into our daily lives to this day. It is mind puzzling that this misinterpretation has been as long-standing as it has. Look at all the pain and hurt it has caused! All of our preconceptions, judgments and attitudes towards sexuality go back to interpreting Adam and Eve's nakedness as sexual nakedness. Its influence is and has been profound shaping our attitudes from religious chastity to abortion and gay rights.

Once we recognize the nakedness of Adam and Eve as a symbol of vulnerability, sexuality is simply a physical function of our bodies and not a sin or insult to God. Why would this physical function be an insult when other physical functions are not? Sexuality belongs to our physical life. This misunderstanding led to sexuality being seen as something to be hidden, harmful and shameful. It has and still is causing much suffering.

Adam and Eve didn't make a mistake or wrong choice! They simply wandered down the path of evolution of human consciousness. Every human toddler takes this step when he/she first starts to refer to him/herself, as *"I want a cookie,"* instead of *"Mary wants a cookie".* It is a step in individuation.

With this step, Adam and Eve became aware of and capable, in their own minds, of both, good and evil. They experienced separation and a loss of connection and safety. They were introduced to human vulnerability and fallibility.

"...the man is become as one of us, to know good and evil."

The God of Genesis became set on preventing Adam and Eve to eat (to know) from the tree of life that would have made them aware of being immortal (experience conscious oneness and invulnerability prematurely?). Just imagine adults stuck at the developmental level of toddlers never transcending the identification with the omnipowers! Not a pretty picture. It is the awareness and experience of vulnerability (nakedness) that moderates the power of good and bad.

Note: experiencing a state of psycho-emotional oneness is not the same as physical immortality.

Every young child moves from preconscious oneness with its absence of awareness of time and separation and vulnerability/helplessness (nakedness), to conscious awareness of self in time and the emotional experience and consequences of separation. The story of Genesis seems to suggest an additional step: *conscious awareness of psycho-emotional oneness beyond time (eternity).*

We must choose between love (good) and fear (evil).

We can imagine the tree of the knowledge of good and evil as a hedge-like tree surrounding the tree of eternal life. This provides a wonderful image for our human experience. The only way to eat from the tree of eternal life then is by first making a path through the hedge-like tree of the knowledge of opposites.

In doing so we gain experience. After all it is the "*tree to be desired to make one wise*". We aid our own evolution. It becomes our task to become self-aware and wisely handle the power of good and evil. We learn to dispel the illusions of separation with its feelings of alienation and lack of safety. Until then, we are all caught in the hedge-like tree of good and evil (fear-based thinking and living) and have to laboriously find our way through its maze.

When Adam and Eve made that first choice they became conscious of their vulnerability and of good and evil. They experienced fear, guilt, shame and separation. When a young child first becomes conscious as being different from its parents, it too experiences vulnerability, helplessness, fear, guilt and shame and becomes afraid of separation.

Humanity has been sent wandering down the path of becoming conscious. It is now up to each individual to choose again, daily. Our choice is between love and fear. Love will ask us to extend ourselves and see all things as part of us. Fear will scream: "Y*ou are wrong and bad!" "You will lose and be hurt!"* Fear will ask us to protect ourselves and see others and life as out to get us. The choice is ours!

Evil is a term describing that which is regarded as morally bad.

Whatever is undesirable, seen as bad, wicked, vicious, doing or intending to do harm, depraved in intention or purpose, causing pain or trouble and offensive, is called evil. In most cultures, the word is used to describe acts, thoughts and ideas which are thought to bring about withering and death—the opposite of life. As such it is the antithesis of good. However, we have begun to regard evil as if it was a *thing or an entity. Evil becomes d[evil], an entity that is out to get us.*

Before God became all-good and the d(evil) represented the all-bad, good and bad co-existed. In reality they still do co-exist within us as an ongoing daily choice.

An interesting word play is possible. When one reads the word evil backward, from right to left instead of left to right, the word reads *live*. Whenever our energy does not extend towards life (from love) but withdraws from life (out of fear), it may be called *evil.*

Evil is an energy that has been distorted and misdirected. It therefore stands in opposition to love and brings misery. It is a wrong choice or faulty interpretation made by our minds that is enacted. It is energy directed away from what is life-giving.

Emotional suffering is the outcome of fear-based thinking and living.

Each individual has to sort out the truth from the misinterpretations (based in fear) that have attached themselves to their experiences and interpretations. Only then can one reach a new level of connection, identification, integration, forgiveness and ultimately inner peace and joy...*new life.*

Emotional suffering is the outcome of this confusion around truth and misinterpretation. In all its countless manifestations, emotional suffering is a form of fear.

It is not the suffering itself, but the fear of pain and suffering that is the culprit. The resulting loss of awareness that we are loved, lovable and loving and as a result deserving has the power to disconnect us from our inner being. We experience ourselves as vulnerable (naked). An utter feeling of vulnerability and helplessness rests at the bottom of every unresolved trauma. Physical or emotional suffering cannot disconnect us from the reality of who we are.

The story of Jesus Christ is one example of this. Seeing our source on the outside, fearing ourselves to be separate and alone, fearing loss and fearing that those we love can be harmed, makes us vulnerable to experience ourselves as disconnected.

The truth of who we are has never changed and is always part of any situation. A form of this truth exists on several levels. The most upper level is the truth of what is: *factual truth*. Underneath this level is our *personal emotional truth,* a result of interpretations based in past experience and decisions. On a deeper level is the truth of *who we are* (*eternal memories*).

It is our deep-seated fear of vulnerability and helplessness that gets us into trouble.

Psychologically speaking this is the case for every young child, when the child loses its awareness that it is loved, loveable and loving (eternal memory). At the moment when fear enters, the recognition of vulnerability and potential loss enters as well. The child is psychologically tempted to symbolically eat of the fruit of knowledge of good and evil. The child is tempted to divide experience into good and bad and side with one half against the other half.

As adults, we repeat this experience daily. We are never only angry or unsettled by the facts in a situation. We become afraid, angry and judgmental, hurt and lose awareness of reality, when factual truth becomes surrounded by personal emotional truth. We lose sight of the eternal memory of who we are (invulnerable and whole) and who others are.

Doubt enters. With doubt comes fear of loss. It is followed by instinctual self-protection and choosing sides which leads to a sense of separation intensifying our fear. At that moment in time, we begin to wander in the world of the shades. We *"die"* to the awareness of who we are, as first experienced (in Christianity) by Adam and Eve.

Jesus seems to have known about this underlying sense of vulnerability.

"...Therefore I tell you, do not be anxious about your life,..., Look at the birds of the air: they neither sow nor reap nor gather into barns, and yet your heavenly Father feeds them. Are you not of more value than they?" Matthew 6:24-34 (Luke 12:24-27)

Our life becomes governed by the experiences of swinging between the opposites.

We may not consciously remember when and how the original split occurred. However, we can recognize that it occurred by our life experience. We are caught in a frantic struggle to escape the negative side of an opposite in our life. Yet, the teeter-totter of superior and inferior, important-unimportant or worthy-unworthy etc. has an iron grip on our life.

We typically at first attempt to only experience the positive side of the particular opposites we are dealing with. This may lead us to become very capable, knowledgeable and/or wealthy in an attempt to avoid the negative side. Yet, the positive and negative are the opposite sides of the *same coin (experience).*

We cannot escape or annul the shadow manifestation completely. When we least suspect, it will assert its existence.

We may blame others for not treating us as equals (important, worthy, included, etc.). We do not realize that the fragmentation exists inside and therefore can only be truly solved inside. We may fear that others don't see us as equals (etc.) and overreact attempting to protect ourselves from what has not happened. We demand, avoid and compensate.

Once we begin to look inside by choice and find a place beyond the particular pair of opposites that we are dealing with, we begin to *"eat from the fruit of the tree of life"*.

We have to face our *personal demons:* the not assimilated pain we carry inside (personal emotional truth) and sort out the truth from the misunderstandings that surround it (gaining eternal memories).

Acceptance allows for change and new life.

When we have found our truth in a situation our energy extends itself in a calm manner of certainty. Truth is an inner experience and leads us to the acceptance of what is, painful as it may be at the moment.

The truth about *who we are* is part of life's mystery discovered as we evolve (given to us by the lake guardian as we answer/respond correctly). We can lose our awareness of *who we are* but that does not change *who we are.*

Truth often rests at the balance point between the opposites. It is identified with both extremes through the energy of understanding, acceptance and forgiveness. We need to first understand (grow in awareness) to be able to accept and finally forgive others and ourselves. This depends on our willingness to surrender our righteous position. It is a *giving to* or better yet, *a receiving of* release. This doesn't mean that in forgiving we condone or *whitewash* what has happened.

We recognize others and ourselves as fallible human beings. We are as subject to good and evil and frightened of our vulnerability as they are. In doing so, we attest to our invulnerability and with it release the other and free ourselves.

We continually make choices about how to interpret experiences and others actions and motivations.

Much of this choosing has become habitual. It has become dictated by internalized automatic meanings and habitual mind patterns. We *nourish* ourselves on gossip, a false sense of closeness based in exclusivity, judgment of others as less, bad and wrong. We nourish ourselves with strange attempts to provide for our safety and security *("drink from the dirty water/eat the fruit of evil").*

Our conscience gives us warnings. Most people rather continue to stay with good and bad, right and wrong, me and not me. They feel reluctant to undertake the at times arduous journey of uncovering the underlying truth in a situation and facing their vulnerabilities.

There is another choice we have. And, choose we must if we are to gain both self-awareness and the experience of oneness. We can nourish ourselves on goodwill, perceiving others (and our own) wrongdoing as a call for love and help. This leads to reestablishing trust that we are loved, loving and loveable. We can embrace and constructively direct our emotions and discipline our minds to make them into the tools they were meant to be.

We will fail, as certainly others will fail us, some more some less. It is not up to us to judge if the more or less makes someone more or less worthy of love. We are all capable of succumbing to the same human temptations. Superiority has no place between brothers and sisters. One day, as our understanding has grown, we will step beyond forgiveness.

Much energy is given to the idea of evil, in particular within religions.

As in the myth, to reach *reality* and receive the eternal memories of our *true self*, we have to pause and answer correctly some very important questions. These answers are truly our response to whatever confronts us today. They are either based in love-based thinking and living, containing truth, or are based in fear-based thinking and living, containing interpretation. They therefore are either life-giving or life-denying.

We have to choose to either nourish ourselves at the *"spring of clean life-giving water"* (love energy) or the *"spring of polluted water"* (fear energy).

The tree of life and spring of life are available to all who do not wish to live trapped in the world of opposites, wandering in the shadows lost (habitual interpretation). The tree of life and the spring of life are symbols for the ultimate destiny of mankind.

The polluted spring, the awareness of nakedness and the tree of knowledge of good and evil are a symbol of our present-day human affairs. They are a symbol for living lost in fantasy (personal emotional interpretation and fear), denial and punishment, thrashing around in a bad dream.

Hourly and daily, we are challenged to choose who we are going to be within the circumstances we face.

The bad dream we live in and reality (heaven) are two exclusive states of consciousness. We cannot be in both of them at the same time. We can have one or the other. Adam and Eve lost their ability to eat from the tree of life once they had become aware of their nakedness and eaten from the tree of the knowledge of good and evil.

Truth and misinterpretation are equally exclusive because they are consuming and all encompassing, each in its own way. The one rules out the other. We must choose.

A fascinating wordplay is to read the word evil backward. It reads live; in other words, when life force energy is used in the wrong way (backward), it becomes evil. It becomes energy that is life denying.

When we experience a feeling of love notice how our energy extends itself, it wants to flow outward. We experience ourselves as open and compassionate. When we experience a feeling opposite to love (due to our interpretation of what is), our energy wants to withdraw. It wants to protect us from whatever threat (based on fear/loss/harm) we perceive. We experience ourselves as closed. Defense turns into attack. We all do this, only the degree varies.

May you be the one to throw the first stone who has never felt tempted to respond like this!

Our interpretation of what is determines our stance with regard to it.

The fascinating thing is that we can undo the choice we made just a moment ago (with regard to interpretation). We can decide to change our mind about how to interpret and therefore what stance to take and with what attitude to approach what is happening. We have the power of being able to reinvent ourselves minute by minute.

If we are willing to mop up after ourselves for past wrong choices, we will be led unerringly towards a more peaceful and happy outlook on life. That by itself is worth taking this approach for. We feel happier and more loving and peaceful when our energy is extended, if we are ready to believe in a God and spiritual reality or not.

Adam and Eve had a choice, a curse and a blessing. Every human being has been given this power to choose. Choose we will and choose we must, consciously or habitually. Our present life is an accumulation of choices made in the past and choices made in the present.

Responsibility understood rightly is the realization that the quality of my present day life is the result of the choices I made and make. Satisfaction is a state of "being", not a state of "having".

About the Author

Gudrun Christeane Carstairs is a consultant and counselor with a background in education and psychotherapeutic work. She received her degree in Social Pedagogy and Education in Germany and is a Registered Clinical Counselor in British Columbia, Canada. Her innovative work uses a multidisciplinary approach drawing on conventional Western schools of Psychology and contemplative Eastern schools of thought.

For the past 25 years fellow counselors and lay people alike have attended her workshops seeking her insights and unique ability to identify the inner dynamics that typically manifest as outer frustrations. An experienced and dynamic educator, counselor and public speaker, Gudrun assists others in integrating ideas, situations and issues in ways that others may not readily see as workable.

"Finding the key to unlock our inner world unlocks our outer world simultaneously. The laws of the psyche are as predictable as the laws of physics. Beyond that, every living being is a mystery and as unlimited and unknowable."

Gudrun is a wife and mother. Originally from Germany, she lives with her family in San Diego County, California.

For requests about workshops, lectures and other products by Mrs. Carstairs or any personal correspondence please go to: www.GudrunCarstairs.com

This book is also available as an e—book.

Bibliography

Bradshaw, John. *Healing the Shame That Binds You.* Deerfield Beach, FL: Health Communications, 1988.

Campbell, Joseph. *The Power of Myth.* New York: Doubleday, 1988.

Chopra, Deepak. *Quantum Healing.* New York: Bantam Books, 1989

Forward, Susan, and Buck, Craig. *Toxic Parents.* New York; Bantam Books, 2002

Foundation for Inner Peace. *A Course in Miracles.* New York: Penguin Group, 1996

Gendlin, Eugene. *Focusing.* New York; Bantam Books, 1982.

Gibran, Kahlil. *The Prophet.* New York, Borzoi Books, Alfred A Knopf, 1923

Goleman, Daniel. *Emotional Intelligence.* New York; Bantam Books, 1997.

Greenfield, Susan. *The Private Life Of The Brain.* New York: John Wiley & Sons, 2000.

Haim, Ginott. *Between Parent and Child,* New York: Three Rivers Press, 1965

Hay, Louise. *Heal Your Body.* United States: Hay House, Inc., 1984

Houston, Jean. *The Search for The Beloved,* Los Angeles: Jeremy P. Tarcher, Inc.

Johnson, Robert A. *We. Understanding the Psychology of Romantic Love.* San Francisco: Harper One, 1985.

Lerner, Harriet. *The Dance of Anger.* New York: Harper & Row, 1985.

Mahler, Margaret S., and Pine, Fred, and Bergman, Anni. *The Psychological Birth of the Human Infant: Symbiosis and Individuation.* New York: Basic Books, 1975

Miller, Alice. *The Drama of the Gifted Child.* New York: Basic Books, 1981

Pinkola Estes, Clarissa. *Women Who Run With the Wolves.* New York: Ballantine Books, 2003.

Pipher, Mary, and Ross, Ruth. *Reviving Ophelia.* New York; Penguin Books, 2005

Satir, Virginia. *The New Peoplemaking.* Mountain View, CA: Science and Behavior Books, 1988

Shapiro, Debbie. *Your Body Speaks Your Mind.* Boulder, CO: Sounds True, Inc., 1997

Viorst, Judith. *Necessary Losses.* New York: Ballantine Books, 1986

Printed in the United Kingdom
by Lightning Source UK Ltd.
136141UK00001B/124/P

9 781601 456533